AN ENGLISH JOURNEY

An English Journey

RICHARD WEST

MANCHESTER–OLDHAM–ROCHDALE

BOLTON–WIGAN–LIVERPOOL

MORECAMBE–HEYSHAM–LANCASTER

WINDERMERE–GRASMERE

NEWCASTLE–CHESTER-LE-STREET–DURHAM

DARLINGTON–YORK

BRADFORD–BARNSLEY–BAWTRY

LINCOLN–ELY–KING'S LYNN

EAST DEREHAM–NORWICH–LOWESTOFT

SOUTHWOLD–ALDEBURGH–WOODBRIDGE

FELIXSTOWE–BURY ST EDMUNDS

CAMBRIDGE–LONDON–ROCHESTER

CANTERBURY–FOLKESTONE–RYE

BRIGHTON–CHICHESTER–PORTSMOUTH

SOUTHSEA–WINCHESTER

SALISBURY–BATH–BRISTOL

WORCESTER–BIRMINGHAM

WALSALL–LICHFIELD

CHATTO & WINDUS–LONDON
1981

PUBLISHED BY CHATTO & WINDUS LTD
40 WILLIAM IV STREET
LONDON WC2N 4DF

CLARKE, IRWIN & CO. LTD
TORONTO

BRITISH LIBRARY CATALOGUING IN PUBLICATION DATA

West, Richard
   An English journey.
   1. England – Description and travel
   I. Title
   914.2′0485′7   DA631

   ISBN 0-7011-2584-5

PRINTED IN GREAT BRITAIN
BY EBENEZER BAYLIS & SON LTD
THE TRINITY PRESS, WORCESTER, AND LONDON

Contents

The author would like to thank the following for kindly granting permission for the use of copyright material included in this book: John Calder Ltd. (*Nothing to Declare* by Michael Gillard and Martin Tomkinson); the Estate of the late George Orwell (*The Road to Wigan Pier* by George Orwell, published by Secker & Warburg Ltd.); Macmillan Ltd. (*The Best of Friends* by John Aspinall); Penguin Books Ltd. (*English Society in the Early Middle Ages* by Doris Mary Stenton); and A. P. Watt Ltd (*William Cobbett* by G. K. Chesterton, and 'The Secret People' from *The Collected Poems* of G. K. Chesterton).

Introduction

This account of a journey through England requires some introductory explanation. The choice of a subject may sound presumptuous on the part of a writer who, as far as his name is known to the public at all, is known as a correspondent from Africa, Central Europe and South-East Asia. I have indeed spent much of the last twenty-five years abroad, partly from *Wanderlust* and partly because it was cheaper than working in England, but I trust I have never become, in that time, a stranger in England.

I started as a reporter in 1955 on what was still called the *Manchester Guardian*. For the first two years I spent most of the time travelling about the north of England, with less frequent assignments in southern England, Scotland and Wales. During my third year, I was the *Manchester Guardian*'s Yorkshire and North-East correspondent.

Again, in the early 1960s I worked for the weekly *Time and Tide* as a kind of provincial roving reporter, writing a series of long, fortnightly pieces on towns and cities in Britain. At this time I grew interested in and concerned about the destruction of ancient cities, the growth of the property boom and the slow corruption of local politics – particularly in the Labour Party.

When *Time and Tide* changed hands, I continued to write on topics like these for the *New Statesman* which then (but no longer, alas) was a radical journal.

Often, abroad, I day-dreamed of writing a book about England: I once read Defoe's *Journey*, all one sleepness night in Addis Ababa. Nothing came of the project and soon I was off to Saigon once more.

And so I was pleased when, this year, Chatto & Windus suggested this book.

In planning this journey, I soon decided to leave out Scotland, Ireland and Wales, which have their distinctive problems, and anyway would require more space than was feasible in a book of this kind. Besides, in treating of England alone, I hoped to consider those differences – sometimes imagined – which are said to divide the north from the south of the country. Certainly, it is more in the North than the South that one sees the decline of industry; but largely because there was more to begin with.

I chose to begin and finish my journey in Manchester, since that was the place I started off as a journalist, twenty-five years ago. Also, Manchester has endured to the full almost every one of the follies besetting England – from city centre development, to local government reorganisation, to being the seat of the Equal Opportunities Commission. I am also very fond of that city.

From Manchester I continued through what was the great industrial region of Lancashire, to Liverpool, one of the saddest places in England and on, through the Lake District, to Newcastle. In northeast England I turned my attention to something that is epitomised in this area: the moral collapse of the Labour Party and trade union organisation. In Darlington, home of the *Northern Echo*, I try to discuss the troubles that have overtaken the newspaper business of which, of course, I speak with particular feeling. Then down through Yorkshire and Lincolnshire to East Anglia.

East Anglia is becoming once more the richest and liveliest part of the country – though lacking the glory it had in the Middle Ages. Here the journey grows much more cheerful and stays so in Kent, the South Coast and even in Bristol, one of the few cities not quite ruined and uglified over the last twenty-five years.

A week in Birmingham put me in sombre mood once again. There will be those who accuse me of having written of England in sour and dyspeptic mood. After all, they may say, it is still a remarkably pleasant country compared to most. To which I can only say that it is much less pleasant than twenty-five years ago; and wantonly so. It has disimproved, as the Irish say, in a way that most countries have not.

My experience as a foreign reporter has taught me that not all countries change for the worse. Some, like France, Holland and

Germany (West), seem to be actually pleasanter each time I go there. Cities destroyed in the Second World War have been rebuilt and made attractive: in England, cities untouched by the war have been vandalised by crooks and property men. We in England like to imagine that things like vast local bureaucracies and mad trade unions are universal phenomena of the time: they are not. England is, rightly, a worldwide object of scorn and pity. Because I have spent much time abroad I am able to see England partly through foreign eyes; and what I see frightens me.

This book is the record of a continuous journey: I was in each place on the day I said I was, though sometimes I came back to London to spend a night with my family. Although I have cut and tidied up part of the manuscript, it remains as a journal – with some of the faults that entails. In the places I went to, I had time to touch only on certain aspects of life. I have not attempted a survey of modern England. This is not an objective or even a fair book. In many places, I dare say, my reactions were subject to private mood, or chance encounter.

I have, over the past twenty-five years, written on most of the places and topics that feature in this book. Several passages have appeared in more or less similar form as articles in the *Spectator*, that fine radical weekly, to whose editor, Alexander Chancellor, I am most grateful. Although I have everywhere returned to places to take a fresh look, I have nowhere changed earlier writings just for the sake of it.

There are no revelations in this book; no exposés; no investigative journalism. That kind of thing serves a useful purpose, but libel laws make it dangerous even in newspapers; almost impossible in a book. The one book of that kind I wrote earned me a total of £500. The lawyer who read it for libel got £1000. The lawyer who wrote in to the publishers to complain on behalf of his client was probably paid about £5000. From the point of view of the author, that is a mug's game.

Richard West
London, March 1981

From Manchester to Liverpool

MANCHESTER – OLDHAM

ROCHDALE – BOLTON – WIGAN

LIVERPOOL

24 September – Manchester   My journey round England began at what used to be called the Gateway to Manchester – London Road Station – where I had stepped off the train as a novice reporter twenty-five years ago; to a North of soot-blackened but busy workshops and warehouses, of back-to-back nineteenth-century cottages, bomb sites where the urchins played at football, wise-cracking whores under the street-lights, and pubs where short, taciturn men in cloth caps and shiny faces played cribbage or darts, and put out saucers of beer for the dog. At first I hated the place; then grew to love it, and still love what little remains.

London Road Station has gone. The sound Victorian building was pulled down and replaced by a bare, featureless concrete box – deprived even of benches in case it attracted the down-and-outs. Even the name London Road has been changed to Piccadilly, although it is hundreds of yards from the Manchester square of that name. The managers of British Railways (now British Rail), who for the last thirty years have pursued the government's plan of running down our railway system in the interests of the motor industry, have treated Manchester with their usual brutality. No plaque or memento that I could see is left to remind the public that this was the terminal for one of the first trunk railways in the world; the first to be joined by an electric cable so that the progress of the trains could be signalled along the line.

London Road was not as majestic as Euston, where British Rail not only tore down the arch (quite wantonly as it turned out) but refused

1

to number the stones, in case any sentimentalist wanted to put it together again. Its chief glory remains the colossal series of arches, a viaduct which supports the track and the trains from beneath; it is worth a visit – and getting fouled by the thousands of pigeons there.

The station itself was a place to rush through while 'getting out of Manchester' – that emotive phrase which I shall mention again. The only occasion I spent much time there was one evening in 1955 when the IRA had rung up to warn they had planted a bomb. The bomb scare was a hoax. They almost always were in that early 'campaign', as the IRA like to call their squalid murders. Perhaps they were short of explosives; perhaps, in those days, they felt compunction for their sins. A few weeks later they rang up the *Manchester Guardian* to say they had planted a bomb in our local pub, The Connaught; all the reporters on duty helped to cover that story till closing time.

Stepping out of the Piccadilly Station, I took a look at the Manchester skyline, a different one from that I remember: many more blank spaces now, and not thanks to the Luftwaffe; a few warehouses now, but little soot; a few workshops, but nobody working in them; a great many high-rise buildings, including the infamous home of the new Greater Manchester Council – of which more later. Piccadilly, once the central part of the city, is cluttered with tall, gawky, ugly buildings that overshadow the statue of Queen Victoria. She looks firmly in the other direction. At the side of the ramp from the station down to the street, I noticed a curving office block in the shape of a shallow S. It is the work of Colonel Richard Seifert, the architect-entrepreneur who has blotted the face of London with piles such as Centre Point, the *Sunday Times* building and, worst of all, the National Westminster Bank, that temple to Mammon which overshadows St Paul's. The Colonel's work can be found all over the country, especially in Birmingham – on which he has stamped his character and aesthetic standards as did Sir Christopher Wren on London.

The Colonel, according to *Who's Who*, has served on the British Waterways Board, whose chairman, Sir Frank Price, the Birmingham politician and property millionaire, is an old business colleague and friend. The Colonel's building here at Piccadilly Station stands near the junction of three of the country's oldest and finest canals – the Rochdale, the Ashton and Cheshire – which run, if that is the word for canals, past fine eighteenth- and early nineteenth-century mills and warehouses, sometimes passing on aqueducts over the streets and houses. Probably few people coming to Manchester know of this eerie and beautiful world beside the canals, so close to Piccadilly Station: I did not know of it when I lived here during the Fifties, but now I go there for solace after the hideousness of the rest of the city. I went there today, lugging the shoulder bag of clothes and books that I am taking on this journey.

Apart from stray, savage Alsatian dogs, the towpaths along these canals offer excellent walking. Most of the warehouses are shut, but some can be visited and admired by connoisseurs of industrial arch-aeology. (This is a thriving hobby nowadays. Other countries have industry: we have industrial archaeology.) The canal locks are in working order. One of the keepers told me: 'I can remember the time when the barges brought in lime, cotton, port and Jamaican rum. Now it's open again to pleasure boats.' The barges, or butty boats, live on only in memory – in the Butty Boat Bar of the Manchester Midland Hotel – just as the textile industry lives on in the King Cotton Bar of the Piccadilly Hotel. The lime, the cotton, the port and Jamaica rum are carried by lorry. What kind of economics is this when finite fuels are running out? Bring back the barges! Bring back the horse!

The wealth of Manchester started with the canals, which brought cheap coals from the pits of the Duke of Bridgewater; one of the series of Ford Madox Brown paintings in the Town Hall – purporting to show the history of the city – depicts a barge of apple-cheeked, laughing maidens, decked on a barge like models on a carnival float. In fact the canals were filthy dirty. Now they are clean again and en-joy what is called 'a leisure, amenity value'. Even the fish have returned, and with them the anglers. I saw a young man float-fishing with maggots as bait and asked him what he expected to catch. 'Roach, tench, perch and pike,' he said. Then, noticing that I looked rather sceptical at his mention of pike (which seldom take maggots), he added defiantly '. . . and trout. I've had two trout as big as this' — and stretching out his right arm he indicated a length of at least eighteen inches: a huge fish. He was pulling my leg, in usual Lancashire fashion, but nevertheless I have heard that coarse fish, if not trout, grow to considerable size in these former industrial canals. You can see people fishing from Princess Street, right in the heart of Manchester.

One of my first ever jobs on the *Manchester Guardian* was to investigate a story that a fish, a bleak I think it was, had been found in the River Irwell. The fish was dead and, as far as I can remember, some scientist said that it came from another, cleaner river and must have been thrown into the Irwell as a joke. I doubt if a fish could live in the Irwell even today, though as late as 1740 salmon ascended as far as Manchester. Then came the Duke of Bridgewater's canal, cheap coal, and the world's first industrial slum – the first housing estate for factory workers. It was built at the confluence of the Irwell and Irk, and was graced with the beautiful name of Angelmead. An early writer called Angelmead 'the chimney of the world . . . the entrance to hell'; and the misery of its hovels roused Friedrich Engels to fury and socialism. Hundreds of factories vomited smoke, tar and sulphuric acid into the foggy, marshland air; the Irwell was choked by millions of tons of cinders; its surface was streaked azure, crimson and bile-green with the effluent of a dozen dye-works. It still has a putrid, bluebottle sheen.

Angelmead was well described by the young Engels, who had come to Manchester as a clerk for his father's textile company:

Passing along a rough path on the river bank, in between posts and washing lines, one penetrates into this chaos of little one-storied one-room huts . . . most of them have earth floors – cooking, living and sleeping all takes place in one room. In such a hole, barely six feet long and five feet wide, I saw two beds – and what beds and bedding – that filled that room, except for the doorstep and fireplace. In several others I found *absolutely nothing*, although the door was wide open and the inhabitants were leaning against it. Everywhere in front of the doors were rubbish and refuse, it was impossible to see whether any sort of pavement lay under this, but here and there I felt it out with my feet. . . .

The inhabitants of these hovels – men, women and children – worked twelve hours a day in mills and sweatshops that were often still more unhealthy than their homes, because of the steam heat. Epidemics of cholera ravaged Angelmead. Often those who survived the epidemic dug up the corpses of those who had died and ground up the bones to sell as fertiliser. The smoke and the damp made Manchester famous for TB and bronchitis until quite recent times.

In *The Condition of the Working Classes in England*, Engels remarked that 'there are few strong, well-built and healthy people among them – at least among the industrial workers who generally work in closed rooms . . . they are almost all weakly, gaunt and pale.' The industrial revolution produced a new race of physically stunted people. When the Boer War broke out in 1899, two-thirds of the Manchester volunteers were refused outright as unfit and only a tenth accepted. Those figures took no account of the men who were so obviously unfit that the doctors did not bother to examine them. During the First World War, Manchester and its neighbourhood produced the smallest soldiers in the British forces. About 90 per cent of the Bantam regiments (minimum height for entry, five feet) came from this area. In Manchester at that time twelve-year-old children who attended private schools were, on average, five inches taller than those who attended state schools.

The cleaning of the canals has followed the cleaning of the Manchester atmosphere; the campaign for clean air began in earnest during the 1950s, and may have had something to do with the running down of the coal mines in Manchester, since miners got cheap or free coal and therefore opposed smokeless fuels. Even when I first came here, the city and even the southern suburbs were frequently blanketed in a sour, acrid fog that was agony to anyone liable to bronchitis. People smoked cigarettes to hide the taste. Earlier in the century, and perhaps as late as the 1950s, old women in Salford over the Irwell would ward off the threat to their lungs by tying rashers of bacon over the chest each autumn. And of course people believed that 'where there's muck there's money'. The saying is probably true: I have heard that the operatives of a great Japanese steel company sing a song which boasts how 'the smoke from our foundries blots out the sky'. There is a famous anecdote in Engels about how he had taken a walk in Manchester with a middle-class, Liberal manufacturer gentleman to whom he had described the horrors of working-class life. 'He listened to all this patiently and quietly,' Engels concluded, 'and at the corner of the street at which we parted he remarked: "And yet there is a great deal of money made here. Good morning, sir." ' Although Engels raged at what he called bourgeois hypocrisy, I rather suspect that the businessman was pulling his leg. After all, did not he, Engels, also exploit the system and spend his profits on keeping an Irish mistress and drinking champagne?

But bad as the conditions were in Angelmead and the worst

industrial slums, the prospect of wages attracted thousands of land-less labourers from the countryside in the nineteenth century. The industrial revolution also attracted thousands of overseas immigrants, especially the Jews, whose culture and influence are stronger now in Manchester than perhaps any other city in Europe. The first Jews to arrive in Manchester were of two very different kinds. There were textile importers from Germany, like Nathan Rothschild, who wanted to get some control over the produce at source, and there were poor Jews who came as refugees from religious persecution. The former were from the start made welcome and tended to integrate with the non-Jewish Germans. The poor Jews, often illiterate, tended to live by begging or peddling cheap watches and jewellery, a trade that frequently caused them to come up in court charged with receiving stolen goods. The largest immigration of Jews to Manchester started about 1875, soared after the Russian pogroms of 1880–81, and lasted until the First World War.

The sub-proletariat of industrial-revolution Manchester was formed of immigrants from South and West Ireland, where poverty and even death by starvation were commonplace. The Irish immigrant would arrive from the ship barefoot, accompanied by his pig which, as Engels remarked, 'he loves as the Arab loves his horse, with the difference that he sells it when it is fat enough to kill. Other-wise he eats and sleeps with it, his children play with it, ride upon it, roll in the dirt with it, as one may see a thousand times repeated in all the great towns of England.'

This Irish sub-proletariat was prepared to do jobs, like handloom weaving, that could not provide a living for even the most desperate English workers. Many starved to death at their work, in conditions that beggared description even by Engels. Because they were poor, Roman Catholic, often nationalist, the Irish were feared by the English, who called them the 'Celtic incubus'.

They were always quick to riot. During the cholera epidemic of 1849 an Irishman went to the hospital to inspect the corpse of his grandson and, opening the coffin, found that the doctors had cut off the head to use for research, placing a brick as a makeweight. Within minutes an Irish crowd had besieged the hospital and smashed the windows. The biggest police station in Manchester was set in Strangeways, the giant and sombre prison topped by a vast chimney, the work of the architect who later built the Town Hall. Generations of Irish rebels have served 'under the chimney', and come out bitterer than they went in.

Engels's researches provided Karl Marx with some of the raw material for his revolutionary writings, but on the one occasion the older man came up to Manchester he spent all his time in Chetham's Hospital Library, where he and Engels had first met. The two men regarded Manchester, the site of the first industrial revolution, as the logical site of the first proletarian revolution they so keenly awaited. Certainly Manchester had a history of political radicalism dating back to the time of the French revolution. There were frequent Luddite revolts by handloom weavers who feared the introduction of new machinery that would put them out of work. After the victory of Napoleon at Waterloo, the growing industrial regions of England clamoured for more representation in Parliament, where power still lay with the landed classes. In 1819 the Reform agitation came to a head with a meeting in St Peter's Fields in Manchester, where 60,000 had gathered on what was to be the site of the Free Trade Hall. The local magistrates, in a nearby house on the site of the present Midland Hotel, sent in mounted yeomanry to arrest the principal speaker; regular troops were sent in to rescue the yeomanry, who had been trapped in the crowd. Panic set in, and the yeomanry fired into the crowd, killing eleven people and wounding many. An officer of the regulars reproached the yeomanry – 'For shame, gentlemen, what are you about? The people cannot get away' – but the damage was done, and the 'Peterloo Massacre' stands as the most bloody encounter in modern English history; an indication, perhaps, of how peaceful that history has been.

I walked to the Midland Hotel and asked if they had a room, but found that it cost too much for my budget. If somebody else was paying I would love to stay at this plush Edwardian pile, whose guests seem to be mostly from the Granada TV company; you can find yourself sitting among the entire cast of *Coronation Street*. Some of the south rooms face onto a wilderness of rubble in which stands a solitary pub, Tommy Duck's, which is also worth a detour, as Michelin says. The ceiling is covered with dozens of pairs of knickers. And behind the Midland Hotel to the east, and as far as the Granada TV studios, are railway ruins older even than London Road. This year marked the 150th anniversary of the opening of the

Manchester–Liverpool line, on which occasion the hapless Cabinet Minister Huskisson was knocked down and killed by the train he had come to see. Later the Duke of Wellington travelled the route and was stoned by the crowd when he came into Manchester. The station now is, of course, another museum. This year, to mark the anniversary, three new trains were built as replicas of the originals. Two of them broke down and failed to complete the journey. Such are our modern engineers that they cannot even build a primitive train.

25 September – Manchester   Last night I stayed at a hotel with a night club. Today I have moved to a pleasant Armenian boarding house in the Fallowfield–Withington district of southern Manchester. It was Engels, a far more perceptive and a livelier writer than Marx, who explained, in *The Condition of the Working Classes in England*, how Manchester's bourgeoisie would move ever further south and west of the factories – mainly to get up-wind of the smoke – and how in the process they actually could not see the proletarian slums from the main road. In Engels's time the slums were as close as Irish Town – where he went to find his colleen mistresses – and there were still slums at Chorlton-cum-Medlock when I first came here twenty-five years ago. By then some of the old bourgeois districts had turned into slums: Hulme, All Saints and Moss Side, which was a West Indian quarter. All these have been flattened and replaced by a wilderness of high-rise estates and car-parks. Beyond the University, which has been modernised and made hideous, you come to Chorlton-on-Hardy, Fallowfield, Withington and Didsbury, all of which remain rather pleasant leafy suburbs of bed-sitting rooms, small flats and boarding houses. It is a pleasant segment of peace between the motorways that radiate out of Manchester. The Palatine Road, which leads south from Withington village, used to be nick-named the Palestine Road after the many Sephardic Jews who came to this area at the turn of the century; they were then considered a cut above the Ashkenasi Jews of North–East Manchester, who were refugees from the pogroms and prejudice of East Europe. The Sephardic Jews, mostly from Spain and North Africa, suffered a fall in fortune during the 1920s which had something to do with textile exports. When I first came here, Withington was then no longer a smart place to live for a family man. Even Didsbury, once the Hampstead of Manchester, had declined. The successful people,

Jewish or gentile, had moved over the border into Cheshire, thus ful-
filling Engels's prophecy.

There is a plaque to Engels now on the site where he lived – a
block of flats known as 'Toblerone' because its triangular shape
resembles the bar of chocolate of that name. Over the last fifteen
years, ever since Marxism was once more taken up by the English
middle classes, as many as four different people have run conducted
tours of 'Engels's Manchester'. One of these tour leaders was an
orthodox Russian Communist; two were from different Trotskyist
sects; a fourth was a most attractive girl who has also written a book
on sex for schoolchildren. Engels would not approve of our modern,
liberated girls. He liked women for sex alone, 'as sex objects'. He also
enjoyed champagne and fox-hunting. In fact one gets the impression
he hated the Manchester bourgeoisie because they were puritans who
did not enjoy the fruit of their wealth. He also disliked the Jews,
which put him at enmity with most of the Manchester German
colony. He sneered at the money they spent on building a shrine to
Schiller.

But Engels did contribute to the fund to build the Town Hall and
the Albert Memorial standing before it. When the Town Hall was
opened in 1877, the Lancashire statesman John Bright said that 'no
building in Europe could equal it in costliness and grandeur', and
the Tory Disraeli called Manchester 'the most wonderful city of
modern times . . . Manchester is as great a human achievement as
Athens. It is the philosopher alone who can conceive the grandeur of
Manchester and the immensity of its future.' Even twenty-five years
ago there was something grand about the Town Hall and those who
held the position of mayor. The grandest of these was Alderman
Leslie Lever, also the Labour MP for Ardwick, who used to proceed
round Albert Square like a king, bowing and waving acknowledge-
ments to the real or fancied cheers and greetings of Manchester
citizens. Whenever he gave you a lift in his mayoral car, and you
thanked him for it, he used to brush away your remarks with the
pious answer: 'Why shouldn't we do good to one another, here on
earth?' He loved to shake hands, or to 'press the flesh' as Americans
say – especially with churchmen. It was said in his constituency that
he attended as many as five different church services every Sunday,
including concerts of the Salvation Army; at the re-opening of the
Anglican Cathedral (it had been bombed during the war) Alderman

Lever stopped the procession down the aisle to shake hands with the Archbishop of York; he was a friend of Matt Busby, the manager of Manchester United, always a Catholic Irish team, and he became the first Jew in England to gain a Papal knighthood.

All Manchester people loved Albert Square. They gathered there each New Year's Eve to sing Auld Lang Syne and to kiss the girls; and every New Year's Day the *Manchester Guardian* carried a light-hearted article on what the statues of Albert and Gladstone thought of such debauchery. Today the statue of Albert is crumbling away and may not be saved in spite of the money raised to restore it; the acrid fumes and the fog have been too much for it. The Town Hall too seems to have lost some of its grandeur, in spite of, or maybe because of, having been cleaned. The old muck really suggested money.

The Manchester motto, much displayed in the Town Hall, is *Concilio et Labore* – through council and work. Bees, the symbol of work, are seen in the floor mosaic. The pride of Manchester Art Gallery is an enormous painting called 'Work' by Ford Madox Brown, who also did the historical series in the Town Hall. The frame round the canvas – of brawny, sweating men and their no less diligent womenfolk – is inscribed with biblical maxims: 'I must work while it is still day. For the night cometh when no man may work'; 'Seest thou a man diligent in his business. He shall stand before Kings'; 'In the sweat of thy face shalt thou eat bread'; 'Neither do we eat any man's bread for nought but wrought with labour and travail night and day'. While looking at this painting, I once heard a voice behind me exclaim 'Work! They don't know what it means today. Ergophobia, that's what we suffer from.' It was an elderly gentleman, much displeased with the younger generation.

When I lived in Manchester I grew heartily tired of the locals who lectured me, as a southerner, on how hard they had worked in their youth, rising at five to work in the mill and spending their evenings at night school. I loved to catch them out in laziness. For example, a friend of mine who worked for a Yugoslav newspaper was asked by a Manchester businessman to visit his factory at half-past eight the following morning. The Yugoslav arrived at the set time and was told by a secretary that her boss never got in till half-past ten, and then only three days a week. A facetious sign in a Manchester club once read: 'In the interests of economy, will the last businessman to leave

Britain please switch off the lights'. Not surprisingly, Manchester
people have tended to drink deeply, first to relieve the misery of their
lives and later, simply to get drunk.

As Engels said, 'Drink is the only thing which makes the Irishman's
life worth having, drink and his cheery carefree temperament.' The
Irish were notorious for the consumption of rot-gut 'potheen', potato
spirit made in illicit stills; but drink was an escape for everyone in
Manchester. A hundred years ago, it was reckoned that every man,
woman and child in England consumed thirty-four gallons of beer a
year, not to mention gin and other spirits. Consumption was far the
highest in Manchester, where the city's population of 400,000 was
served by 475 public houses and 1143 beer houses. Even in this
century, when conditions had much improved, it was customary for a
man to drink eight pints of beer a day *at work*, so that most workshops employed a boy full time just to carry the drink from the pub.
The feast of St Monday (a holiday with a weekend hangover) was a
feature of Manchester life – and still is in Sydney, though there it is
known as a 'sickie'. When I first went to work in Manchester, I was
often puzzled at hearing the locals say that 'Manchester is easy to get
out of', because in fact it required a long journey to reach proper
countryside. Only after a year or two did I understand that 'to get out
of Manchester' means to get drunk. They used to have an expression
here – 'he'd sup out of a sweaty clog'. The American journalist
Negley Farson, who started life as an engineer in Manchester, has
described in his autobiography, *The Way of a Transgressor*, how
proud of their work and their product were his colleagues; he also
begins one chapter: 'It was in Manchester that I learned to drink.'

People in Manchester still drink, but they no longer work, or at
any rate not at anything useful or profitable. And yet it was work,
however oppressive and exploited, that made Manchester famous
throughout the world. Work, and muck and money. The very name
of Manchester has become symbolic, so that often abroad I have
been welcomed to some industrial city proudly described as the
'Manchester of Poland' or 'the Manchester of Korea'. The spinning
and weaving of cloth was never as big in Manchester as in neighbouring towns, but now the garment industry too is in decline. The textile
machinery works have long been closed, as have most of the other
engineering firms; the docks have declined even faster than Liverpool's; the number of people engaged in all kinds of manufacture has

11

fallen by 50,000 over the last twenty years, and not for want of capital for investment.

Engels, of course, wanted to see the ruin of Manchester capitalism, and prophesied that 'King Cotton' would steadily lose territory to foreign competitors. Indeed, it survived in the first half of this century only through tariffs on imports from rivals such as Japan and the suppression of rivals from within the Empire. The Indian Independence movement was feared and disliked in Manchester, so that when Gandhi came on a visit before the last war, there was fear for his physical safety. As late as the Fifties the cotton trade unions were petitioning their local Members of Parliament about the import of textiles from Hong Kong, produced by 'sweated labour' – in other words, in the same conditions of work that had prevailed in Manchester only a few decades earlier.

Today the wheel has come full circle. What remains of the Manchester textile industry has been taken over by just those Asians it used to exploit. Indians and Bangladeshis have taken over the warehouses and the wholesale garment stores. Pakistanis control the market in watches and jewellery that once was controlled by the Jews. All along Great Ducie Street and the Bury New Road, the shop signs are changing from Goldblatt, Solomon or Levine to Singh, Rajah or Bannerjee. A huge mosque has been built in Victoria Park, once a wealthy Jewish housing estate.

Many of the Pakistanis (they are the largest group) arrived in this country very poor, as the Jewish refugees did – indeed some are also refugees from General Amin's Uganda. After saving some capital by working perhaps in a curry restaurant, they buy into a business of wholesale goods, such as oriental souvenirs.

The author of that scholarly book, *The History of Manchester Jewry*, Bill Williams, once told me: 'The Asians started off like the Jews in cheap jewellery, and then they have gone into the production of clothing. Now you get the Asian equivalent of the old Jewish sweat-shop with the women and children hidden away from the factory inspector.' Many of the Asians, like the Jews of the last century, are established merchants in their own countries who have come to Manchester to control their imports at source. The prestige of the Asian buyers was shown in 1976 when, on the centenary of the birth of Jinnah, a banquet was held in the Manchester Club, attended by the Pakistani High Commissioner, the Lord Mayors of

Manchester and Stockport, the Chief Constable of Manchester, and other top dignitaries. The Asian presence is everywhere. As an old Mancunian friend told me, 'One day you'll be walking to work and you'll see a second-hand furniture shop, and the next day you'll find it's a Pakistani bank or a Pakistani sweet shop – you know those sticky cakes they love.' A little Chinatown is growing up behind the Manchester Art Gallery. And, on most days of the week, one can see groups of Japanese tourists photographing the ruins of the industrial revolution.

At this year's meeting, in Salford, the British Association published a lecture by an economist, H. B. Rodgers, on Manchester and its economic troubles, 'A New Industrial Revolution (Deferred)' the thesis of which was that 'the investment surge of 1960 to 1980 had been directed not so much towards reconstructing the economic base . . . as towards rebuilding the urban fabric and remodelling its transport flow' – in other words, knocking down a handsome city and building motorways, tower blocks and the monstrous Arndale Centre, a yellow, grotesquely hideous office and shopping 'complex' that squats on the dead body of Manchester like an enormous spider. Nicknamed 'the largest public lavatory in the world', it comprises two hundred shops, seven major stores, a market hall, bus station, multi-storey car-park, all in a windowless skin of putty-and-chocolate coloured tiles.

Such is the secrecy of our local government, that we may never know how or why this centre was given permission to go ahead; which is a shame, for the complex is not only an eyesore but a frightful waste of money. Only the chain stores can pay the rent and the rates; the absence of windows means an immense cost in electric light; and while the complex was under construction, the people who used to shop in Manchester started to patronise stores in suburban towns like Sale, Stockport, Bury and Rochdale.

The destruction of Manchester was done with intent: the planners and city architects of the late 1950s set out to 'wipe the slate clean' — their phrase — by demolishing every building and starting the city afresh. This plan, the ideal of every greedy architect, did not succeed, but much of historic Manchester was destroyed. The terraced cottages of the poor were the first to go, and good riddance one might say. Certainly some of these houses, especially those from

13

before the year 1880, when damp proofing was introduced, were noisome and even dangerous; in 1955 I went to interview the family of a child who had just been killed when a house fell on top of him. But most of these houses were not slums at all and could have been made into pleasant homes by the addition of bathrooms, lavatories and the like. Even in the 1950s there were quite a few middle-class people who tried unsuccessfully to buy these old working-class houses to do them up, as the middle classes have done in London quarters like Islington or, still more boldly, the Paddington district of Sydney. (Sydney and Edinburgh are the only two cities of the English-speaking world that have almost escaped destruction.)

The planners made no attempt to restore old houses. They bulldozed mile after mile of terraced cottages and built in their place the high-rise, municipal flats which are frequently just as damp as the nineteenth-century slums, as well as being dirty and ravaged by hooligans. A recent report claimed that the 15,000 people who live in the high-rise 'complex' of flats in Hulme, near the old centre of Manchester, suffer seven times the national suicide rate, thirty-one times the crime rate, and forty-one times the murder rate. Drug addiction and racial feuding are rampant. Dozens of residents of these flats have told me that they now wish they were back in their nineteenth-century slums, where at least they knew their neighbours. Manchester's Chief Constable, James Anderton, started work as a constable on the beat in Moss Side, which used to be rather a rough quarter with brothels, drug sellers and West Indian clubs, but he tells me that crime prevention then was easy compared to the present day. If somebody rings from an upstairs flat in Hulme to say that someone is trying to murder him, it is not physically possible, Anderton told me, for the police to go to his help. Remarks like this have made Anderton most unpopular with the Left but very popular with the people of Manchester. He understands clearly the evil done to this country by ideologues who have broken up the traditional system of education, group or religious loyalties, and above all the family, in order to scatter people in 'nuclear families', with no friends and relations, no neighbours, policemen or priests, and only the dubious comfort of crass young social workers.

The destruction of Manchester was not confined to nineteenth-century houses. Most of the old mills and warehouses have gone, to be replaced by skyscrapers. Most of the good pubs have gone: The

Bodega, The Theatre Tavern (with its majestic display of sandwiches), Sam's Chophouse, The Connaught – and even the medieval Wellington. Oliver Cromwell no longer stands on that place by the Irwell where, so it is claimed, the first man was killed in the Civil War. During university rag weeks they used to paint white footprints from Cromwell's statue down to the nearest gents; that tradition is over now, and nobody seems to know where Cromwell's statue has gone; perhaps to some yard like the one I discovered behind a suburban police station in Warsaw filled with gigantic statues of Stalin and Red army soldiers. The Arndale horror now covers the site of the old *Manchester Guardian*, whose owners and editorial staff, instead of exposing this outrage, sold their old offices before moving to London only to lose a lot of money as well as the character of the newspaper. Serve them right!

Even those buildings which have survived demolition have changed their function and purpose. The three great old theatres have been turned into bingo halls while a hideous metal theatre-in-the-round has been placed in the Royal Exchange, a graceful hall across the road from the old *Manchester Guardian*. Even in my day, businessmen in the Royal Exchange still bought and sold cotton around the world; looking up from the theatre to the top of the wall, one can still see the list of closing prices in New York, Hamburg and Sydney. The insertion of this repulsive theatre, which quite destroys the grace of the Royal Exchange, was done, needless to say, at the expense of the tax- and ratepayers. The shift of investment from commerce and industry into building and property speculation is both the cause and effect of decline in Manchester. In Hong Kong, which has taken over from Manchester as the main producer of textiles in the world, the people understand the danger of making money from property, even though land and living space there is in short supply. When, a few years ago, Hong Kong Spinners shut down one of their mills to redevelop the site with a skyscraper building, a Chinese paper rebuked them thus: 'How can hair grow without skin? Industry is the skin, and real estate the hair.'

Talent, as well as investment, has been diverted from industry. The clever, ambitious, or merely greedy young are no longer keen to get into commerce or industry, preferring a soft, well-paid and secure job in the local bureaucracy, which comprises not only the old Manchester Council but Greater Manchester Council, which is housed in a high-rise building behind the Town Hall. The enormous staffs employed by the two councils, as well as the whacking rates they charge, have brought the name of Manchester into ridicule and disgrace. The motto *Concilio et Labore* still hangs in the old Town Hall, and the bees still buzz in the floor mosaic, but few of the bureaucrats do any work. When I was here as a journalist in the 1950s, one could instantly get to see one of the top Town Hall officials, or Leslie Lever, the Mayor himself, but now it is hard to get an interview even with one of the Public Relations officials who, like all their tribe, are adept at preserving secrecy. I called one Friday afternoon about three o'clock at the Town Hall annexe and asked to see one of the Information Staff, only to be informed by the commissionaire that everyone had left for the weekend.

The deterioration of local government, in Manchester as in the rest of England, is almost entirely the fault of Edward Heath and his henchman Peter Walker, who broke up the old counties and brought in the 'two tier' system. I am told by an old friend that when the commission on local government organisation came here to Manchester they considered a plan for re-forming the boroughs and counties according to local support for football teams – so that Manchester would be split into City and United districts. So frivolous, even lunatic, were the men who advised Peter Walker. Today I bumped into an old friend who works in Manchester for the Tory Party. I asked him and his colleague from London if they could give one single justification for Walker's local government reform, and they both said, quite honestly, that they could not. But they do not advocate undoing the mess; restoring the old counties, or sacking the hundreds of thousands of useless bureaucrats. So we, the Secret People, of Chesterton's poem, are doomed to perpetual servitude under Peter Walker and his kind.

They have given us into the hands of the new unhappy lords,
Lords without anger and honour, who dare not carry their swords.
They fight by shuffling papers; they have bright dead alien eyes;
They look at our labour and laughter as a tired man looks at flies.

26 September – Manchester   There are other bureaucrats in this city as useless and harmful as those who work on the councils. The Chief Constable, James Anderton, made a speech last night in which he denounced what he rightly described as the race relations industry, strike picketing rights, and the Sex Discrimination Act. The latter's executive body, the Equal Opportunities Commission, has its headquarters in Manchester – or Personchester as it was dubbed by the wits. A few years ago I called on the offices of the Commission in Quay Street, near to the Free Trade Hall, with a view to writing an article for the *Spectator*. I got to the notice board which carried several appeals by the Society of Civil Servants – 'Fight the Cuts. Save jobs' – and found what is called an Enquiry Office. After explaining who I was to a pleasant lady behind the desk, I was met by a Mr Bob Platt, who told me he worked in the Information Unit. The Unit, Mr Platt explained, was responsible for receiving certain dignitaries such as the head and deputy of the Northern Ireland branch of the Equal Opportunities Commission – they had been in Manchester on the previous day – but it did not provide information to journalists. 'My hands are tied,' Mr Platt told me gravely.

Who could I then speak to, I went on; for nothing so whets the inquisitiveness of reporters as finding that nobody wants to talk to them. I was told:

'Our Press Officer, Bobby Vincent-Amory, who is in London.'

'When is he coming back from London?'

'It's a she. She's permanently in London. Haven't you come across her? She seems to know everybody in London.' I said that no, sadly I had not met Bobby, and that anyway I wanted to speak to people in Manchester; apart from anything else, I wanted to know how civil servants enjoyed being dispersed from London into the provinces.

At last Mr Platt telephoned London – 'Hello, Bobby, this is Bob' – to explain who I was and what I wanted. At one point in the telephone conversation he turned to me and said, 'She wants to know if you're freelance,' to which I said 'Yes, I am.' He said down the phone 'Yes, he is,' and then, turning to me, 'she thought you were,' I felt that in some odd way I had been caught out in an indiscretion. Then Bob handed over the phone to let me talk to Bobby. She impressed upon me the great range and complexity of the work of the Equal Opportunities Commission. She said that I really needed a thorough briefing about its work but this was difficult to arrange as they were short of staff in their publicity department. 'I don't want to sound rude,' she said, 'but there are thousands of people waiting for interviews and we'd prefer to give priority to a paper with a bigger readership than the *Spectator.*'

I said I was interested in the work of the Commission in Manchester and nearby. Bobby said that they were now engaged in the Tameside Inquiry (on the decision by that North Cheshire local authority to resist the replacement of grammar by comprehensive schools), presumably over allegations that not enough girls got grammar school places. However, Bobby explained that as an inquiry was under way, any comment upon it could lead to a fine of £400.

The telephone conversation ended when Bobby said that I might be granted an interview with Mr Nandi of the Commission in Manchester, provided I first wrote a letter to say what kind of questions I wanted to ask. I declined this offer. No journalist should agree to write out his questions beforehand and anyway, I had read of Mr Nandi in *Private Eye*, from the days when he worked on another senseless quango, the United Kingdom Immigrants Advisory Service.

The Commission is useless and risible; also, I think, really harmful. It puts down women by making them feel ashamed of their natural enjoyment of caring for children, housework and skills such as sewing. It tells women they ought not to work in the textile industry but instead should be engineers or truck drivers; but most women because of their nature *enjoy* and are specially good at work with textiles. By filling the heads of women with grievances about equal rights, the Commission has actually made it harder for women to get jobs, since employers resent being obliged by law to pay out pregnancy leave, for example. The meddling of the Commission has broken down the goodwill and the private arrangements which used to obtain in most firms between employers and women employees.

The Commission is not just harmful but actually wicked in its attempt to abolish 'sexual stereotypes' among children. Take, for example, its leaflet issued to primary schools entitled 'Do you provide Equal Educational Opportunities?' It tells teachers to consider 'aspects of early activities' very carefully. These include

sex-stereotyped play activities. (Are the doctors, astronauts, Red Indian chiefs, pirates, policemen etc. always boys? Are the nurses, hairdressers, shop assistants, aeroplanes stewards, teachers etc. always girls?) . . . Do boys always carry the milk crates? In thematic work, do girls always investigate clothes, food, home life etc?

And so on. We, the sophisticated readers, find this amusing, perhaps at the worst annoying. We tend to forget that a whole generation of children have been subjected to propaganda based on a false view of human nature which can be upsetting, will tend to make them humourless prigs, and, worst of all, will deprive them of childhood, that world of imagination and fantasy, so remote from the joyless bureaucracy of the Equal Opportunities Commission.

27 September – Manchester   Manchester City and United are playing each other today. 'Which ground are they playing on,' I asked at the pub, and was told, 'You don't want to go there. Football's ruined. I haven't been to a match for seven years. My mother, she's eighty, she lives near Maine Road [the City ground] and I'm worried whenever they have a match there, you'd never believe the damage they do – windows smashed all down the street, worse than the bombing, and Maine Road had its share of bombs. I'm not an admirer of Russian communism but I do wish we had their penal system. Send the football hooligans off to Siberia for five years, to work their knackers off. They wouldn't come back for more. When I was a boy we used to take sides for City and United. We'd bet with conkers, three conkers that City would win, but we didn't fight about it. Now the young fellows just go for the punch-up. They don't care if their own side wins or loses. They just want a fight – knives, darts, stones, what have you. And the football players are all stars – £500 or £700 a week. Can you imagine Bobby Charlton getting that money? Do you know in Millwall in London, some of the football hooligans are tied up with the National Front? I think that all the National Front should be shot, along with the IRA and all those right-wing terrorists.'

28 September – Manchester   The Sunday papers have taken up the remarks of James Anderton concerning the race relations industry, and how it is infiltrated by people who want to provoke hatred between the West Indians and the whites, as represented by the police force. What he says is correct: the Anti-Nazi League and the other militant spokesmen of British 'blacks' – as they call both Asians and people of African origin – have always presented policemen as enemies. Last summer one of their lawyers declared that immigrants

19

should refuse to take part in police identification parades, or give the police any other assistance in bringing criminals to justice. Statements like this, which suggest that the West Indians want a separate law for themselves, can only serve to make them more unpopular. Immigrants to any country, especially if they are identifiable by their colour of skin, have to be extra careful to abide by the custom and law prevailing there. In the case of the Jews, the Irish and, more recently, those from the Indian sub-continent, the provenance of a person was clear from the name. The *Manchester Guardian*, in 1836, reported the case of 'an Israelite named Reiss who defrauded a lodging-house keeper of £3.' The newspaper got a laugh out of a Jewish pedlar who stole a ham, and also out of the pickpocket Isaac Jacob, who told the police 'Me hungry belly, no moneysh; so me took tic-toc.'

The modern *Guardian*, like most newspapers, refrains from stating the racial origins of a person appearing in court; indeed one might be open to prosecution for printing words that could arouse ill-will against some ethnic group. I think it wrong and dangerous that fear or dislike of an immigrant group should not find expression in print. It was largely because of the bad publicity, of the kind that I quoted from the old *Manchester Guardian*, that the Manchester Jewish community purged itself of ill-doers, of Fagins. Jewish criminals learned to fear Jewish jurors. Habitual beggars and thieves were packed off to America. As a result the Jewish community won the respect of the people of Manchester. Nor did they think it odd that the *Manchester Guardian* made fun of Jewish criminals, though they resented the *MG*'s rabid anti-semitism during the Boer War. They accepted the shame of their evil-doers, just as they took a pride in Jews who won honour and fame – like Leslie and Harold Lever.

The present ban on mentioning racial differences undoubtedly has something to do with shock at Hitler's massacre of the Jews; but it is nevertheless unwise. Although we may no longer write about it in newspapers, the Jews remain a distinct people in English life, in most ways admirable but in some ways different. And just as, in the 1830s, the Jews tended to be pickpockets and fences, so in modern England, they are heavily represented in property speculation, trading with eastern Europe, and Harold Wilson's resignation honours. They are also prominent in the Trotskyist parties and in the sex industry.

There may be an explanation of why some Jews go in for such anti-social behaviour, but I think it a pity that these days one cannot even discuss the question. All attempts to ban expressions of racial prejudice are bound to inflame that prejudice. Because the newspapers decline to print the race of, for instance, muggers in South London or Birmingham, many readers assume they are all West Indians, whose origin does not come across in their names; I have heard this said by many people throughout the country. The foolish or mischievous folk of the race relations industry do no good to the young West Indians by telling them that their crimes are not their own fault but that of 'society'; that they are therefore accountable to a different law from the rest. Such differential treatment of a minority in this country can only annoy the rest of us and make us resent the immigrants. But that, as Mr Anderton rightly said, is the aim of some people engaged in the race relations industry.

29 September – Manchester I spent the end of the morning pleasantly occupied in a pub near the art gallery, in conversation with the barman, a Scot and former seaman, another Scot, a young man from Rochdale, a postman and a commercial traveller with a big grin and a hopelessly ill-fitting set of false teeth. The conversation started off with last Saturday's football match and the evergreen topic of why the Manchester fans include so many hooligans. As usual the public blamed the players for setting a bad example – 'the trouble begins on the pitch' – and went on to say that most United fans were not from the city at all, 'You've got them in Malta,' the barman said, 'and 10,000 out in Australia. I've seen them in Brisbane.' We went on to talk about the phenomenon of football managers, who now have the glamour and publicity that was once reserved for the players. This first manifested itself in the shape of Matt Busby, the manager of United, who was badly burned in the plane crash in Munich in 1956. His fight for life, his recovery and the way he rebuilt the team made him a national hero, although I must add that the first game played by United after the crash was the foulest and most brutal I ever saw. From then on, Busby and Leslie Lever became joint monarchs of Manchester, representing the coalition of Irish and Jewish interests in the city.*

* Busby himself is a Scot.

21

Conversation turned to the next generation of football manager stars such as Revie, 'Big Mal' Allison* and Brian Clough — successes and failures, sexual adventures, court disputes and trips to work in the Persian Gulf. Like Chief Constables, football managers seem to be bobbing up in the press and the TV to talk about things like religion and trade union reform which have only tangential relationship to their work.

The conversation turned to the war over oil between Iran and Iraq. The barman made the point that Russia and South Africa stood to gain from the crisis, since any threat to the oil supply sent up the price of gold. The war reminded somebody of that fought by Peru and Chile over a desert of phosphate and bird-dirt. 'Yes,' someone added, 'and all the generals and admirals on either side had Irish names.' That was good for a laugh. In spite of the IRA and the centuries of war and hatred, the English still think of the Irish as funny. Even after the pub bombings five years ago, there was only occasional anger displayed to the Irish in this country. They remain a very well-liked minority group and I think they enjoy living in England, as well as making a living here, which is why they have tended to turn in the IRA bombers and gunmen.

The mention of South American Irishmen prompted the ex-sailor to tell of a bar called O'Reilly's in Panama, whose manager of that name was a huge coal-black Negro. And then he told us a very good Irish joke: 'Did you hear about the Irish onion? When you peel it, it makes you laugh.' Then somebody told a joke about Negroes in the southern United States; the tone of the joke was friendly. This summer I met some people from Manchester who were on holiday in Miami and asked me about the Test Match: although they supported England, they wanted Clive Lloyd, the West Indian captain, to make a century; he plays for Lancashire and is very popular here. Altogether one hears less racialist talk in Manchester than in London; and less than I can recall from twenty-five years ago.

The conversation this morning turned to the current Labour Party dispute at the Blackpool conference. It was pleasant to find that the random group of people shared my own distrust and dislike of politicians of all political parties, and all shades of opinion, from Wedgwood Benn to Ian Paisley. 'How do they think they're going to get us

* A few weeks later I learned of Mr Allison's sacking from City under the headline 'BIG MAL AXED'.

out of the Common Market? Labour got us in the bloody thing. And they're not going to give it up when all those jobs and tax-free perks are there for the picking. Look at Barbara Castle! She opposes the Common Market and then becomes a Euro MP. She's done well out of politics, she has.' The commercial traveller said: 'There was a boy at school with me who was in a special class for backward children. Now he's an MP, and quite famous. What a horrible lot of people.' This was a few hours before the debate in Blackpool, when Benn and his equally horrid enemies in the right wing of the party were mouthing their rival brands of stale but dangerous slogans. Is Benn bad and mad, or just mad? The debate goes on. He was the man who landed us with Concorde, and subsidies to the *Scottish Daily Express* as well as the Meriden motorbike works which, I see from today's paper, is finally going bust. Good riddance.

30 September – Manchester – Oldham   In the late evening I go on to Oldham, a once proud mill town that now has been merged into Greater Manchester – although taxi-drivers charge time and a half for this 'out of town' drive. William Cobbett was once MP for the town and so, much later, was Winston Churchill; elections here used to be rowdy and stirring. Now it is deader than Manchester. When I worked for the *Manchester Guardian*, Oldham was one of the places you came to see life: the worst old slums, the back-to-backs, with their outdoor communal lavatories. Conditions in some of these hovels were rightly denounced, but even in those days we knew that high-rise blocks of flats were not the proper alternative; I can remember writing a story in Oldham about a high-rise block which had been vandalised and some of its residents terrorised and depressed within a few months of its opening. I don't claim that I saw the danger clearly as early as that: like most people I wanted to think that anything would be preferable to the old slums; I hoped that people would get used to life in the high-rise flats. It was not till the early 1960s that some of us journalists – like the young Christopher Booker – came to see clearly the madness of planners and modern architects. Twenty years later, even some of our politicians have grasped the truth.

There seem to be acres of open land in Oldham, perhaps where the slums were destroyed and nothing put in their place. As a result, the wild life has come back in force; the dawn chorus of birds outside

B

my hotel seemed to contain a huge range of voices, among them the night-jar. A night-jar in Oldham! The town seems rather empty compared to what I remember. I was last here on a Saturday early in 1958. The local football team, Athletic, were playing at home, and I had been detailed to write one of those folksy bits that the *MG* liked on the eating and drinking habits of people before and after the match. It seemed that the favourite drink was sarsparilla; the favourite food, raw tripe sprinkled with vinegar, and eaten out of an evening newspaper. The speciality of the North was something called 'slut tripe', grey in colour, which looked like an old and filthy bath towel, cut into segments. At times like this I came to believe in the concept of North and South as two different nations that never could understand one another. I liked the tripe you used to get in the chain cafés, but raw slut tripe was too much even for one whose palate and stomach can face most tests.

1 October – Oldham   The day in Oldham began with a rainy mist that twenty-five years ago would have brought with it fog, bronchitis and burning throat. But now the mill chimneys have gone with the sarsparilla and tripe. The chimneys are not just inactive; they have been knocked down, although I am told that some sentimentalist in the region has taken to buying up and preserving mills, hiring steeplejacks to keep the chimneys in constant repairs.

Consider these statistics: at the outbreak of the First World War, this town of Oldham alone had as many cotton spindles as France and Germany put together and half as many as all the United States of America. At that time 600,000 people were employed in spinning, doubling and weaving, as well as a further 100,000 in cotton-related trades, so that about one quarter of all the United Kingdom's exports, in value, was due to cotton yarn and cloth. Now the United Kingdom ranks pretty low among European textile producers; let alone Asia.

The German socialist, Friedrich Engels, predicted clearly what was to happen. In a new preface to the British edition of *The Condition of the Working Classes in England*, written in 1892, he explained how the boom of the 1850s and 1860s had come from the opening up of new markets for English goods: 'In India millions of hand-weavers were finally crushed out by the Lancashire power loom.' But, he went on,

The Free Trade theory was based upon one assumption, that England was to be the one great manufacturing centre of an agricultural world. And the actual fact is that this has turned out to be a poor delusion. The condition of modern industry, steampower and machinery can be established wherever there is fuel, especially coals. And other countries beside England – France, Belgium, Germany, America, even Russia – have coals.

Perhaps even Bright, the very embodiment of the Free Trade theory, had gloomy moments and lost his faith in continued progress, as when, at the opening of the Manchester Town Hall in 1877, he warned that great cities had fallen long before Manchester was even known. Once, after seeing round a ruined castle, Bright asked himself 'How long will it be before our great warehouses and factories in Lancashire are as complete a ruin as this castle?' Almost exactly a hundred years is the answer.

It is popular wisdom here that the textile industry was destroyed by unfair competition, coming from India after the First World War, Japan, and, after the Second World War, from other East Asian countries like Hong Kong, South Korea and Taiwan. It is also assumed that when we lost our African empire, we automatically lost that sale of gaudily coloured Lancashire cloth, as well as of Birmingham metal trinkets, which Stanley had said was England's reward for clothing the shameful nakedness of the pagan Negro.

This argument simply does not stand up. The Far Eastern countries still hold only a small part of the world trade in textiles, which mostly comes from Western Europe and the United States. These countries have to compete with Hong Kong on the same terms as Britain, but make little fuss about it. The countries of Africa still do not produce their own cloth; they import it, but no longer from Lancashire.

Whatever is wrong with the Lancashire textile business cannot be blamed, for once, on trade unions, South-east Lancashire has never been cursed by the inter-union squabbles, political agitation and sheer bloody-mindedness which brought south-west Lancashire to a state of collapse. For one thing, the great majority of the work force in the textile industry have always been women, who stay admirably hostile to all attempts by middle-class feminists and political agitators to fill them with grievances about their rights. There has always been a tradition in Lancashire that girls go to the mills until they marry and then return to them as a kind of relief from the boredom and loneliness of the home. Anyone who has tried to employ a char – that is a working-class, middle-aged woman of the traditional kind – will find that they ask twice the money to work on their own as to work in the company of their friends. Lancashire women enjoy the comradeship of their work-mates and, like those gangs of cockney chars that you see on the buses in London, can turn the air blue with their language. Young men who went to work in a Lancashire mill were frequently debagged and treated to coarse jokes by these lecherous ladies.

Even today, in a time of recession, Lancashire women boycott employers they do not like. They will work very well for a boss who offers crèches, days off work for family problems, and general kindness and sympathy. Today's Rochdale *Observer* carries the story that '32 girls at Bowker Bros., Whitworth, have taken a 50 per cent pay cut for two months to help save their jobs. The firm's chairman Mr J. Bowker said: "We are just like a family. The girls are doing everything they can to help save the firm."' It gives one reason to hope that ordinary Lancashire women have not swallowed the poisonous notions presented to them by the Equal Opportunities Commission.

So what is wrong with the Lancashire textile trade? From reading the trade press, especially the magazine *Asia Textile*, which gives the view of the Hong Kong producers, I get the impression that what is wrong with our textile business is much the same as what is wrong with the country at large. As I mentioned a few days ago, much of the money and human talent that might have gone into industry has gone respectively into property, and unproductive jobs in bureaucracy. In the textile industry, as in the car industry, brewing and newspapers – not to mention the nationalised industries – there has been an unhealthy tendency towards mergers into bigger and bigger units, whose bureaucrats and centralised management have little aptitude for change or initiative. The craze for 'economics of scale' was rampant in the 1960s with both the Conservative and the Labour Party, and encouraged a number of takeover bids in which the big fish swallowed the small. The big six breweries took over all but a few of the thousands of family firms; provincial papers were merged or closed as the Fleet Street giants grew fewer and more gigantic; the Leyland company, much praised then for its 'dynamism', took over, and most of the other motor firms – with the result we know. In the textile industry, especially during the change from cotton to man-made fibres, most of the old family firms were bought up by Courtauld's and ICI, the second of which then tried to take over the first. This 'rationalisation', as it was known in the jargon word of the time, does not seem to have helped the textile industry: at least eight Courtauld textile factories have been shut in the last few weeks alone.

When I rang up the Courtauld public relations department in London, and asked the reason for the closures, a grave voice answered 'We do not comment at times like this. It's been very traumatic.' In other words, a private enterprise public relations person, just like his fellows in government, believes it his duty *not* to inform the press and public what has gone wrong; rather to cover up the company failings. So one has to turn for news to *Asia Textile*, in which I read of a recent report by the International Labour Organisation:

Whereas Japan, West Germany and the NICs [new industrial countries] are capable of altering their industrial patterns and building on their advantages, Britain seems tied to an out-of-date and old-fashioned system. Post-war governments are roundly criticised for putting too much effort to make things easy for the declining industries and doing too little to encourage the growing ones ready to absorb the displaced labour. By contrast Germany, which does not featherbed its threatened industries, has gained 20 jobs by exporting goods to the Third World for every job lost through cheap imports.

So much for the threat from Hong Kong.

Asia Textile also contains a report by the Clothing Industry Productivity Resources Agency in Leeds suggesting that

the British clothing industry could reduce its prices, increase its profits and pay better wages, simply by using better manufacturing methods, employing fewer indirect staff, making wage systems more sophisticated, and by having better control. In a study made . . . one German company included for comparison was able to compete in the British market in spite of paying wages twice as high as the British average.

That last point is the one that tells. It is not true, as some Conservatives think, that British industry has been priced out of the market by greedy trade unionists. Some of our workers are poorly paid compared to those on the Continent or even further abroad. The textile workers of the East are no longer sweated labour. In Hong Kong early last year I learned that a woman straight off one of the refugee boats from Vietnam, can easily get a job at £25 a week, tax free. In Thailand, a less prosperous country, the women workers get two US dollars (80p) an hour minimum wage – which is not bad compared to the £1.30 an hour which is what you see advertised here in employment exchanges.

2 October – Rochdale My mind was full of such matters even before coming to Rochdale, the birthplace and long the home of Bright. His statue is everywhere; in the Town Hall (only a shade less huge and magnificent than that of Manchester itself), on a plinth in the main park, and even in waxwork form in the John Bright Room of the Rochdale Museum. This room is full of presents and testimonials given to him by businessmen for getting rid of the Corn Laws; it displays his letter of resignation to Gladstone; his face, intelligent but a bit austere, even priggish, appears in several portraits. I feel I know Bright best from the portrait of him in Trollope's Palliser books. He was the mentor of Phineas Finn and encouraged him to resign on the question of Irish land reform; how right Trollope was to see that particular question was far more important than all the noisy debate on reform in England itself.

In case one is tempted to think that Bright was merely a windbag and demagogue – a kind of nineteenth-century Benn – one has only to seek out the Everyman volume of his speeches. In that book nothing is finer or, to a modern reader, more poignant than the address Bright gave to the workers of Rochdale on 2 January 1877. He told them about the struggle, thirty years earlier, to repeal the Corn Laws and other taxes on imported goods; of the suffering of those days when the 'Corn-law rhymer' Ebenezer Elliott wrote:

> Bread-taxed weaver, all may see
> What that tax hath done for thee.
> And thy children vilely led,
> Singing hymns for shameful bread.
> Till the stones of every street
> Know their little naked feet.

He went on to tell them of the enormous benefit they had gained from the banning of import duties; how the consumption of butter had risen from 1lb to 5lb for every person, of cheese from 1lb to 5½lb, of rice from 1lb to 11lb, of potatoes from nothing to 16lb (he was harking back to the Irish potato famine), of sugar from 15lb to 53lb, and of wheat flour from 42lb to 197lb. Nor were the gains simply material. 'Look at what has taken place in this country with regard to the means of education,' Bright went on. Now everyone had a news-paper if he so wished, thanks to the end of the excise duty:

Take the *Evening News* published in Manchester, or the *Manchester Examiner*, or your paper here, the *Observer*. Every paper of that sort cost 7d then; now it costs ½d, or 1d at the most . . . And now what an excellent machine, what an admirable thing a good newspaper is!

he continued, listing their coverage of all the affairs of moment throughout the five continents. He praised the efficiency of the trains, of the posts and telegraph.

Bright went on to warn those who thought that trade unions would set everything right:

I am of the opinion that trade unions may be useful if they will not depart from sound economic principles, and if they will not interfere with the indi-vidual freedom of their members or the freedom of those who have the employment of capital. Last year . . . I pointed to the fact that there is no class of persons whose wages have risen more in the last twenty years than the class of [women] domestic servants, and amongst domestic servants there are no trade unions, no committees, no orators to expound their interests and maintain their causes

– and no Equal Opportunities Commission.

Today the unions clamour for import controls, especially on tex-tiles. When it was learnt this summer that House of Commons barmen were issued with jackets made in Hong Kong, the Labour MP for Blackburn, Jack Straw, complained that 'when Lancashire mills are closing at the rate of one a week, this is an incredible insult to management and workforce who are struggling so hard.' The general secretary of the Tailors and Garment Workers said that guests to their annual dinner would have the labels on their clothes inspected and those wearing foreign-made dresses or suits would be made to 'feel uncomfortable'. As a representative of the Hong Kong workers put it (I quote once again from *Asia Textile*), 'They [the countries of the western world] do not like to give up the industries of the eighteenth century and they still want to monopolize the industries of the twenty-first.'

The Cotton Board used to try exhortation – 'Britain's bread hangs on Lancashire's thread' – and here in Rochdale I saw some of the fatuous 'Buy British' slogans prepared by British Leyland and paid for by the taxpayer. If propaganda is backed by import controls, the mass of the public will suffer. The British Retail Consortium, speaking for our shopkeepers, said this year that import controls (from countries in Asia) had favoured higher price imports from Europe, had hurt the high-street consumer and in particular pushed up the price of children's clothing . . . *Till the stones of every street/Know their little naked feet.*

3 October – Rochdale – Bolton – Wigan   People in Rochdale are worse off now than they were; but at least some of them now seem to know the reason why. At a queue in the bus for Bolton, a group of old ladies wanted to know what the fare was; I was the only paying passenger. 'It must be 30p or 40p' said one (it was actually 80p). 'I really pity the people who work. I don't mean the skivers, I mean the people who have to pay tax and insurance stamps and their fares to work. That's why so many people choose to skive. But Maggie's got the right idea for this country.'

Last night I went to a pub in the city centre and found that the top bar was almost empty. The barman, who came from Northern Ireland, said that half the time he was on his own. 'Not long ago, we'd have all three bars full from opening time in the morning till closing time at night. But now they stay home. It's not the pub – you can see just the same at The Flying Horse, where you're staying – it's simply the price of beer.' The conversation turned to the film *McVicar* – which concerns prison life in England – and one of the two other customers proved to be an authority on this subject: 'You know what they say about child molesters getting attacked by the other prisoners? Well it's true. I've recently been in Strangeways [Manchester prison], and the screws tipped us off when a child molester was coming. The lads poured water all over his bedding to stop him getting any sleep. They beat him up in the shower with wet towels.' From there the conversation turned, as it often does in this part of the world, to the 'Moors Murderers', the man and woman from Manchester who tortured children and then buried their bodies out in the countryside. The murderer, Myra Hindley, found a champion in the Earl of Longford, but I have never heard anyone in the Manchester region who thinks she should get a pardon. One of the reasons for the popularity of the Manchester Chief Constable, James Anderton, is that he has tried with some success to ban the kind of sadistic pornography (much of it dealing with children) on which the Moors Murderers fed their imaginations.

These remarks came back to me in Bolton when I read in today's papers of how a social worker in charge of a council home in Haringey in North London had distributed marijuana to children in care and had gone to bed with a thirteen-year-old girl. It turned out that when he was hired by Haringey Council he was on parole after serving a five-year sentence for armed robbery under arms. I wondered how even Haringey Council could have given such a job to such a man until I opened the *Daily Telegraph* and saw from the picture of the convicted man that he was a Negro: perhaps this was a case of Haringey applying 'reverse discrimination', or preference to a coloured person, regardless of qualification? It does seem hard, though, on children in council care, especially when they are often taken away from their parents for no reason except to appease the lust for power of professional social workers. There was a case in the newspapers two years ago of a woman whose child was taken into care because, at the age of three, it still could not talk and was lacking in what the social worker described as the proper 'motor skills'. This monstrous sentence upon the mother, who even the magistrate admitted loved her child, took place in Winchester. Probably there are dozens of cases each week when children are seized in this fashion by the state; it is a commonplace in Sweden. The councils in London which go in for seizing children into care, as it is misleadingly called, will not provide even the simplest information about which children are taken and why. One learns of this only when somebody comes up in court like today's criminal social worker. Sometimes it is the children in care who come up in court, like the West Indian boys last year who got drunk in their council home and raped one of the resident lady social workers. Was I the only person in England who found that story grimly amusing?

The talk of child molesters and hanging reminded me of what I was told I should see in Bolton: this was The Last Drop Inn, so called I was told at Granada Television, because it was kept by the hangman Albert Pierrepoint. I dimly remembered from years ago that Pierrepoint had kept a pub, from which he would journey to all those parts of the world, notably Singapore and some of the ex-British West Indies, where capital punishment stayed in force and his expertise was desirable.

Pierrepoint was a much respected man in Lancashire. Hanging was widely approved as punishment for convicted murderers. So was flogging. Lancashire people often point to the Isle of Man as a place where they know how to deal, by birching, with young offenders. Although I knew of this predeliction for punishment, I did not expect to find that The Last Drop Inn had become an hotel and shopping centre, complete with the Bumbles Bistro, a flea market, art gallery, antique shop, village tea shop, hair designers and North-West Tourist Information Centre. The rooms are booked up weeks in advance, largely by people from the United States and Australia; there is a framed letter from Mrs Thatcher thanking The Last Drop for all they did for her during her stay in 1978.

The hour I spent at The Last Drop caused me to brood on the English passion for hanging. Why did the public approve this especially gruesome form of execution? Why was its abolition so bad for sales of popular newspapers? I used to know an elderly former convict, a confidence man, who made a living by getting interviews with convicted murderers: he normally posed as a clergyman but he found he could also pose as a personal friend, an ex-army chum, or a schoolmate. I remember meeting him once in his favourite Fleet Street pub – since destroyed – still wearing his clerical collar after a day at Wormwood Scrubs and holding a letter from a murderess awaiting execution in Manchester. 'Dear Reverend,' the letter began, 'I shall be on my knees tonight praying for you.' 'Silly bitch!' he exclaimed and borrowed a pound from me to get some more drink. He had letters from most of the famous murderers since the war, from Haig, Heath and Christie: 'a funny little man, the day before he was topped, he was worried about his income tax.' He made a living as long as the death penalty stayed in force; he was billed in one of the Sunday papers as 'Britain's top psychiatrist', but abolition destroyed his career. 'I'm not a believer in hanging,' he told me, 'but this means financial ruin'. I wonder what happened to him; perhaps he returned to his previous work of selling cleanliness certificates to Greek and Italian restaurants.

Asking around, it seems I was misinformed by my friend in Granada Television: The Last Drop had never been owned by Pierrepoint, whose pub had been called The Struggling Man and was variously sited at Oldham, Whitfield and Blackburn. The Last Drop of the title was meant as a reference to an empty glass and had wrongly acquired the sombre significance of the gallows. All this I was told in The Man and Scythe Inn which dates back to the thirteenth century and has its own claim to fame in matters of capital punishment: James, Earl of Derby, spent here the night before his execution on 15 October 1651, and the chair he sat on is still preserved in the pub.

There is an Arndale Centre here, but quite a bit of the old Bolton was spared by the developers. Here, as in Rochdale, Oldham and Manchester, I found the buildings that remain as great a cause of melancholy as the ones that have gone: they remind one only of vanished glory and purpose.

The immense Town Hall is fronted by statues of Chadwick and Dobson – two of the city fathers – and bears in the pediment over the portico the figure of Manufacture holding a distaff, Earth with a cornucopia, and Africa as a piccaninny with a basket of cotton. The main door is locked and inscribed with the aerosol slogan 'I hate JR. and I hate wogs', a reference to the TV villain and to the people of Africa. I entered the Town Hall by its side door and found it still more depressing. The lobby is plastered with dozens of pamphlets issuing from the public relations department of Bolton, of Greater Manchester and of something called the Association of Greater Metropolitan Authorities, the senseless bureaucrats who have been imposed on London, Liverpool, Manchester, Birmingham, Leeds, Sheffield and Newcastle. Their poster says that 'the old industries on which the prosperity of England was built were largely based on these areas. The decline of these industries has left behind formidable problems of dereliction, pollution, unemployment. . . .' But surely the basic problem is the decline of industry? Why has this happened? In large part thanks to the setting up of colossal expensive bureaucracies such as Greater Manchester. All the energy that went into producing wealth is now given to 'job creation' – setting up sinecures – and tidying up the muck which went with producing the money. Here are some of the schemes of a body calling itself 'The Greater Manchester Clean-up Campaign': 'Fill an 'ole in Oldham. Make a play area in Prestwick. Clean a river in Rochdale. Paint a house in Hyde. Grow flowers in Flixton. Use waste ground in Whitefield. Pick up litter in Leigh. Fill a skip in Stockport. Recycle bottles in Bolton. Clear a canal in Collyhurst. Demolish an eyesore in Eccles. Make Manchester immaculate.' But not, of course, cleanse the graffiti on Bolton Town Hall. At 10.15 I looked into the Town Hall chamber and found it empty. I looked into the bar – for 'staff and councillors only' – and found it packed. Arts Council pamphlets quote the asinine words of its chairman to the effect that most people need arts as they need food and drink. True: but the arts, like food and drink, have to be paid for. Why did Bolton need to build the preposterous Octagon Theatre, opened in 1967 by Princess Margaret; or indeed the Pedestrian Precinct, which so I am told, won awards from Heritage Year, the Manchester Society of Architects and the Concrete Society. What in the name of heaven is the Concrete Society? Bolton is well aware of its heritage: there are all kinds of booklets and books on industrial archaeology. They keep up the tomb of Samuel Crompton, who made the first spinning mule, and the shop where Richard Arkwright worked as a barber before he invented the spinning jenny. There is even a Samuel Crompton bistro; but no more mules in action.

An engineer I met in The Man and Scythe invited me to a drink at the Socialist Club. This turned out to be in the house where William Lever, later Lord Leverhulme, was born. The irony did not escape my socialist friends. But the atmosphere of the club was despondent. They were all unhappy about the Labour Party nonsense in Blackpool this week, and the unemployment. 'The whole of Bolton is going to close down. You'll find that gloom all over. Yet we've never had trouble here like in Liverpool. No strikes. No communists. If you go for a job you have to show your union card, but that's the end of it. It's not like Liverpool where they've brought the trouble on themselves.'

Two young men in the club have been working in Holland as fitters. 'If you go into a bar there, you'll find the man next to you is English. Then it turns out that the whole lot are. We do the night shifts and week-ends, the jobs that the Dutch won't take. You come in at half past four on Friday night and work through till Saturday morning and then you get Heinekened. Beer's a pound a pint but it's much stronger than ours. And also there's mad grass – as much as you want. Sometimes I'll go to bed three times a day. I wouldn't work in Germany. There, if you're five minutes late, they dock you an hour's pay.' These migrant workers felt very superior to the Turk, Yugoslav and Portuguese migrant workers in Holland. 'That lot'll work for peanuts,' they said.

In the Socialist Club in Bolton I said I was going on to Wigan and somebody gave me detailed instructions of what to do there: 'Get out at Wallgate Station. There's a good pub on the left. Have one to settle yourself after the ride. Then there's a wine lodge on the right, and just down the road there's a lot of them – all exceptional. Then there's the Ship Hotel. That's where you want to stop.' Needless to say, I never found the Ship Hotel or anywhere else I was told to go. I have never, in all my visits to Wigan, found the pier. I still do not know if there actually is a pier or whether the whole thing is one of those straight-faced Lancastrian jokes that have made Wigan famous. Wigan is the origin of the joke about the miner, Jack, who one year goes for his holiday, not to Blackpool like his workmates, but to Paris. Back at work, Jack is secretive about the experience. But, at last, on a Saturday night at the working men's club, two of the younger men are deputed to ply Jack with beer and get him to talk about Paris. For many pints he is silent, and then he says, 'I'll tell you one thing about Paris. Fooking's only in its infancy in Wigan.'

The bedroom of the Grand Hotel has fire instructions in French and German as well as in English: 'Ne vous affolez pas. Soyez calme et rapide, vous sauvrez peut-etre des vies. Den Kopf nichy [*sic*] verlieren. Ein ruhiges verhalten und sofortiges handeln konnen leben rettes.' The bar of the same hotel has a comic plaque purporting to be from the Grand Hotel, Cairo, saying 'Will guests requiring of partners for sleeping purposes, male female both please most kindly request the desk of reception.' The barmaid filled me in on what has happened to Wigan since I was last here twenty-odd years ago. 'They've closed down the old Empire dance hall, they're knocking it down. It's going to be a municipal leisure centre. They've closed down four of the cinemas and turned them into discos. The last mine's been closed and there's a disco over that. They've even got a disco on the pier.'

Did she not find, I asked, that all these discos were terribly noisy? If you go to a movie these days the volume is turned up to a painful volume because the disco age group is deaf. No, the barmaid said, she did not mind the noise. 'In my family they've got the stereo, the radio, TV and cassette all going at once. And during the day I work in a factory making speakers, cassettes, the space invader machines and the slim-line video machines. We play them all back to test them.'

I went to a pub with a TV set in order to watch the replay of the boxing match between Ali and Holmes. There was a couple watching the fight; they brought in a baby and sat it upon the billiard table. Then two young women in ankle-length skirts wanted to play billiards and parked the baby on one of the chairs. All this time, a very old man in a cloth cap, National Health glasses, and ditto teeth was watching the fight. Every time that Ali was hit, which happened constantly in this fight, the old man uttered a cackle of laughter; his whole frame shook as though from a cough. The baby went off to sleep and the two girls laboured away at their billiards, missing every second ball and frequently scratching the cloth.

I have just re-read *The Road to Wigan Pier*, and once again I find little resemblance between the Wigan that Orwell described and the Wigan I know. Of course many years have passed since the time of his visit, 1936; but Wigan has not much changed since I first went there in 1956 to write an article about Orwell's book. I cannot remember what I wrote, but I came away with the strong sensation that everyone I had met in Wigan was pulling my leg. I get that feeling everywhere in Lancashire but most strongly of all in Wigan. Yet George Orwell does not seem to have had this sensation. He takes everything he is told with the utmost seriousness, yet I am sure that everyone in the town must have been hooting with mirth at this strange, tall Etonian in frayed clothes who wanted to live in a filthy boarding-house and to eat revolting bread and marge, complete with the thumb-prints of the landlord.

There is a very funny passage – unconsciously funny, however – in which Orwell describes the arrival of a Londoner, a commercial traveller:

In the morning as we were dressing (he had slept in the double bed, of course) I saw him look round the desolate room with a sort of wondering aversion. He caught my eye and suddenly divined that I was a fellow-Southerner.

'The filthy, bloody bastards!' he said feelingly.

After that he packed his suitcase, went downstairs and, with great strength of mind, told the Brookers that this was not the kind of house he was accustomed to and that he was leaving immediately.

George Orwell assumed that this Cockney had come down in the world and was used to staying in commercial hotels. I think the Cockney had quite sensibly known that cheap lodgings do not need to be filthy; that landlords should wash their hands before passing out slices of bread. There was a masochistic streak in Orwell. He sought out the nastiest places to eat and sleep, and seemed to demand the company of the lowest class, although, as he says himself, he found them physically repulsive. He writes pages on whether the working class smells, and on how he could not be accepted because of his upper-class accent; he chose the hardships and loneliness of his stay in Wigan, apparently as a kind of penance for having been born to the middle classes.

I find Orwell's attitude incomprehensible. I come from the same social class and speak with the same kind of accent, but I have never felt an aversion to people in places like Wigan; on the contrary, I find them far better company than the kind of people you meet in Surrey or Sussex. As a journalist with a middle-class 'Tory' accent, I have found it always easy to cover events like strikes and elections in which one has to interview working-class and presumably Labour supporters. I have only once encountered antipathy, and even on that occasion a Communist objected not to my accent but to my newspaper.

The one weakness of *Wigan Pier* and all George Orwell's writing is over-seriousness. One gets the impression that no one in Wigan made him laugh, yet I find it the funniest town in England. But in spite of his seriousness and his middle-class guilt, Orwell wrote a magnificent and a prescient book. He had not yet understood that socialism, like any political system, is bound to produce a new set of tyrants; he did understand, as early as 1936, that the socialist movement had come under the domination of middle-class ideologues, of feminists, 'vegetarians with wilting beards, of Bolshevik commissars (half

37

gramophone, half-gangster), of earnest ladies in sandals, shock-headed Marxists chewing polysyllables, escaped Quakers, birth-control fanatics, and Labour Party back-stairs crawlers.' That is still a perfect description of the Left, though Orwell might have added yacht-owning trade union leaders, Oxbridge Trotskyites with lingua-phone Geordie accents, 'Right to Choose' ladies, sex education maniacs, race relations workers, sociologists and social workers. Most of these people today are the children or grand-children of just that middle class which, in Orwell's day, ran the country and the Empire; the only difference is that now they have lost the ideals of patriotism, religion and honour that made them a decent, if not very efficient, body of government. The working class are still out of power and, here in Lancashire, out of work – just as in Orwell's day. And what is more they hate and despise the new middle class far more than they did the old; their views on matters like sex, religion, the Royal Family, crime and punishment, education and the police, are closer to those of the old middle class than to those of the new. They remain impervious to the kind of pernicious nonsense preached by the *Guardian's* Women's Page.

4 October – Liverpool   By train to Liverpool, where I discovered without surprise that the dockers are once more in danger of closing down the port and all the ports of England. Apparently they are in sympathy with some dockers made redundant at Grimsby and Immingham, but it is only weeks since the Liverpool dockers threatened to cause a national strike. The owners did not want to go on paying 150 men for doing no work at all, and instead suggested they take a 'fall-back' pay of £72 a week for doing nothing. The dockers refused, and it must be said that for once they were in the right; they were guaranteed full payment for life in a pact drawn up in 1972 by the cowardly and disastrous Heath regime. The Liver-pool dockers say in their own defence that the port was destroyed by containers; they would not adapt to unloading this form of transport, and so the ships went instead to new ports like Felixstowe on the Suffolk coast, which I hope to visit later this year. Even the ships from Iceland go to Felixstowe rather than Liverpool, which is mad, as can be seen from the map.

The great docks remain as monuments to the time when Liverpool people worked. Gladstone, Alexander, Langton, Hornby, Brocklebank, Canada, Huskisson, Sandon, Wellington, Bramley-Moore, Nelson, Waterloo and Princes still are in partial use, but the greatest of all are closed: Canning, Salthouse, Albert, Wapping, Queens, Brunswick, Toxteth, Harrington, Herculaneum. The Canning now has a maritime Museum, complete with dummy cases of rum and bales of cotton, and the figurehead of a buxom woman clutching a rose. There have been all sorts of plans for the South Docks. The property man Harry Hyams and Colonel Siefert, the couple who gave London the Centre Point Building, have long had a plan to knock down the Albert Docks and build a hundred-storey office block. But who needs office blocks in a city where no business is done? The vast classical offices of the shipping and insurance houses already look too big for the work they do. In Liverpool, even more than in Manchester, one sees the physical evidence of this country's collapse; and here, by contrast to Manchester, one must put most of the blame on the lunacy of trade unions.

Merseyside used to be one of the world's great shipbuilding centres until the 1950s, when there began what came to be called the 'hole-boring dispute'. Two rival trade unions claimed the right of boring the holes in plates of steel. The argument dragged on for years until at last the shipbuilding companies closed their yards except for minor repairs. Successive governments have attempted to shore up shipbuilding. The Tories offered a tax concession to owners of ships, which businessmen used as a way of supporting other more lucrative businesses such as property speculation. The last Labour government offered the Poles immense sums of money to buy ships from British yards rather than Gdansk, whose union troubles are worse even than ours, though of a different kind.

Dozens of firms have tried to set up factories in the Liverpool area — only to see the workers running mad-cap labour disputes, sit-ins and strikes. The chairman of one company blamed it on Communists, especially of the Trotskyist faction; now, when he takes on staff, he vets their political leanings, although he did not tell me how. He tried to impress on me that things were not as bad now as a few years ago. 'Our docks aren't as bad as Southampton's. Our car workers aren't as bad as Linwood's in Scotland. Our pickets aren't as bad as at Grunwick. Our shipbuilders aren't as bad as at Glasgow.' This rather negative catalogue did not entirely convince me, but I hear that some of the foreign businessmen have had success in their labour relations. The Japanese zip-manufacturers YKK, have had only three one-day strikes in the last seven years, which must be a record for Merseyside. The managers work eight hours on the shop floor; they unload the lorries; and every year they take the shop stewards on holiday to Japan to see Mt Fuji, the temples, and the massage parlours.

Merseyside is especially known for the high rate of unemployment among school leavers – the figure is now about 15 per cent – but even this problem is not quite as serious as we are led to believe. For one thing, most of them live at home and, what with the dole money, are suffering no actual physical hardship. The main cause of the unemployment is simply that here in England, unlike in, say, Japan, young people starting jobs expect to obtain a wage almost as big as someone who has been working for twenty or thirty years. In local government, thanks to the unions like NUPE and NALGO, young people start at the standard rate for the job. This was not always so. An apprentice mason who started work on building Liverpool's Church of England Cathedral during the Thirties received for the first few years a mere 8p a week, in modern money. The apprentice system was widely accepted as fair, since single young men do not have the responsibility of a wife and children. Moreover, in jobs that require experience and training, a starter is worth little. Employers understand this today, which is why, given the choice, they prefer an experienced worker over a school leaver. And apprenticeships, or training schemes, do not work today, because few boys or girls are going to work for only a little money, when they can get more on the dole.

In more ways than one, these school leavers are victims of just the people who claim to be helping them: the trade union militants, the Trotskyists and all those older people who want to instil in the young a sense of grievance. There was an outburst of fury when Margaret Thatcher very sensibly said that young people should travel to find work. Here in Liverpool, a city that grew from immigration, the response was adamant: jobs must be provided on the spot. The BBC runs a series of TV programmes designed for young people 'presently in an on-going unemployment situation' – they really do talk like that. The import of these programmes is teaching the youngsters that not they but 'society' is responsible for their plight. It does not encourage them to seek a job; indeed by its representation of typical

40

'kids' as ill-spoken, ill-mannered and stupid, its makes it more hard for them to impress employers. The programme producers actually seem to encourage these children in their grievances against society, the employers and the police. The fact is that unemployment is, paradoxically, now just another industry – like race, sex and equal rights – providing money and work for social workers, left-wing TV producers and all that tribe. If the young people of England were all to find jobs, these people would themselves be unemployed.

The absurdity of the youth unemployment was brought home by something that happened to us in London. Wanting to fix some door handles and windows, my wife called for a carpenter and was sent not one but a pair. They worked well and during a pause – while one of them went out to buy more screws – the other asked my wife if he might have a look at Ronald Knox's essay on Meditation. These two young men were graduates of one of our old universities; they had taken a course in carpentry, and were now doing good business. Something is wrong in a country where Oxford graduates turn into carpenters, and the carpenter class appear on TV to complain about life on the dole.

I once saw an advertisement from the Merseyside Development Board saying: 'William Ewart Gladstone, born 1809, would have been proud of the new Merseyside.' On the contrary, I think he would sink into black depression. At any rate, I have. More even than in Manchester, one gets the feeling of purpose and glory gone. The slums of the inner city are mostly boarded up, vandalised and inhabited by old people or squatters; the inhabitants have gone off to still more horrible new slums like Kirkby. The streets of the old bourgeoisie, including the one in which Gladstone was born, have turned into exotic offices: the Western Acupuncture Academy, the Euro Exhaust Centre, the Private Chauffeur Club, the Chinese Martial Arts Centre, the Indian Vice-Consulate (sharing a house with a sauna club).

The Swiss psychologist Jung has described in his memoirs a dream about Liverpool, which he visited in the company of some business-men – in his dream, that is, for he never went to the city. To him it symbolised both the liver, a vital organ, and life itself – he called it the Pool of Life. There is a statuette of Jung in a shop in Matthew Street, near to the cellar in which the Beatles played for the first time, in England, the music that made them and Liverpool famous.

The Cavern was a place of pilgrimage, not only to music-lovers but to trendy journalists from the Sunday papers who wrote on the Beatle phenomenon. That was seventeen years ago. Now nobody comes to Liverpool if he can help it. The Beatles have broken up and even the cellar in which they played has gone.

The melancholy of the place I find overwhelming, perhaps partly because my late father and his father came from here and therefore, for want of another, I think of Liverpool as my ancestral city. I went to a concert in the Philharmonia and that only made the melancholia worse. They played the Enigma Variations, Elgar's lament for what he remembered of England in childhood and youth . . . I could not take it, and went to a pub.

5 October – Liverpool This morning, a Sunday, I went to the two Cathedrals which have given the city fame, or notoriety, in the Christian community of this country. Designed by Giles Gilbert Scott at the start of the century and still not complete at his death in 1960, the Church of England cathedral is, whether one likes it or not, a wonder of twentieth-century architecture. Its sheer bulk – it is the fifth largest church in the world – is both its peculiar strength and a cause of unending controversy. In an article in defence of his plan, written in 1904, Scott explained that the city would have a Gothic Cathedral

but of a quite different type to that of our medieval cathedrals; in fact there is no Gothic building in the world to which it can be compared . . . and if the citizens of this great port succeed, as no doubt they will, in completing the huge fabric, they will indeed have cause for pride.

What Scott could not envisage was that long before the Cathedral was completed, the port itself would be no more. Instead of a city without a Cathedral, we have a Cathedral without a city; a diocese without a flock. At several stages during the building, and as late as the 1960s, it was considered abandoning the grandiose plan and compromising with something smaller. The Dean of the Cathedral, Edward Patey, has told a Liverpool writer: 'When I first came [in 1964], to be absolutely honest, I began to wonder whether it was my job as Dean to discourage the completion of the Cathedral.'* However, the job was finished, and Sir John Betjeman has called it 'one of

* *Today's Cathedral* by Joe Riley. London, 1978.

42

the great buildings of the world . . . the impression of vastness, strength and height no words can describe . . . Suddenly, one sees that the greatest art of architecture, that lifts one up and turns one into a king, yet compels reverence, is the art of enclosing space.'

Greatly though I admire Sir John's judgment, and greatly though I admire the Cathedral when seen from a distance, I found the interior strangely dead: it fails to inspire the awe and joyfulness that I feel at, for instance, Ely or Winchester. But I may have been put off the building by some of the things I saw and heard there, not least Dean Patey. He is a very trendy cleric, perhaps the origin of the Peter Simple Bishop of Bevindon, the Revd Spacely-Trellis. As Mr Riley says of him in his book, he has made the Cathedral 'a multi-racial, multi-media, multi-conscious, multi-denominational laboratory'. Oh, has he? He has smiled approval as youngsters jived in the central space to the music of a pop group. He has backed the Campaign for Homosexual Equality. He has got in different ethnic minority groups to talk on International Women's Year. After the Battle of the Atlantic Service one year, a man wrote to complain that all he had heard was 'left-wing politics' when he had come to honour the dead, to which Patey wrote back that 'the best way to honour the dead was to live in a more just society than that which caused them to be killed. If you think that's left-wing, then, okay, it's left-wing.'*

That is not left-wing, so much as nonsense. Those who died in the Battle of the Atlantic were not killed by 'society'. (Whose society, anyway, Britain's or Germany's?) They were killed by submarines in defence of their country; some of them would have said their God and country. A few weeks ago, I attended at this cathedral part of a day of discussion, at which the leading speaker was Christian Howard, a leading light in the World Council of Churches. Her remarks on the Third World were sensible compared to those of the Dean who joined with her in discussion. He talked of 'liberation theology', how the church must be on the side of change and revolution, of how in an 'unequal, unjust world, we celebrate a God who gave his son for the world'. Having spent many years in South-East Asia, Africa and Latin America, I have seen a lot of bloodshed and misery caused by armed 'liberation', which never in practice makes the world more equal or more just; quite the reverse. In every

* Dean Patey organised a memorial service for John Lennon, the former Beatle murdered in New York in December.

country where 'liberation' has been applied – in Palestine, Cyprus, Algeria, Indo-China, Southern Africa, South America, not to mention Ireland – it has led inexorably to dictatorship, civil war or partition; or all three.

Walking round the Cathedral, one soon sees evidence of political posturing, the craze for equality and what the Dean calls justice. The literature of the Liverpool Industrial Mission tells of the work of the Revd Bert Galloway, the Revd Bob Dews, the Revd Russ Naylor, the Revd Ben Pratt and the Revd Mike Diggle. You find the Revd Jack Burton's pamphlet *Driven to Prayer* concerning his ministry as a bus driver. Perhaps they are doing a splendid job but I rather suspect that Bert, Bob, Russ, Ben and Mike are regarded as condescending. Why should a factory worker, any more than the rest of us, expect a priest to ape his manners, to shorten his name, or to drive a bus? The job of a priest is to care for our souls, to comfort the sick and dying and, yes, to reprove our sins. A priest should command respect, and even a touch of fear. In countries, like Ireland, where the churches are still powerful, a priest or a Presbyterian minister may be popular with his flock, even a bit of a card, but he never lets people forget his special position.

The Roman Catholic Cathedral is a sweating, cement, conical building, well described as 'Paddy's Wigwam', also the 'Mersey Funnel.' Inside it is dark, dank and rather creepy; it suggested to me a theatre-in-the-round built somewhere in eastern Europe. The Stations of the Cross which surround the central stage are represented not by images of the torment of Christ but by news-photographs, sub-titled with captions of weird theological import. The first picture, for instance, shows a group of raggedy slum-children – in Europe or the United States, but it seems rather a long time ago – over the caption 'Jesus was condemned to die because of the world's sins. He was innocent like these children, condemned to a life of poverty'. Now wait a moment! . . . But it is no good. One could no more explain the fallacy of that argument to the man who wrote it, than the fallacy of Dean Patey's remarks on 'society'.

It is no surprise to find that the two Cathedrals get on famously. In the Fifties in Liverpool there used to be riots between the Catholic and the Protestant communities; and once the Bishop of one was stoned by hooligans of the other. Now it is very 'ecumenical'; the Anglican Bishop and Catholic Archbishop like to point out that the

44

two Cathedrals are joined by Hope Street, and that the Catholic Cathedral was built by a Protestant, while Scott was a Catholic; they even issued a joint statement condemning Mrs Thatcher's suggestion that unemployed Liverpool youths should travel to work. Even the many graffiti upon the buildings show the signs of an ecumenical spirit: 'Paddy's Wigwam' is covered with slogans for Manchester City Football Club – always a Protestant faction – which compensates for the Irish beggars outside the door, and the empty Guinness bottles beside them.

Ecumenism in this case seems to unite the churches horizontally rather than vertically: it joins what might be called the progressive faction of each, the people more interested in politics than religion, but does not unite the people of both churches who lay more stress on questions of faith. This point was made in a recent *Guardian* letter by two Americans writing to warn the English about the coming visit by Pope John Paul II. 'This Pope is an arrogant, self-serving cleric,' they said, 'and ironically of a similar mentality to that fear and fate-preaching fundamentalist interviewed by Polly Toynbee (*Guardian*, 8 September). The Protestant Reverend David Samuel and the Roman Catholic John Paul II are the Janus faces of a neurotic, masculine theology.'

A few weeks ago, the Papal Cross in Dublin erected to mark his visit last year was scrawled with the slogan 'If men got pregnant, contraception and abortion would be sacraments'. One might have thought this blasphemy and a national insult, comparable to the Nazi slogans on synagogues, would have been condemned by newspapers such as the *Guardian*. Not so. Two of its regular Women's Page writers, Angela Phillips and Jill Nicholls, gloated over this protest by the demented scrawlers. 'Right on, Sisters!' they cackled, and the *Guardian*, which once stood so hard for the independence of Ireland, printed this insult to Irish religion and pride.

6 October – Liverpool I asked reception at the Adelphi Hotel why the charge for a single room was only about two-thirds that of the Midland Hotel in Manchester, which is also managed by British Rail. 'We've got too much competition,' she said; and too few businessmen coming to Liverpool, she might have added. The poor old Adelphi is only a shade of its former splendour. In the days when the trans-Atlantic liners left from Liverpool, this was the place where the first-class passengers said farewell to their families and friends. It was the meeting place of the shipowners, the merchants, the shipbuilders and the insurance brokers. It was a place of colossal dignity, except on Grand National night when the rich young bloods formed rugger scrums in the hall.

During the Sixties, during that Indian summer of fame given to Liverpool by the Beatles, the Adelphi acquired an extra if rather dubious glory as the abode of Harold Wilson during general election campaigns. His own constituency, Huyton, covers the infamous Kirkby housing estate, just to the north of here, and Wilson has long been rather a local hero. Phonetic experts have told me that when he is over here, his natural Huddersfield accent is modified to a kind of Scouse, but the slur is not really justified since Wilson's family moved to this part of England when he was still young. I well recall the climax of the October 1964 election, which brought Wilson to power. At a party in the Adelphi on the day of the poll, we heard the news of Khrushchev's fall from power, and Mr Wilson, who fancies himself as a Kremlinologist, produced an explanation of what had happened. We journalists who had been with him on the campaign presented Wilson with, if I remember correctly, some book or books by Trollope. He was cheerful and sprightly as ever, although not very hopeful about the result. At the hall in Huyton where we were watching results on TV, Mr Wilson grew still more gloomy and fortified himself with a glass of brandy, having first got one of his flunkies to hold up an open paper to hide the sight from the press photographers. The only time I have seen Mr Wilson lose his temper was when a German TV cameraman tried to film him drinking beer on a train.

The Liverpool Press Club now has premises underneath the Adelphi; but even this is a sad place today. Only two of the national newspapers now consider it worth having a staff reporter in Liverpool; during the 1950s two or three were employed by each of the daily papers, including those that are now no more like the *Herald* and the *News Chronicle*. All afternoon in the Press Club the journalists drank and made up stories: the man-killing spider off a banana boat, the wolves escaped from a local zoo, and the long police hunt for a limping sex maniac. The police themselves invented half these stories, for they too enjoyed the atmosphere of the Press Club.

This evening in the Press Club, I met a man whose job is inspecting the kitchens of British Rail hotels; but he has an alternative job which I found much more interesting 'My hobby is the breeeding and selling of birds such as linnets, gold-finches and bull-finches. There's a tremendous business here in the North-West. You catch birds with tottle, that's a bird lime made of resin, a very strong and tactile substance that looks like treacle. Naturally when the birds have this substance on them they need washing before sale. But next month every bird born in this country must have a ring on it to show it was born in captivity. Before that I could sell the birds wild. But there's still a business in breeding birds. If you breed a gold-finch with a canary you get a marvellous song bird'. Papageno had come to life.

The North-West and the Lakes

MORECAMBE – HEYSHAM – LANCASTER

WINDERMERE – GRASMERE

---

7 October – Morecambe　I came on to Morecambe to find it almost deserted, although the illuminations are on, and early October ought to be still in season. The economic depression and the weather have made this one of the worst summers in memory, which is sad, for Morecambe has much to offer as a resort – much more, I have always thought, than Southport or Blackpool. It has, for one thing, a quite incomparable view over the bay to the north shore and, in the distance, the hills of the Lake District. The air is bracing – today it is too bracing, with gale force winds and rain – and you can walk for miles on the front. I can never understand why Yorkshire and Lancashire people now feel snooty about their seaside resorts; I met many northerners in the hell of Miami Beach, where they all complained of the heat, the price of drink in the bar and even the hotel rooms. A Liverpool man said it was worse than Butlins, while his friend, who had Mum and Dad tattooed on his arms, said that he could not judge, for he had never been in an hotel before. Many of those I met were unemployed or working on short-time: but still they had found the money to go to Miami.

I looked out an article that I wrote about Morecambe in 1962, beginning: 'Some locals complain that Morecambe is having its worst season for 50 years . . .' It seems I was told by a tourist official that trade had been 'pretty rotten in parts of Scotland, Yorkshire and Lancashire', and rain had done more than anything else to keep people at home. Apparently the Conservative government was to blame for recession; in the Starlight Club they sang a music hall song:

> Hats off to Harold Macmillan
> Though some folks are after his blood,
> Famous for making that wonderful crack
> About never had it so good,
> And now he explains it was only in fun,
> He should go in review now the Crazy Gang's done.

The comedian echoed the hopes of most of the working class when he went on:

> Hats off to the Labour Party,
> They're pulling together again,
> For certain Hugh Gaitskell's new postal address
> Will be Downing Street, Number Ten.

But Hugh Gaitskell died, or was murdered by the KGB as some people now think, and the Labour Party is still not pulling together.

The Madame Tussaud's was shut, so that I could not confirm whether General Montgomery was still shod in suede purple 'brothel-creepers' as he was in 1962 and again in 1975, when I was last in Morecambe. The town invented and still manufactures rock and potted shrimps, but otherwise it is not very prosperous.

Morecambe is rich in comedians, including Eric Morecambe himself; George Formby came from nearby, and the film of *The Entertainer* was shot with the pier as a background. The pier still survives, but is often vandalised. This week's *Visitor* carries a story about a two-year-old who was drowned after apparently falling through a hole in the pier. The coroner said that, from the evidence given,

more than a casual act of vandalism would have been required to open the hole. He would be most surprised if such an act of vandalism had occurred in daylight when there were always people on the pier. It seems to me it could well be the hole had existed longer than members of the pier staff had considered it was there; it may have been vandalised during the hours of darkness other than that day.

The story does not speak well for Morecambe and its visitors. When the little girl disappeared and was seen to be in the ocean, her father jumped in to rescue her but himself got into difficulties and had to release her. None of the bystanders went to the father's help while he struggled to save the infant. Nobody threw him a lifebelt because, so a pier official explained, all the lifebelts were stolen. 'Each time these were replaced' he said, 'they were thrown into the sea'. Except of course when a child was drowning.

8 October – Morecambe   When the Liberal Party was meeting in Southport this year, some of the delegates issued a protest about the traditional saucy postcards, which, so they said, were degrading to women. When Orwell wrote his essay 'The Art of Donald McGill', the feminist movement had not yet swelled into the clamorous and ubiquitous army of 'women's libbers', forever campaigning against their exploitation by men, against the sexual stereotyping of children, against inequality, against the conception of woman's duty as housewife and mother. They have written a lot on the sex act itself. One New York lady, Kate Millett, wrote a book denouncing the concept of men as the source of sex pleasure; she herself prefers women. Another New York lady composed a pamphlet entitled *The Myth of the Vaginal Orgasm*; a third produced a survey purporting to show that most women got sexual pleasure only from masturbation, alone or with female partners. It is taken as a proven fact by feminists in this country that women did not enjoy sex in the nineteenth century ('shut your eyes and think of the Empire') and may not have enjoyed it until about 1965. Almost every women's magazine contains an article on how to increase sexual pleasure; how to conquer inhibitions; how to obtain the rightful number of orgasms. It is a lucrative industry for psychiatrists, sexual counsellors and the whole new breed of 'agony aunties'.

But seaside saucy pictures portray an entirely different attitude towards sex among British women – who form the great majority of the purchasers. The basic joke, which has scarcely changed since before the war, is woman as sexual predator, with man as the (usually disappointing) sex object. Some of the jokes show women discussing among themselves: *Woman to salesgirl in furniture shop*: 'I want something good in a double bed, Miss' – 'Try our Mr Jones here, he's smashing even in a single bed'; and there are any number of pictures of women looking up at kilted parachutists, and examining statues of naked Roman gladiators.

A still commoner joke concerns men's inadequate sexual performance: 'They say he hasn't any scruples' – 'Blimey I'm sorry for

his wife'; *Huge wife dragging husband into sex aid shop*: 'Let's see if
they can do anything for you'; or, *Girl in newspaper small ad department to elderly man*: 'How many insertions do you want, Pop?' –
'Crikey luv, I doubt if I could manage the first one'; or, *Naked bride
sitting up in bed and telephoning as tired bridegroom gasps at her
side*: 'Hello mum, I see what you mean about women being the
strong sex'; or, *Wife to husband trying to open bottle*: 'You can't
even screw a cork successfully'; or *Husband to wife*: 'The plumber
says I need a new ball and cock dear' – 'Well it didn't take an expert
to find that out.'

These jokes are as old as the saucy postcard and only slightly more
explicit; women enjoy the joke, the double entendre, rather than any
explicit sexual portrayal. The joke of the Roman gladiator depends
on his facing the other way. I suspect that this bawdiness among
working-class women goes right back to Victorian times or indeed the
Middle Ages. In a delightful memoir on his childhood in Salford, *A
Classic Slum*, Robert Roberts says that husbands and wives in the
early years of the century would admit to each other, and even to
neighbours, that when they made love they shut their eyes and
thought of a film star; not the Empire, but Valentino. Thirty years
ago, when I was in the army, I was queueing up in the NAAFI for egg
and chips and I couldn't avoid hearing the conversation between the
waitress serving me and her colleague. The colleague was telling
bitterly of a man the night before who was too shy for more than a
kiss or cuddle, to which my waitress replied consolingly 'Yes, some of
the young soldiers these days think it's for stirring the tea with.'

Founded on the experience of neurotic middle-class New York
misfits, the women's liberationist movement has little relevance to
the majority of women, either in England or, I should think,
America. They continue to grow up with romantic ideas of love and
marriage and bearing children, and at the same time a bawdy streak
which deflates and mocks the romantic pretentions. If a husband
turns out not to be Valentino in bed, if only as he gets older, it is far
more natural (and therapeutic) to turn it into a joke, rather than
seeking divorce or undergoing analysis as is the custom in New York.
Sometimes, in London, I get depressed by the sour angry faces of
women demanding free abortion, pay for housework, unisex hospital
wards, the abolition of sexist children's books and all the other non-
senses of the angry feminist middle class; then I think of those saucy

postcards and know that not all women are mad.

9 October – Heysham – Lancaster – Windermere   Today I walked
along the beach to Heysham, which is pronounced here 'Heesham',
to see the church of St Peter and, behind it on the cliff, the ruins of St
Patrick's chapel, one of the oldest and most awe-inspiring creations
of man in this country. As the name suggests, the chapel was founded
by Irish missionaries to this country, perhaps in the early eighth
century; with a west wind as strong as the one today, they could have
come over here in a day or two. The two walls that stand are said to
bear the mark of Irish masonry; there are Celtic crosses; and, something I had not seen before, graves marked by holes in the shape of
coffins, cut in the living stone of boulders, six graves in a row on one
side of the chapel and two smaller ones, for children perhaps, set
rather apart. These holes in the rock are full of water after the storm.

Looking out to sea from behind this chapel and graveyard, it is
easy to think back to the eighth century, to what is mistakenly called
the Dark Ages. Relations between this country and Ireland were much
more cordial then. The British Christians in this part of the country
looked to the Irish as allies against the English or Anglo-Saxon
invaders from Germany; and all three peoples were later to make
common cause in face of the threat from the Norsemen or Vikings.
To make matters more confusing, some of the Norsemen's attacks on
northern England during the tenth century were launched from their
Irish settlement in what is now Dublin.

Irish history books tend to suggest that all the traffic between the
two islands consisted of Britain sending her armies to conquer the
Irish, and Ireland sending her saints to convert the British. Neither is
really true. The Irish often invaded Britain; they occupied Galloway
in the south-west of Scotland; and one Welsh prince of Caernarvon
was given the title of Irish-slayer because he had managed to drive
back one of their many invasions.

Some of the Irish missionaries came to this island in the wake of
the invaders; St Columba went to the Irish colonisers of Scotland and
founded the monastery at Iona. Although it became unique and
wonderful, the early Irish church had, after all, started as an off-
shoot of the British church. After the Synod of Whitby in 664, when
the Roman or papal faction triumphed over the old or Irish church –
the quarrel concerned much more than the date of Easter – some of

the Irish monks went home, accompanied by a number of English supporters. There were English bishops of Mayo during the eighth century. As Dorothy Whitelock says in *The Beginnings of English Society*, 'Many Northumbrians went to Irish monasteries, to add the merit of exile from their native land to their renunciation of the world's pleasures.'

The Irish Church was characterised by piety, austerity and a tireless zeal for converting heathens. It was opposed to the Roman faction which wanted authority for the bishops, as well as the pomp and regalia that go with office. In some ways, it was temperamentally akin to later Puritans and non-conformists, so that Ian Paisley, a hard opponent of Rome, might be said to be more in St Patrick's tradition than some of his Catholic countrymen. Certainly when one thinks of those Irish priests with bundles of fivers at Cheltenham races, it seems that the church has altered since the time of the monks here in Heysham. Was not Henry II told by the Pope to invade Ireland in order to stamp out fornication among the clergy, particularly in what is now County Clare? But if the Irish Church has lost some of its ancient austerity, it has never lost its ardour for missionary work all over the earth. It is fascinating to read how, back in the Dark Ages, the Irish were constantly travelling not only all over England but all over Europe too. You could hardly enter a monastery in the depths of Gaul without meeting an Irishman, just as today you will find him in any bar from Hong Kong to Nairobi.

Heysham remains one of the ports for Irishmen coming to England. The IRA used to use these steamers for sending across their agents and weapons; the Birmingham pub bombers were caught here attempting escape. The thought of that terrible crime brings one brutally back to the twentieth century. So does the observation that someone has carved the initials JR on one of the eighth-century tombstones. Where are the slogans demanding abortion? Does nobody in Heysham read the Women's Page of the *Guardian*? I left the church and walked to the top of the hill to the South, and what I saw there caused me to cry out in horror. There, on a spit of land in the bay, was a nuclear power station, huge, silent and menacing. I should have remembered that it was there for only this morning I read in the *Visitor* that in the event of a nuclear war this was a prime Soviet target. If so it is not the first time that the Russians have caused trouble in this part of Lancashire. Across Morecambe Bay lies

Barrow-in-Furness where the Bolsheviks in 1918 attempted to start a revolution and take Britain out of the First World War; or so John Buchan suggested in *Mister Standfast*. The Government nearly sent Richard Hannay there in order to sort out the Reds.

I went on to Lancaster. A friend of mine who used to teach in the University here said that people would approach him in the Senior Common Room, introduce themselves as Professor or Lecturer in such-and-such a discipline, then add in a furtive way: 'I also work for the such-and-such insurance company. Would you be interested in taking out a policy?' After a walk round the town, I decided to go to Windermere, which is not the pleasantest town in the Lakes but is the only one you can get to by train. Everywhere in the Lake District is pleasanter when the tourists have gone and the locals come back into their own. A group of them in the hotel bar are discussing that favourite topic of conversation – the use of brutality by the police. They are all in favour of it but only as long as the wrong-doer is 'bashed' rather than 'brained'. They all seemed to agree on and understand this distinction.

10 October – Windermere – Grasmere   I was pleased to read in the *Westmorland Gazette*, under the headline 'Planners reject Kendal scheme', that 'Plans for a huge new £3 million supermarket and hotel development in Kendal town centre have been thrown out this week.' Planning permission had been refused by the South Lakeland Council's Development Control Sub-Committee. Bully for South Lakeland Council: I almost began to forgive it for having assumed the powers and title of Westmorland – one of the English counties that vanished completely under the Heath regime. But then I discovered that, having first looked at the Kendal story, I had not noticed the front page lead, saying 'Superstore hits new opposition. A guest house proprietor is planning to lead a campaign against the proposed £1 million development of Windermere railway station.' Apparently the *Gazette* had revealed last week that the British Rail Property Board, in conjunction with E. H. Booth, a Preston firm, were planning to turn the station into a 12,500 sq ft supermarket, plus 7500 sq ft of storage space and staff rooms, plus an overhead road or ramp leading up to a park for 200 cars. A man called Peter Moakes (described as 'BR's Property Board Estate Surveyor and

Manager') is quoted as saying about this horrendous project: 'Any plan that brings £1 million of investment and 100 new jobs to a town like Windermere must be good news for everyone.' Any plan, Mr Moakes? A plan for a motor car racetrack? An open cast mine? A nuclear power station? A concentration camp?

I hurried to see Mr Ronald Dunn, the proprietor of the guest house referred to in the *Gazette*. At the back of his house is the small wood and orchard which will be bulldozed under the BR plan and turned into a ramp to the giant car park. At least six firms will be put out of business, he said, and he contradicted the claim by BR of providing a hundred jobs locally. Most of the foremen and managers would come from outside. He was appalled by the prospect of people coming to Windermere (which boasts of being the Gateway to the National Parks) and stepping out, quite literally, into a giant supermarket. The plan would greatly increase the number of cars in Windermere – where, in summer, it can take an hour to drive across town. Worst of all, it would ruin the Windermere shops which provide the town with every conceivable need and are, moreover, friendly and personal. Here Mrs Dunn chipped in to tell about how, when she wanted some plates for a dinner, the local shop had lent them free. 'Can you imagine a supermarket doing that?' she added. Her husband referred to the promise made by E. H. Booth's that theirs was a foodstore only and would not be stocking things like hardware; but was such a promise legally binding? 'I dread to think what will happen to our shopping centre, the two streets. It will have to close down like other small villages where supermarkets have been allowed. All we'd have would be souvenir shops, estate agents, accountants and building societies.' He is right; that has happened to dozens of small towns afflicted by shopping centres and supermarkets. And in the end, prices rise too.

From the Dunn's, I went to James Gibson, a blacksmith who runs the Victoria Forge, which is also due for destruction under the BR project. 'I've been a blacksmith since I was fourteen, at six shillings a week with annual increases of two shillings a year. I took over this place twelve years ago when it was not doing well and now I employ a trained man and one who's in the middle of his apprenticeship. We'll be wiped out. I've been under the weather since I heard about this plan. It's absolutely knocked the bottom out of everything. I'm

c

a very worried fellow, I can tell you.'

It is hard to decide whether British Rail or South Lakeland Council is worse of the two villains behind this scheme. There was a photograph in the newspaper the other day of Sir Peter Parker, the chairman of British Rail, as he smiled for photographers on some new-fangled train going at 150mph. But who *needs* to travel at that speed? What the country badly needs is the restoration of branch lines with frequent trains at competitive prices, so that the public are not forced to use cars. There are many political difficulties, such as the power of the motor car lobby, but Sir Peter should turn his attention to them, sack his public relations staff, abandon his 'bullet train' and, above all, get out of property deals like this one at Windermere.

It may sound fanciful to suggest that such a plan would never have been conceived had Westmorland not been turned into South Lakeland; but it is true. For about a thousand years the county of Westmorland was administered by sheriffs and, latterly, by a county council, which governed badly or well, but always in view of the public. Their debate and decisions were known. Today things are different. The plan concocted by British Rail and E. H. Booth was only revealed last week to the people of Windermere; there was no prior discussion in public.

My mood did not improve in the bus going to Grasmere on a road which even at this time of year was noisy with cars. The South Lakeside Council enforces a law that no café or boarding house in the National Park may put out a sign, however small, to advertise bed and breakfast or teas, as this would spoil the 'visual amenities'. Yes, but since these signs are meant to be seen from the road, they would spoil the view only from motor cars, which are the real visual offence to the rest of us. Would it not be wiser to ban cars from the National Park except for the people who live here; and let the visitors come by train? I know that Wordsworth opposed the opening of a railway line, but then he had not seen its still worse successor the car. Nor did he live to see speed-boats, and water-skiers on Windermere. What is the sense of calling a place a National Park, an absurd title anyway, and then scaring the birds, the beasts and the fish with such hideous and unnatural behaviour? In August, I read that the Countess of Arran was aiming to reach, and has just reached, 100mph on Windermere, and wanted to be the 'fastest woman on water'. My thoughts about that are unprintable.

11 October – Grasmere Why attempt a description of Grasmere when this has been done so often and so magnificently by its most famous resident?

> But I would call thee beautiful, for mild,
> And soft, and gay, and beautiful thou art,
> Dear Valley, having in the face a smile
> Though peaceful, full of gladness. . . .

There are those who have said that Wordsworth was sentimental about the countryside, that he invested Nature with human emotions and fancies, that he was making a dream world of escape for the capitalists of industrial England. There are those too who claim that Grasmere has been commercialised; it is easy to make fun of the Japanese tourists who photograph one another outside Dove cottage. But the tourist season is over now and the valley and Grasmere village itself are looking again as described in Wordsworth's poems and the enchanting journal kept by his sister, Dorothy. Their writing and Grasmere have given me great happiness, which is why I have lingered three days in this quiet corner of England.

It would be pleasant to stay at Grasmere even without reading a line of Wordsworth, just as one might enjoy Bayreuth while disliking the music of Wagner, but anyone who does this is missing the opportunity, in England almost unique, of comparing the works of a major poet with what was his inspiration. Little remains of Shakespeare's Stratford, Dickens's Yarmouth, Keats's Hampstead or Chaucer's road to Canterbury. Jane Austen's Bath is much the same physically, but little remains of Society as she knew and disliked it. But the valley of Grasmere remains as Wordsworth described it; the wild life is not much depleted; the country people probably speak in the accent that Wordsworth spoke; and as for the tourists and smart owners of second homes, well they were here even in Wordsworth's day.

Dove Cottage where Wordsworth and Dorothy, and sometimes the Coleridges, lived for a time (the house was taken over by de Quincey) is well preserved, as is the Wordsworth Museum next door. Indeed, so excellent is the whole arrangement that I wish they would stop describing it as the Wordsworth Heritage Centre, a phrase that smacks of the Arts Council, the tourist industry and the public relations trade. The cottage itself is sparsely furnished but pleasing for its associations; I liked best the sign reminding visitors to the garden that this had been made by William and Dorothy Wordsworth, so please could we treat it with respect. There is so much about gardening in Dorothy Wordsworth's *Journal* that it came as almost a shock to realise that the shrubs and flowers are, so to speak, the descendants of those she planted and raised.

There is a separate library of Wordsworth manuscripts, and the museum itself gives more attention to Wordsworth's circle of friends, and to reconstructing the fashion of his age. Because he spent so much time in the Lake District, we tend to think of Wordsworth as a solitary, almost a recluse, so it is good to be reminded that he was also a public man, who knew almost everyone interesting in his age. He was a friend and admirer of Charles James Fox, in spite of their different attitude to the French Revolution, and he wrote a tribute to Fox shortly after his death. We see the original of a funny letter to William Godwin, the anarchist, who had sent Wordsworth a very small parcel hoping to save expense in cash on delivery. Wordsworth wrote back explaining that there existed a uniform charge of 4s 6d, for the tiniest parcel as for one of twenty times bigger. He compares Godwin's behaviour to that of the unmarried girl who confesses to having a baby but adds that it is only a small one. There is a letter from Benjamin Robert Haydon recalling that famous dinner when Lamb had got tight and wanted to measure people's crania, and Keats had proposed 'confusion to the memory of Newton'. 'Upon your insisting on an explanation before you drink it,' Haydon reminded Wordsworth, Keats had said ' "Because he destroyed the poetry of the rainbow by reducing it to a prism".'

Re-reading Wordsworth and tramping about these glorious hills, I recalled the joy with which I had read the poems first as a boy with the good fortune to grow up in the countryside – although a flatter, greener and tamer countryside. He exactly expresses the wildness (a favourite word) of walking for miles alone in the hills, of climbing trees for birds' eggs (Wordsworth too was guilty of this) and of fishing. He was a keen but not always lucky angler for pike, as Dorothy writes in her *Journal* for 9 June 1800: 'We went to R. Newton's for pike floats and went round to Mr Gall's boat, and on the lake to fish. We caught nothing as it was extremely cold. The reeds and bull-pipes of a tender, soft green making a plain whose surface moved with the wind. The reeds not yet tall. The lake clear to the bottom but saw no fish.'

Towards the end of my schooldays, I stopped reading Wordsworth and turned to the younger romantics like Keats, Byron and Shelley, then later still Eliot, Tennyson, Kipling, above all Yeats. I fell for the fashion of thinking Wordsworth solemn and stuffy and even banal. 'Two voices are there:' goes J. K. Stephen's famous parody of his poems, 'one is of the deep; . . . And one is of an old half-witted sheep . . . And Wordsworth both are thine.' And indeed, in his efforts to capture accurate details of everyday life among common people, Wordsworth frequently was banal, though not as banal as our modern 'working class' authors and poets, from Lawrence onwards. Yet only today, after climbing a fell, I became aware, by physical mishap, of how one of his most famous banalities was not as banal as I thought. Becoming aware of pain in my right ankle (caused, I think, by a too tight sock) I reached down to feel if the place was swollen, and at the same time there entered my mind that line about some elderly labourer 'the more he toiled, the more did his weak ankle swell'. I now feel a bit guilty for having laughed at the old chap's affliction.

As a foreign correspondent returned to England, I felt a particular poignancy in the lines

> I travelled among unknown men,
>   In lands beyond the sea;
> Nor, England! did I know till then
>   What love I bore to thee.

Equally simple and moving are the lines addressed to the six-year-old Hartley Coleridge:

> O blessèd vision! happy child!
> Thou art so exquisitely wild,
> I think of thee with many fears
> For what may be thy lot in future years.

That poem was written for one of the children of Coleridge, who touched on the same theme in his 'Letter to Sara Hutchinson' – an

earlier draft of 'Dejection: an Ode' – which was addressed to the
Grasmere household, and read out loud to Dorothy at the cottage:

> Those little Angel children (woe is me!)
> There have been hours when feeling how they bind
> And pluck out the wing-feathers of my mind,
> Turning my error to necessity,
> I half-wish'd they never had been born! . . .
> With no unthankful spirit I confess.
> This clinging Grief, too, in its turn, awakes
> That Love, and Father's Joy; but O! it makes
> The Love the greater, and the Joy far less.

Even those of us who are not, like poor Coleridge, unhappy by
nature, must sometimes feel the same way about bringing up
children in 1980, under the threat of a nuclear war.

While Coleridge grew increasingly melancholic, Wordsworth
acquired a kind of serenity as he grew older: he came to terms with
himself and the world – perhaps to the detriment of his poetry. He
hints at this in the wonderful 'Intimations of Immortality':

> But yet I know, where'er I go,
> That there hath past away a glory from the earth

I apologise to those readers who anyway know and understand
those verses: but there are many, I think, who cannot grasp Wordsworth's vision of God in nature. Even the conservationists, the
Green Movement, often talk as though saving whales or guarding
natural resources was simply a way of preserving a balanced ecology
in the interests of mankind; not as interference with nature. Even
some of our spiritual leaders seem to have missed the point, as I saw
from a newspaper story the other day. The Bishop of Warrington,
The Right Revd Michael Henshall, is reported to have condemned
harvest festivals as 'irrelevant'. He deplores the 'massive senti-
mentality' of hymns in which congregations pine for gold corn in
Canaan's pleasant land. He prefers such modern hymns as 'God of
concrete, God of steel'. The Bishop applauded a demented clergyman who had put an anti-tank gun in his chancel for his harvest
thanksgiving, and replaced onions hanging from the pulpit with
grenades, so as to preach about 'the misuse of the arts of creation'.

The attitude of the Bishop of Warrington is probably representative of a church and a society which still believes that things like steel, concrete and armoured cars are somehow more 'real' and more 'relevant' than harvests of corn and onions. Wordsworth thought otherwise. He would have seen that a harvest festival is fundamental not only to Christianity but all religions in which men give thanks to God for the gifts of nature. This is why there are so many people these days who look for religious inspiration to the poets or to the great musicians, like Beethoven, rather than to the Churches.

The rascally poetaster Leigh Hunt was one of the many who turned on Wordsworth during his lifetime, first for accepting the sinecure of distributor of stamps for Westmorland, and later for taking the Poet Laureateship. Never mind that Hunt was not a good enough poet to get the Laureateship; never mind that, as a notorious sponger – he is caricatured by Dickens as Harold Skimpole in *Bleak House* – Hunt would have taken any sinecure and today would be taking an Arts Council grant; he and the rest of the jackals got Wordsworth labelled a turncoat.

It is true that Wordsworth at first supported the French Revolution and later condemned its result, but the change of mind was not dishonourable. It was just that he came to see the evil of terror and war as instruments of political change; his sonnet on Bonaparte expresses this perfectly. He saw clearly how revolution, based on the concept that man is born free, will end up inevitably with man in chains, under the tyranny of a Bonaparte, Lenin, Stalin, Hitler, Mao or Pol Pot.

Wordsworth became a Tory, but not in the sense we know it now. He would have detested socialism, but still more what we have come to call capitalism, the industrial revolution which, in Wordsworth's lifetime, changed the world more than the revolution in France. He fought a long battle to keep the railway out of the Lake District; one hates to imagine his feelings about the motor car.

> Little we see in Nature that is ours;
> We have given our hearts away, a sordid boon.

In recent years there have been attempts on the part of the modish intelligentsia to do dirt on the reputation of Wordsworth, suggesting that he had a sexual relationship with his sister Dorothy. I saw a bit of a worthless TV film on the Lake poets, made I believe by the crass and pretentious Ken Russell. He has bought a house near Grasmere, which bodes ill for the district.

Of course Wordsworth loved his sister Dorothy as he loved his other sister and brother; and Freud declared that familiar love was sexual. The answer to that is that Freud himself was not only a charlatan but a man of grotesquely unusual sexual habits – he foreswore intercourse with his wife at the age of forty, and thereafter spilled out his fantasies through the 'case-histories' of his neurotic patients. Retrospective psycho-analysis can be amusing and may occasionally hit on the truth, but Wordsworth is not a good subject. He was not a secretive or repressed man. Even during his lifetime, he published references to his love affair with a French woman, and he wrote a beautiful sonnet to his illegitimate daughter.

The poison has spread even to Grasmere. 'We're not interested here in Wordsworth', a young man told me, 'or in his torrid love affair with his sister.'

But Grasmere remains almost as marvellous as it was in Wordsworth's day and will, God willing, survive to a day when nobody can remember Ken Russell, or Sunday newspaper serials on the private lives of the great. The lake has, as yet, no motorboats, and still very few fish. 'There's trout and perch and eels,' I was told 'but you can waste all day trying to catch them. The only way to get perch is with minnows. I used to get eels to sell to the hotel but that's no good nowadays.' Wordsworth might have written some lines on the Solitary Eel Catcher.

13 October – Grasmere – Newcastle Regretfully, I leave Grasmere, where I have much enjoyed myself. It is an admirable place in many respects: the owner of a five-bedroom house behind the hotel pays rates of £8 per annum, compared to the rates of £800 I pay*, for a smaller place in London. The Lake District must be the only part of England where you can still burn coal in your fire; down in industrial Lancashire, they are so strong against air pollution that in Rochdale it was not permitted to roast an ox to celebrate the Jubilee. In the pub at the back of The Red Lion, I asked advice on how to get by public transport to Newcastle. 'It's impossible', says the proprietor, 'to travel from west to east across England, except between London and Cornwall.' Then everyone starts to talk about

---

* Or rather, do not pay. The profit earned on this book has not been sufficient to pay my debt to Camden's villainous council.

the iniquities of British Rail and British Airways. It seems that the British Rail supermarket scheme at Windermere is not unusual as a commercial deal with private companies. They offer excursions to London in which, if you calculate on the base of normal fares, you stay for £3.50 a night at one of the Maxwell Joseph hotels. And you can now get a half-price fare for two people provided you show the coupons from two packets of Persil. Why does British Rail become involved in these business stunts with companies such as Grand Metropolitan and Unilever – or whoever it is that makes Persil?

To get to Newcastle, I took the bus to Keswick, another bus to Wigton, another to Carlisle and a train from there. At Wigton bus station I saw the graffiti 'Lord God up above gave to me Foxy to love he picked him out from all the rest because he knew I loved him best. . . .'

The North-East and Yorkshire

NEWCASTLE – CHESTER-LE-STREET

DURHAM – DARLINGTON – YORK

BRADFORD – BARNSLEY – BAWTRY

14 October –Newcastle In Newcastle I went to St John's Church, near to the station, and saw this notice on the door: 'To visitors. This Church is the House of God tabernacling among men: Enter therefore and adore him: or else enter not'. A pleasant change from the trendies at Liverpool Cathedral. Another sign says that 'The vocation of the Congregation of St John's is to maintain a place of stillness in the midst of madness'. There is also a placard of SPVC, one of the anti-abortion groups. It is an Anglo-Catholic Church of the puritan sort, on the side of the present Pope. (Who has put his foot in it recently with his caveat against men looking lustfully at their wives. He should study the comic post-cards in Morecambe.)

The Station Hotel is a regular hang-out of T. Dan Smith, I am told by the barman. Another regular of the bar says that 'Grouse is a very smooth blended whisky but if you drink a bottle of it, you'll get a hangover'. What bottle of whisky does not give one a hangover?

15 October – Newcastle I had never known before that Newcastle has a splendid Cathedral, the former parish church of St Nicholas. It was made a bishopric in 1882 but was nearly given promotion as long ago as 1553, when John Knox was the parson. This fate was averted because of the death of Edward VI. Although he said some amusing things about women, Knox was a power maniac, an Ian Paisley of his day. Apparently Charles I attended this church when he was prisoner of the Scots and, one Sunday, had to hear a sermon denouncing his government. When the preacher, to rub in the point, called for

Psalm 52 ('Why dost thou tyrant boast abroad thy wicked words to praise'), the king stood up and called instead for Psalm 56 ('Have mercy, Lord, on me, I pray, for man doth me devour'); and the congregation sang the psalm of the king's choice. This Cathedral, like many churches these days, has a visitors' book. Normally these books are filled with banal comments – 'nice', 'well kept', 'peaceful', and so on, but this one has a taking entry: 'Dear God Please pray for me I have lost my faith in you Help me Get it back I have also lost my money (I believe Police took it from my wallet) as this was for my holidays in two weeks time I don't know what to do. Pray for me. Patrick.' He adds his address 'because I don't think you know about me'.

16 October –Newcastle The local papers have routine articles about youth unemployment. At the party conferences, even the Tory one, the stirring tirades on the horrors of unemployment were made by people from north-east England. This area, Geordieland, has a tendency to self-pity; it is constantly moaning about the injustice and suffering it has endured, though much of the damage was self-inflicted. The misfortune of north-east England once had a basis in bad luck: the coal and shipbuilding industries suffered during the slump of the time between the two wars, and many people really suffered then. The Jarrow Hunger March did express a genuine grievance, even though it has since become a matter of myth and confusion. How many people know that the Jarrow hunger march was thought up and organised by the Jarrow Conservative Party? Strange but true. It was hotly opposed by the Labour Party in Parliament. And on the march, the protesters were given their best welcome by Tory mayors.

Strangely enough, the Tories have always been ready to offer sops to the North-East, to bolster its dying industries, to stuff money into its begging bowl. Harold Macmillan constantly prated about the suffering he had witnessed here in the 1930s, and when he was premier he created a special Cabinet ministry for the area, with, of all people, Quintin Hogg as the minister. Hogg came up here wearing a cloth cap, and made a fool of himself. In West Hartlepool, the waiter at my hotel said of Mr Hogg 'If he'd come to eat here, I'd have poured soup over him.' The Tories will never learn to expect no gratitude from the Geordies; the more money you spend on them, the more they will want, the more they will make you subsidise their indolence and cantankerousness. The children have an inherited knowledge of unemployment; they are taught it at school, as you can see by the essays on the subject appearing as articles in the local newspapers. And here, as in Liverpool, the unemployment is partly fictitious. There are no regular jobs, with pensions and benefits, but there are any amount of jobs on the black economy, which is flourishing here. In one pub I go to, two young men are bargaining with the landlady on getting a contract to paint the walls: cash only, no cheques accepted. Some of the staff of the pub, as well, are paid in cash only. I met two sisters, one a nurse and one in the civil service; they talk of unemployment and do not understand what it means. They talk of unemployed women working as cleaners or barmaids. I cannot persuade them that somebody who is earning money as a barmaid or cleaner is not unemployed. Their thinking is altogether odd. They assume that a woman who goes out cleaning is doing so for amusement, to get away from her husband and children. They are both, in their own words, 'husband hunting', in order to have children – 'the only thing that matters in life' – but also assume that after a time they will go out to work, to have fun. They belong to the world of the seaside postcards; the feminists would despair of them.

17 October – Newcastle The Station Hotel includes a 'Viking' restaurant, and there are other places in Newcastle named after those people. One would think that here in the North-East the Vikings would not be remembered as heroes but rather as monsters of cruelty and rapacity: but no, the Vikings have won a new image from television, especially the programmes of that Icelandic Viking apologist Magnus Magnusson. As it happens, this part of England still looks to the Scandanavian countries and Holland and Germany, rather than to France; it is to those countries that schoolchildren go on exchange visits. Only a few years back this city was crowded with foreigners, mostly from Scandinavia, who came to shop and drink at a bargain rate of exchange. I once went to breakfast at a hotel in Jesmond, the northern suburb of Newcastle, to find that the menu was printed first in Norwegian and only second in English; in the bar that evening I heard an English middle-aged woman demand and obtain £50 to go upstairs with a Scandinavian man. The boat to Stavanger was crowded with shoppers.

Some of the socialist thinking of Newcastle came over the North Sea from Norway and Sweden; T. Dan Smith, the Mayor and at one time 'Mr Newcastle', went to these countries and liked what he saw. (He also said at one time that he wanted to make this city the 'Venice of the North, with ring roads instead of canals'.) Now, the Scandinavians come in smaller numbers: the pound is strong and their governments slap a duty on anything bought in this country. It seems too, that those countries are now in a bad way. Denmark has long suffered the consequences of spendthrift behaviour; now Sweden as well is in big trouble. An article in the current *Spectator*, by Andrew Brown, suggests that Sweden may even be in a worse mess than England. Their vast expenditure on the civil service and local government bureaucrats, such as social workers, means that the public sector spending increases at twice the rate of industrial pro- duction; industrial workers now form a minority even within the trade union movement; while LO, the unions' central organisation, favours the public sector workers 'who automatically receive greater rewards from increased industrial productivity than do the industrial workers themselves.' The same thing has happened in north-east England, where power in the Labour Party, which used to reside with the miners and shipbuilding workers, has passed to the unions of the civil servants and local government employees. This helps to explain one very big difference between the North-East and Sweden where, according to Andrew Brown, 'it is still broadly true (though no longer axiomatic) that civil servants are completely incorruptible: but the point is that they do not need to be dishonest. The system is so spongey and inefficient that the money soaks into it quite legally.'

In the North-East, local government is corrupt in both these senses: tens of thousands of people are drawing salaries and expenses for useless jobs; *and* some of them have been taking bribes on top. I do not want to suggest that the North-East of England is the only, or even the most, corrupt part of the country. It is simply that we know most about it thanks to the bankruptcy of the Pontefract architect, John Poulson, who did much of his business round here. As a result of what came out in the bankruptcy hearings, Poulson, T. Dan Smith and another Labour bigwig, Alderman Andrew Cunningham, were arrested, tried and sent to prison.

The Poulson affair revealed the massive extent of corruption in the obtaining of architecture contracts: it extended through the housing and planning departments of councils, the civil service, the National Coal Board, the National Health Service, education authorities, British Railways and even the House of Commons. To make matters worse, Poulson was not even a qualified architect but, like Mr Pecksniff (another sanctimonious hypocrite), employed his ill-paid subordinates to produce the designs. The block of flats he erected at Felling, across the Tyne, fell into disrepair almost immediately and had to be rebuilt with government money; his Olympic-size swimming pool, built for Bradford, turned out to be inches too short. The physical outcome of architects such as Poulson and planners like Smith are seen in the ruins of Newcastle. *Si monumentem requiris* . . .

It is easy, too easy, to blame the corruption of English life on socialism, although most of the villains were found in the Labour Party, the unions, the civil service, the nationalised industries and the grossly inflated local authorities. Yet the corruption really began not under Attlee in 1945, but under Macmillan twelve years later. It was the Tories, not Labour, who unleashed the catastrophic property boom, in which money that should have been spent on improving our industry, went into high-rise office blocks and flats, ring roads and motorways, hideous new towns and slums. It was the Tories who started, or stepped up, the wave of public spending, of planning, of recruiting hundreds of thousands of public servants. It was in that age that Poulson flourished.

This period saw the rise to power of that infamous tribe, the public relations men, whose job was, and is, to obscure the truth, to put aside questions, to block inquiry, to gag the press. When I started in journalism, public relations men were still uncommon: if you wanted information you went to the man in charge. Only a few local authorities employed a full-time public relations man; now they employ them in double figures. The king of the public relations men was T. Dan Smith. His multitudinous companies were in part 'public relations', as we would understand the term, and in part channels of money for services to such people as Poulson. (I once did a company search on Smith's public relations firms connected with Northampton. My mind reeled from the effort, but I emerged none the wiser.)

Smith's usefulness to Poulson and others, was due to his friends in very high office: Gaitskell, George Brown, Edward Short and dozens of local Labour Party officials. I was, as it happens, the person who found out that Smith had the first public relations account on behalf of the Labour Party – this was in 1963, when PR was not quite respectable. I had met in a pub one of his ex-employees, who told me the gist of his operations for the Labour Party and others. I went to the Town Hall and waited an hour for Mr Smith to leave a meeting. He brushed aside my request for an interview, so I said to his departing back 'It's about your PR account for the Labour Party.' He became very friendly and very eager not to see this fact come out in print. When it did, Smith's first act was to issue a memo to his staff telling them not to talk to the press. That is the essence of public relations!

18 October – Chester-le-Street   From Newcastle, once the fief of T. Dan Smith, I went on to Chester-le-Street, which was once the fief of the much less amiable Andy Cunningham. Whereas Smith, for all his faults, had started life with fine ideals, and remains an engaging, intelligent person, the 'Godfather of Chester-le-Street' is an unlikeable boss of a kind that flourishes in the Labour Party. He was a bigshot in the General and Municipal Workers Union, and was once the finance chief in the Labour Party Executive, and a henchman of many Cabinet Ministers. On the day Cunningham came out of prison, the then Prime Minister, Mr Callaghan, took tea with him here in Chester-le-Street, which shows that Jim is loyal if not very tactful. Can one imagine Clement Attlee taking tea with a crooked politician? No, one cannot, for the Party then was strict in its moral code. The late Herbert Morrison, one of Attlee's principal colleagues, said that although he opposed capital punishment for murder he supported its use for corrupt people in local government: he would cause a holocaust in north-east England today.

At the height of his power Andy Cunningham ran at least five powerful public authorities in the North-East, including the Co. Durham police who later would have the job of arresting him. He wielded power not only as a union boss but as one of the region's main employers; as Chairman of Newcastle Airport Authority, whose workers are almost all GMWU, he was both boss and union organiser at the airport. When the Labour Party in London finally formed a commission to look into the rumours surrounding Smith and Cunningham, one brave soul stood up and said 'Let's be frank. If

Dan or Andy came into this meeting, two thirds of us here would shake their hands because we owe our jobs to them.' A friend who was present described the reaction to this remark as 'silence, broken by mass shuffling of feet.'

When a by-election arose in Chester-le-Street late in 1972, the split in the Labour Party came into the open. The National Union of Miners, who used to be paramount here, wanted a former colliery worker; Andy Cunningham, whose son was already an MP, wanted a GMWU man. He helped to get the selection as candidate of a researcher Giles Radice, who is an NW3 kind of Fabian intellectual. Many of the local Party were GMWU members, or otherwise owed favours and jobs to Cunningham. I reported on that election – indeed I can modestly claim to have broken the story – and well remember the strange, almost melodramatic atmosphere. Since I stayed in The Lambton Arms Hotel, the HQ of the GMWU faction, I had to meet his opponents by stealth: one man gave me instructions on how I should walk out of town on a certain road, and get into his car when it stopped beside me. I also remember Radice saying that with my accent it would not be safe to go into a miners' club; when I did so, the miners spent all afternoon buying me beer and filling my notebook with rude remarks about Cunningham and Radice. After a local freelance journalist had supplied me with much of the (accurate) information I used eventually in my article, I asked him why he did not write the story himself. 'If I used that story,' he answered, 'I would be put out of work.' The ability of the Labour Party to threaten and silence journalists is something I plan to discuss in Darlington, the major newspaper town of the North-East of England.

Chester-le-Street has a very long history. It had a major Roman camp where, I learn from a local historian, there were water closets in use here up to the fourth century AD – and not then again till the nineteenth century. It was also the earliest bishopric in the North-East of England and the repository of the Lindisfarne Gospels. It now uses *The Good News Bible*. It is odd to find that even in the early eighth century, Northumbrian Kings were notorious for their reckless spending in what we call the 'public sector'; in jobs and gifts for adherents. The Venerable Bede, who of course lived in Jarrow, predicted that all this spending would weaken the kingdom's defences.

A few years ago I discovered another claim to fame of Chester-le-

Street: the parliamentary seat is won at a by-election by Phineas Finn, the young Liberal hero of two of Trollope's Palliser novels. He does not call the place Chester-le-Street but describes a smoke-filled Co. Durham mining town; and Finn conducts his campaign from The Lambton Arms Hotel. He wins the seat from a rich, corrupt Tory, but only after a great deal of unpleasantness. And the pleasures of victory vanish entirely when, later in *Phineas Redux*, Finn is arrested and tried for the murder of one of his ministerial colleagues. Some of the critics at the time thought it too far-fetched for a Liberal MP to be charged with murder; at any rate, Finn, like Jeremy Thorpe a hundred years later, was found not guilty.

19 October – Durham 'Welcome to Durham. Home of Postal Bingo.' It is almost twenty years since I saw that sign in the railway station – a useful reminder that most of the folly of modern England dates to Macmillan's regime. The postal bingo sign seemed especially inappropriate to this sombre, menacing town with its great, grim Cathedral up on the hill and its castle, not to mention its high security prison. Throughout its long history, Durham has served as a fortress against a turbulent North, not just the invading Scots but treacherous English noblemen. The Percys, like Harry Hotspur, came from the North and tried to dethrone the unpleasant Henry IV, who had himself risen to power by Northern rebellion. The Pilgrimage of Grace, the rising in favour of keeping the old Mass, began in the North; it was crushed by Henry VIII. In Elizabeth's reign, the Papal faction rose once more, took Durham and smashed all vestiges of heresy in the Cathedral. In all Elizabeth's reign, while she travelled extensively through the South of England from London, visiting almost every year such distant cities as Norwich, Southampton, Bristol and Worcester, she never once ventured north of Buxton, and would not have gone there but for its curative waters. The North took the Royal side in the Civil War. Charles I hid in Durham and Cromwell arrived in the town as a conquering tyrant.

It was oddly enough in Ely, Cromwell's place of work, that I was lectured recently on the new peril of war between North and South. The speaker, a socialist school teacher, conjured up fearful visions of unemployed workers rioting in the streets of our northern cities and even marching on Westminster, if Margaret Thatcher – 'that bloody woman' – persisted in her disastrous policies. This northern revolt, both longed for and dreaded, is one of the fantasies of the southern, middle-class left. And here, in Durham, it might seem to be feasible. This was the only place in England where there was violence in the General Strike: three miners from Chester-le-Street derailed a train. The Durham Miners Gala each year offers the spectacle of the man-power of organised labour. Just up the road from Durham, at Con-sett, the British Steel Corporation has carried out the single largest closure of industry in the island, producing nationwide wrath from the left, and a mass of articles in the press called 'Death of a Town', and the like. 'Who cares about Consett?' demand the posters stuck on the side of the road to Durham Castle.

But seen close up, the North looks rather less menacing. For one thing, the miners, the proletarian vanguard, have lost most of their old power to the parasitical workers in local government and the like, and are much less militant than they were. If a mob should take to the streets it would probably be commanded by Trotskyite social workers, National Health Service clerks and radical feminist librarians. The annual Gala in Durham is frightening not for the militancy but the drunkenness of the miners who normally leave the town in a litter of smashed glass, empty beer cans and vomit. The landlord of a local pub was contemptuous of the Labour Party: 'Some of the Durham councillors come in here. Complete morons. Pissed out of their minds most of the time. One day they were going by coach to look at a bus stop, to see whether they needed to move it 200 yards. Twenty of 'em turned up, for the outing and the attend-ance money.' When the talk turned to Consett, the pub laughter was general. 'Serves them bloody well right. You'd go there and find them all in the pub from eleven till three. Until last year that is. Then somebody warned them that unless they did some work, they'd be out of business. They started work, and for the first time in years they made a profit. But it was too late.' An engineer in the pub, who had travelled all over Europe, said that even the Swedes 'have started to work again. They hadn't worked for fifteen years.' Whatever the Trotskyists and the trade unions say, some people in North-East England know in their hearts that their troubles are frequently of their own making.

The militancy of Durham is found in unexpected quarters. Passing the Town Hall this morning, I noticed a lot of young people coming out and shaking hands with a clergyman at the door. A glance at the

notice board showed that the hall was now in use for services,
pending repairs to the adjacent St Nicholas Church. Nothing odd
about that. But what was odd was the sheer number of people leaving the service – at least two hundred, I think, and all of them
young. Perhaps, I thought, a pop group had been providing the
music before some TV idol preached the lesson: I thought I would go
to evensong. Once again there was a big congregation, 160 by my
count, and again they were almost all young. Some were university
students, but even during the vacations St Nick's, as they call it,
enjoys a big attendance.

The service was strange and rather disturbing to one brought up in
the old Church of England. Extemporary prayer, rhythmic dances,
announcements given by a man in bright yellow trousers, invitations
to talk to each other after the sermon, and overall a kind of joyous
exuberance, even laughter. It was all, of course, done from *The
Good News Bible* and some weird version of the liturgy in which
'Lead us not into temptation' comes out as 'Do not bring us to the
time of trial'. What on earth does that mean? Surely the old line is
more up to date and intelligible even to those who have learned their
English in comprehensive schools. The new Bible and liturgy
frighten me for one special reason: you begin to forget the old text,
or whether the text has been changed at all. The Ministry of Truth in
1984 continually rewrote history and the archives of *The Times*, just
as the pigs in *Animal Farm* changed the original revolutionary
slogans so that in the end the other animals came to believe that
'Some are more equal than others'. I do not suggest (though I do
suspect) that the Bible has been perverted to make it conform with
our modern ideas; I do suggest, indeed I know, that it is very upsetting to find that words you have known by heart are changed into
something unfamiliar. This would be just as true of anything learned
in childhood, such as a nursery rhyme or a Wordsworth poem.

Changing the language of worship is still more frightening and
more alienating (to use that word in its proper sense) because it
deprives one of all the associations of church, of Easters and
Christmases, of childhood, of school chapel services, weddings and
funerals. It robs one of much of a lifetime's experience as well as of
that sense of continuity from the English past that was one of the joys
of attending church. Above all it deprives the believer in God of that
magic or mystery that was part of the old Bible and liturgy, a beauty

in words that was quite as inspiring to worship as any music. Such things make little appeal to the 'born again' young men and women of St Nick's. They are very devout, and most enviable in their certainty; but is their place in the Church of England? In its craze for modernity, and its fear of giving offence, the dear old C of E seems to tolerate every kind of tendency from the Holy Rollers through 'liberation' lefties and clerical 'gays' to the extreme Anglo-Catholics who are more Papal than the Pope. All that does not remain is the Church of England.

20 October – Darlington The Darlington *Northern Echo* is of special interest to all those who care about newspapers. It was edited for its first ten years by the most famous journalist in our history; it has the largest sale of a morning paper in any town outside London; and in 1977 it was the first daily newspaper to be closed by a strike over the right of journalists to enforce a union closed shop. The issues raised by the strike ought to be studied by anyone who believes in press freedom. But first let us examine the story of W. T. Stead.

The *Northern Echo* began on 1 January 1870 as the first morning newspaper to sell for a halfpenny. It soon caught the attention of Stead, then twenty years old, who was employed in Newcastle as clerk to a merchant who was also the Russian Consul. A fervent Christian, Liberal and social reformer, Stead started to send the newspaper letters, leading articles and reports on philanthropic matters. Although Stead had left school at fourteen he was a mighty reader of books and a fluent, even compulsive writer, who later advised aspiring journalists to 'fall in love with a clever woman a dozen years older than themselves' in order to practise their prose on long, passionate letters.

At just twenty-one, Stead, who had never yet entered a newspaper office, was made the new editor of the *Northern Echo*, the additional staff of which consisted of one 'experienced sub-editor'. Between them they produced, six days a week, four large pages of small-print copy, about evenly divided between editorial and advertisements. Stead reckoned that during his first three years in the job, in addition to editorial duties, he wrote more than one thousand leaders, three thousand notes and various other articles, which was comparable to about ten of this book's pages a day. He wrote in his journal in 1874:

There is no paper now in existence which can be to me what the *Echo* is. I have given it its character, its existence, its circulation. It is myself. Other papers could not bear my image and superscription so distinctly. I have more power and more influence here than [anyone] on almost any other paper, for I work according to my inclination and bias.

His boast of power was certainly not a light one: for the *Northern Echo* became a strong voice in the land. Although Darlington was a small town and the *Echo*'s sales seldom more than 5000, it was anything but parochial, as can be seen from the subjects of its leaders: 'Bright unveiling a statue of Cobden', 'The railway strike in the USA', 'The House of Commons and Irish obstruction', 'The local iron trade', 'Egypt'. Since in those days newspapers republished articles from their contemporaries, Stead became known, and the Earl of Derby wrote to *The Times* extolling the *Echo*'s views on the Gold Coast problem.

Perhaps because he had worked for a Russian Consul, Stead was a partisan of the Tsar against the Turks in their rivalry over the Balkan provinces, and was second only to Gladstone in waging the famous campaign against the 'Bulgarian Atrocities': indeed its first meeting was held here in Darlington. By 1877, Stead was an honoured visitor in London, where he made friends with Bright, James Froude, Thomas Carlyle, Albert Henry George (later Lord Grey) and Mme Olga Novikoff, the 'ambassadress of good will' for Russia in English society, who called the *Northern Echo* 'the best paper in Europe'. Lord Grey was later to remark, with some hyperbole, that 'this provincial editor of an obscure paper was corresponding with kings and emperors all over the world and receiving long letters from statesmen of every nation.' After ten years at the *Northern Echo*, Stead went to London to join the *Pall Mall Gazette*, where he introduced to newspapers the interview, illustrations, cross headings and 'by-lines'. He went to prison over his exposé of child prostitution, 'The Maiden Tribute of Modern Babylon'; and would have scooped the world on the sinking of the *Titanic*, had he not gone down with the ship.

Had Stead been born a century later, he could not have enjoyed such a splendid career. Without having passed through a training school approved by the National Union of Journalists, he could not have got the job on the *Northern Echo*, let alone started as editor. The NUJ would have soon put a stop to a man who worked long, 'anti-social' hours, and enjoyed his job. Which brings one to the question of whether journalists need a union, and whether the NUJ is not actually harmful to newspapers. Is journalism a trade, in the sense of something one learns as an apprentice, and works at until old age? The only specific skill, shorthand, that journalists are supposed to need has become of even less importance since the advent of tape recorders. It is a trade in the sense of 'knowing the tricks of the trade', in obtaining information, conducting interviews, and putting an article into the right order, but even these cannot be taught except by experience. The three most important qualities for a journalist – curiosity, quickness and writing skill – cannot be taught at all.

Journalism is, or ought to be, very competitive, with each man striving to get a new story, to get the most interesting 'quotes', to write the neatest headline or the most rousing editorial. The spirit of competition, within each paper as well as against its rivals, ought to pervade the provincial press as much as the glamorous worlds of Fleet Street and TV. The trade union movement does not, to put it mildly, encourage the spirit of competition.

Nowadays the wrong sort of people get into journalism. In the days of the 'Street of Adventure' journalists started as tea boys or secretaries; they worked on a trial basis, getting paid for what was published; they might even start because Daddy knew the proprietor. These days, the aspirant journalist must enrol in a training scheme. In practice all sorts of people now get NUJ cards. One can join at a publishing house, a public relations company, or at one of the small (usually left-wing) magazines, whose 'journalists' are so active now in the NUJ. It is just these people who want to bar, through a 'closed shop', genuine journalists who have worked for years by the pen.

The demand of NUJ branches to have a say in the choosing of journalists for employment has caused injustices and bad blood because often the applicants are considered, not on their merits, but on their political views. Still more unsavoury squabbles occur when the NUJ debates which of the women researchers or typists are eligible for promotion to journalists, and so to membership of the union. Inevitably the issue becomes confused by sentimental feelings, not least if one of the women is the wife or mistress of a union official: there was a comic example of this not long ago in the union branch of England's most self-important and least literate Sunday newspaper. The idle and incompetent journalists who tend to be union activists are by their nature hostile to women becoming journalists, simply because women work harder. The journalist who provoked the strike at the *Northern Echo* by not joining the NUJ was not only a woman but, worse still in the eyes of the NUJ, a product of Cheltenham Ladies' College and Oxford.

The arguments about the likely effects on the press of closed-shop legislation were discussed at length in *The Times* and elsewhere before the Bill passed through Parliament, with Lord Goodman leading the argument against Michael Foot, the author of the Bill and himself a journalist. The principal theme of Mr Foot's argument was that, although a closed shop might in theory be abused, one could depend on journalists to be reasonable and tolerant. A patent fallacy of that argument is that many people in this country regard Mr Foot himself as a dangerous and censorial bigot, the champion of trade unions against the law, the supporter of despotism in India, and a man so greedy for power that only today he has entered the fight for leadership of the Labour Party.

There have been dozens of instances of people using the closed-shop rule to suppress news. Many papers have appealed to the rules of the NUJ so as not to report on National Front meetings or violent incidents between people of different races. Shortly after the passing of Michael Foot's 'closed shop' Bill, the editorial staff of a Barnsley newspaper struck because some of their number had joined the rival Institute of Journalists; whereupon the local trades council, the local National Coal Board, and local miners union officals threatened to withhold information from non-NUJ journalists. The Act is a godsend to every crook in the Labour Party, the unions and local government. When a friend of mine wrote an article on over-manning by one of the London boroughs, a NALGO official wrote in to protest at attacks on fellow trade-unionists, some of whom, as he pointed out, also belonged to the NUJ. This was a reference to the public relations staff of the borough. Because of the closed-shop Act, the newspapers are now part of the vast web of secrecy which enmeshes government in this country. Only today, so I read in the *Northern Echo*, Darlington Borough Council has ruled that only firms which run a closed shop may tender for Borough Council work. This rule, which already applied to building contractors, has now been extended to garment firms which produce such things as hats and uniforms for the busmen. The *Northern Echo* reports the bare facts of this story but does not explore the enormity of its implications – as W. T. Stead would have done.

The effect of the Act has been largely negative and invisible: the newspapers have failed to pursue investigations that might offend fellow trade unionists. That is one reason why no paper, right or left, has ever tried to expose the notorious and quite blatant theft and corruption institutionalised in some of the unions, notably in the docks and Heathrow Airport. The newspapers dare not investigate theft and corruption even among their own print unions: at one Sunday newspaper, on a Saturday afternoon, the canteen tables used to be cleared and transformed into a huge thieves' market. A reporter once purchased there a revolver and two dozen rounds of ammunition: but he could not write about this in his paper.

In an article written in 1977, I wrote that the power of the NUJ was sometimes described as 'industrial democracy'; I did not imagine then how soon and how infamously this power was to be perverted. The people responsible for the worst misuse of union power are those two feminist writers for the *Guardian* who applauded the sacrilege on the Papal Cross. That was only part of the mischief done by Angela Phillips and Jill Nicholls. The first of those women is both a zealous advocate of abortion and an activist in the Freelance Branch of the NUJ. In that latter role she persuaded the union to grant some of its funds to a 'Right to Choose' campaign, and she backed a resolution that Britain's abortion laws should be extended to Northern Ireland.

This was too much for some of the Irish Catholics in the NUJ, one of whom, Billy Quirke, resigned and joined the Institute of Journalists. Since his newspaper in County Wexford had recently been declared a closed shop, his articles were 'blacked', or refused, as were his reports to Dublin newspapers. He made an appeal to a Dublin High Court for the right to work. One might have thought that Miss Phillips and Miss Nicholls would have been satisfied with the damage done to Mr Quirke. Not a bit of it. In a jointly signed article for the *Guardian* (26 August) they accused the Irish NUJ of insufficient severity: 'Instead of retaliating with a clear defence of the industrial importance of the closed shop and the need for trade union democracy, the Irish Area Council lost its nerve.'

Membership of the NUJ gives middle-class socialists the chance to identify with the 'working class', and it offers a way for Trotskyists, militant feminists and the like to impose their minority views on newspapers. One thing the NUJ fails to do is to bring financial benefit to its members. Journalists in this country are worse paid, taking inflation into account, than they were twenty-five years ago. As a young reporter in Manchester, I got £20 a week. The young reporters who went on strike in Darlington three years ago were earning as little as £30. English provincial journalists get about half as much as journalists on the Continent or even in the Republic of Ireland. The blame for this must be shared between managements and trade unions.

Like most British industries over the last twenty-five years, the press has tended to concentrate into fewer, larger units, each employing larger and often excessive staffs. The big papers, like Beaverbrook's *Daily Express*, deliberately raised wages, fringe benefits and allowances to a level that poorer newspapers could not pay so that the *News Chronicle*, *Daily Herald*, *Daily Sketch*, *Reynold's News* and *Sunday Dispatch* went out of business.

If mergers and over-manning have had bad effects on the Fleet Street newspapers, they have been disastrous to the provincials. In the old days when there were two evening newspapers, and one or two mornings, in most provincial cities, the journalist who thought he was worth more money could find a job with the rival or try for a job in Manchester or London. It is illuminating to compare the state of British provincial and even Fleet Street papers with those in Ireland. Dublin, a city of 700,000 people, has three Sunday newspapers, three mornings and three evening. Compare this with Manchester, whose once famous newspapers are now reduced to the *Evening News*, or London, which used to have three evening newspapers and next month will have only one. The Dublin newspapers thrive and pay excellent wages because they have very small staffs, not because of the NUJ, whose minimum claim is way below what the journalists actually get.

The uselessness of the NUJ was shown during the strike here in Darlington. Before the print unions stopped the paper, the *Echo* continued to be produced by only a quarter the editorial staff, those who were not NUJ members, and circulation hardly suffered at all. Three-quarters of the *Echo* staff were simply redundant. During another NUJ strike, in Kettering, the editor went on producing the paper single-handed and actually raised the circulation.

Unless it can gain a closed shop, or can bring out one of the print unions in sympathy, the NUJ can exert no bargaining power whatsoever. All it can do is lower wages. Even after their six months strike, the NUJ here in Darlington failed to establish a closed shop and failed to obtain a new wage agreement (they accepted the one obtained by the IOJ). All they did here was, in the words of one of the journalists, to create 'a very unhappy newspaper'.

It is worthwhile comparing the wages obtained by the NUJ with those enjoyed by W. T. Stead. When he joined the *Northern Echo* at the age of twenty-one he was given £150 a year, or double what he had earned as a merchant's clerk; the following year this was increased to £250, and in 1875 to £300. He said of his job at the time: 'In money, of course, it is not much, but it is enough to keep me comfortable and Bell [the proprietor] has promised me a share in profits hereafter.' At the *Pall Mall Gazette*, Stead got a starting salary of £1000 with an extra £100 for writings additional to his regular duties.

From looking through old advertisements, one gets some idea of what such salaries were worth in terms of contemporary purchasing power. In Darlington a hundred years ago, one could buy a six-roomed house for £225, rent a five-room house for £14 per annum and an eleven-room house for £50. The fees for one term in Darlington's 'Middle-Class School for Boys' were one guinea per term. Down south, one learns from the *Pall Mall Gazette*, things were marginally more expensive, so that a seven-room house in Oxford, with a tennis court, stable and large garden, was up for sale at £1500 or rentable at £100 per annum, a furnished nine-room house near Clapham Junction rented at two guineas a week, and a furnished flat in Victoria for twelve shillings. New books sold at about six shillings, and rum, gin or whisky cost two shillings (10p) a bottle. Allowing for tax, one can say that a twenty-six-year-old journalist on the *Northern Echo* was paid the modern equivalent of £50,000 which is rather more than the NUJ has obtained for its members. Indeed, since managements tend to regard the NUJ minimum rate as a ceiling, the wretches obliged to join in the closed shop are getting far less than they would by free negotiation.

The drop in earnings of journalists has been accompanied by a drop in status. Of course some of them want this. The militant NUJ pickets one sees clutching the *Socialist Worker* and screaming out 'scab' are often from middle-class homes and (unlike Stead) have attended a university. If, for sentimental or neurotic reasons, they choose to think of themselves as down-trodden workers, they cannot complain if the newspaper proprietors pay them wages to match.

Darlington is a Quaker town, hence the name of the football team and this item in today's *Evening Despatch*:

THE CHEATS. Jim lashes front three. Quakers 'cheats' have been privately and publicly slammed by acting boss Jimmy Shoulder. Uncompromising words at a 45-minute dressing room inquest followed the 1–0 defeat against a steady but uninspired Peterborough side on Saturday. That defeat left Quakers firmly rooted in the Fourth Division basement.

21 October – York – Bradford I stopped off at York to take another look at the glorious Minster, now restored. Beneath the church is a good display of the archaeology of the site, including Roman artefacts, a model of Roman headquarters at York and a replica of a bust of Constantine, who was here proclaimed Emperor by his troops. He went on to found Constantinople, legalise Christianity and, in effect, begin the transmutation of the old Roman Empire into the Holy Roman Empire. My musings upon the tradition of York were brutally interrupted by the remembrance of a newspaper report: the National Theatre has put on a play called *The Romans in Britain* comparing the Roman occupation of Britain with modern British 'imperialism' in Ireland – a play complete with modish scenes of buggery, violence and nudity. Surely the tragedy of these isles is that Rome never extended its empire, civilisation and laws either to Ireland or northern Scotland, which have remained to this day largely ungovernable? York itself, when the Romans withdrew, was sacked by a horde of barbaric Irishmen.

It would be interesting to compare the relative cost of the restoration and upkeep of York Minster with building and subsidising the National Theatre. The fund to restore the Minster was started in 1967 and raised £5 million in voluntary contributions. The plan for the gruesome building on London's South Bank was launched at about the same time and was paid for entirely by central or local taxes. The upkeep of the Minster requires £30,000 a year in donations, which is a modest sum compared to what is asked by other cathedrals in England. The National Theatre, so we discovered after the *Romans in Britain* scandal, gets £630,000 a year from the

Greater London Council alone. I could go and find out how much it gets from the Arts Council or other government bodies, but the discovery might depress me further.

The National Theatre is one of the worst of the bad things that have occurred in the past twenty-five years, the period I look back on during my journey through England. Discounting mere tendencies, such as inflation or hooliganism, I soon compiled quite a long list of specific bad innovations during this period: the National Theatre, the Arts Council, the Ministries of the Arts, Overseas Development and the Environment, oil exploitation both on and offshore, motorways, the Beeching railway plan, legalised immigration, commercial TV and radio, comprehensive education, life peers, destruction of old counties (the worst of all), joining the Common Market, abolition of old regiments, Concorde, betting shops, metrification, decimalisation, the Series 3 Liturgy, *The Good News Bible*, one-day cricket, licensed pornography, mixed Oxford and Cambridge colleges (I approve of mixed public schools), all quangos, the merger of BEA and BOAC, state and municipal lotteries, the abolition of Sunday post, all new universities, referenda, test-tube babies, heart transplant surgery, abortion on demand at twenty-eight weeks, VAT, the Ombudsman, the Race Relations Act, the Equal Opportunities Commission, the *Manchester Guardian*'s move to London, and the abolition of property qualifications for jury service.

Oddly enough, almost every one of these bad things was done either by, or during the period of, a Conservative government.

I spent twice the time compiling a list of the good things that have happened during the last twenty-five years: the restoration of York Minster, the abolition of hanging (for murder: it might suit other crimes), the Campaign for Real Ale, improvement in Rugby Union rules, the Welsh, Scottish and Kent opera companies (see *Southsea* and *Bristol*), *Private Eye,* and the *Daily Telegraph*'s Peter Simple column, I am at present reviewing, for the *Spectator*, *The Stretchford Chronicles*, a selection of Peter Simple, marking the twenty-fifth anniversary of the column. The author of most of these pieces is Michael Wharton, the funniest and the wisest man in England and, I am proud to be able to say, an old friend. This chronicle of the last twenty-five years is in about equal parts hilarious and depressing; and nowhere more depressing than in his paragraph on York Minster, written in 1968. 'A plague of demonstrators is now infesting every part of life. At York they have been picketing churches which are said to be redundant. At the back door of the Minster, some carried a placard reading "Why? A rich church, a poor world".' After disposing of the fallacy that the sharing of church wealth would help the poor, Peter Simple proclaims the truth that when York Minster was built,

few people, if any, thought it a waste of money or an affront to the poor. It was a visible symbol of the splendour of God, and this, if it is anything, it still remains. Far from being an affront to the poor, it is an affront to the rich, to the powerful, to the secular rulers of this world who, believing that no other world exists, must measure everything in terms of this world's use, whether in peace or war.

The West Riding is Wharton's birthplace, and Bradford has inspired one of his greatest characters:

There is an old prophecy in Bradford that at a time of supreme peril for the city the 22-stone, iron watch-chained, indigo waist-coated Alderman Foodbotham will awake from his age-long sleep in his granite mausoleum on Cleckheaton Moor and ride forth in a spectral tram to save his people. When, not long ago, the beautiful smoke-blackened heart of Bradford was torn out to make way for cheap, cardboard skyscrapers, many thought the Alderman's moment had surely come . . . But now Alderman Foodbotham has a personal rather than a civic reason to awake at last. The Conservative Party Conference at Brighton has actually passed a monstrous motion urging the Government either to abolish aldermen altogether or to ensure 'fair representation for substantial minorities'.

(The abolition of aldermen is another to add to my list of bad things done since 1955.)

Fourteen years later, Wharton described how local government workers were chosen in Bradford by Alderman Foodbotham,

the 25-stone, crag-visaged, grim-booted, iron watch-chained perpetual chairman of the Bradford City Tramways and Fine Arts Committee, and for many years Lord Mayor.

There must be people still living who remember the local government hiring fairs which were held every Monday morning in Town Hall Square, in the shadow of the vast smoke-blackened building with its bell-booming towers piercing the rainy skies and indeed, as some believed, actually precipitating the rain.

At the hiring, Alderman Foodbotham 'would go along the line of waiting men, occasionally stopping to poke a likely-looking accountant in the shanks with his stick, or peer into an open mouth, or address a stern yet kindly word to some veteran ledger-clerk or departmental sub-head who had known better days.'

As always, Nature has aped Mr Wharton's art. On the train from York, I read that a Mr Edward Adams, seventy-one, a retired school caretaker from Sussex, had come to Bradford.

to sample its delights as a package holiday centre. Mr Adams of Mann Street, Hastings, was accorded star treatment by the Lord Mayor and other civic leaders as the first person to book a £91 package tour of Bradford next summer. Cllr Arnold Lightowler, wearing full mayoral regalia met the pensioner and his daughter when they arrived by train. Then he presented the first of many hoped-for visitors with a giant stick of rock, suitably inscribed Bradford, as the local Hammond Sauce Works brass band struck up a lively version of 'Ilkley Moor B'aht 'At'. The rock, a local delicacy when soaked overnight in vinegar, was made specially for the occasion by a firm of confectioners at Keighley.

My delight at Alderman Foodbotham, Councillor Lightowler, the Hammond Sauce Works brass band and the rock soaked in vinegar, was promptly dispelled on arrival at Bradford. The first thing you see is a poster calling for help in catching the Yorkshire Ripper, whose tally of murdered women now stands at twelve; and the next thing you see is Bradford itself – a maze of ring roads and hideous blocks and flyovers and desolation. Manchester looks almost untouched by comparison. Bradford is far worse even than Liverpool or Newcastle and may prove worse or at least as bad as Birmingham. And they have cleaned the Town Hall.

I decided to get drunk but walked about twenty minutes before finding a pub, where a gloomy man told me at length why he had not liked Australia. So I went to a concert, sat through the Wagner and the Sibelius, then went to find another pub before the Berlioz. The pub I discovered was decorated with an immense impression of Bradford Town Hall, and a police photograph of a murdered woman. The wanted man is not the Ripper but one of the other criminal maniacs round here.

22 October – Bradford – Barnsley 'Anger over County's sale of souvenirs' is the headline over the story that West Yorkshire County Council plans to compete with local shops in selling souvenirs at

Haworth, the Brontë village. I hope Mr Wharton has spotted this and will tell us the comments of Julian Birdbath, the man of letters and the discoverer of a fourth, hitherto unsuspected, Brontë sister, Doreen. She had little patience with her sisters' literary pursuits. 'Her own interests were mainly in dog-breeding, ballistics and light engineering. Mr Birdbath reproduces a design for a primitive kind of machine-gun which anticipates Maxim . . .' The bus to Barnsley travels at first on a motorway through a moorland of flyovers, exit roads and giant electric pylons. We turned off the motorway and stopped at a town that I did not recognise as the Wakefield that once was a kind of headquarters for covering Yorkshire. It was the seat of the old West Riding County Council and also the legal capital; it was therefore the place where the Poulson bankruptcy hearings took place. That was the last time I went there. But Poulson got his revenge. He or his kind had destroyed the town that destroyed him. Oddly enough, the one place in Yorkshire I know that has almost completely escaped the process of Poulsonisation is Poulson's own home and headquarters of Pontefract, which remains a pleasant eighteenth- and nineteenth-century market town.

It was raining in Barnsley, but not enough to disguise the visual horror I now expect on returning to towns I have known of old; I have not been here in almost twenty years. The town hall is still there, with treble the number of workers no doubt, but its eminence is contested by the Granada Bingo building. Barnsley used to be run by the Co-op. The story went of a stranger in town who asked a policeman 'Where's the Co-op?' and the reply came 'Every bloody where'. The two hundred shops of the Barnsley and British Co-op Society did a trade of £250,000 each week and employed 3000 people out of a population of 75,000. The Co-op was a law unto itself. If one of the staff was caught out stealing, he or she might be tried and punished in private court; the licensing magistrates, all of them Co-op members, might turn down the applications of private enterprise firms; but an old miner told me, twenty years ago: 'I remember the three day week during the thirties. We were really glad of the divvy [dividend] then and the local Co-op would always help out with a bit of credit. Like the rest of the mining families we pretended not to take this help. But we had to or starve. And Barnsley won't let the Co-op down now.'

Or will they?, I wrote at the time. And needless to say, they have.

The BBCS continues, but only in competition with all the multiple stores of a giant shopping complex. There used to be an outdoor market. In my earlier report from Barnsley I wrote that 'Barnsley people swarm to the old outdoor market which cannot have changed much since its foundation in the thirteenth century. The pedlars here know a racy line in sales-talk ("I've admitted it, luv, these potatoes fell off the back of a lorry" or "At Selfridges, London, this costs you nineteen guineas") and do good business on dry days.'

Twenty years later, I find that the outdoor market is still doing good business in spite of the fact that now it is under a three-storey car park. Otherwise nothing has changed. You still see mounds of excellent vegetables and fruit such as Howgate Wonders, the cooking apples almost as big as footballs, and the sales talk now is anti-Common Market: 'English tomatoes! Get your English tomatoes! Guaranteed English Golden Delicious apples!' and so on. You can buy trifle dishes, home brewing kits, and plastic packets of herbs or sweets: 'Please don't squeeze the bags, they might complain'. The biscuit stall offers wonder: Butter Thins, Keil Fingers, Foxes Ginger, Jacob's Fig, Burton Fig, Fully-coated Mis-shapes, Brontë Mis-shapes. The outdoor market under a car park flourishes. The shops of the 'complex' do little business. Good!

The Queen's Hotel has been taken over and now offers very good food. When I was last in Barnsley, on Good Friday of 1961, the waitress produced what she said was a hot-cross bun, and I said in a joking way that it was uncrossed and cold. I thought she was going to hit me. Another journalist I know was actually hit by a night porter for having requested a sandwich. But if the staff are friendly now, some of the clients are not. Last Saturday, in the fine old bar of The Queen's, supporters of Barnsley and Millwall, the visiting team, broke thirty glasses and chucked a chair through one of the windows. No arrests were made. 'If you or I were to do that, there'd be hell to pay,' said one of the hotel staff 'but with hooligans the police just seem to accept it. They don't want to know. They call it keeping a low profile.' One can hardly blame the police. They succeeded in catching the youth in a neighbouring town who had shot another young man with a crossbow, the bolt going through a thick leather jacket and deep into the shoulder. The assailant was fined £150, or 'beer money' as people said in the bar here.

Once, in The Queen's Hotel, I spent a good evening with some of the local miners and Barnsley's MP, Roy Mason. I dimly remember we ended the evening in one of Barnsley's Chinese restaurants and one of its smartest casinos. I liked Mr Mason, although I remarked in my diary at the time that his manner would make him unpopular; he did a quite good job as the Secretary of State for Northern Ireland. The Ulster people thought him rude, but nevertheless they respected him. His handling of the Ulster problem did him both harm and good in his Barnsley constituency. There are many Irish Catholics in the South Yorkshire coalfields, but Barnsley is also the main recruiting ground for the Artillery Regiment, which is now an infantry unit and suffered many casualties during a stint in Ireland. Even some of the Irish Catholics here support Mr Mason, or so I am told. There were two in the bar tonight from County Tyrone, in Northern Ireland. They were drunk, and I thought it unwise to go into politics.

Because of his past, Mr Mason now has a bodyguard. 'It's not because of the IRA,' I was told in the bar, 'but because of the Labour left-wingers.' I see that, writing in 1961, I said that 'since all politics here are socialist, the bars divide into left and extreme left.' The latter is now led by Arthur Scargill, the miner's leader whose friends have taken control of the local Labour Party and want to depose Mr Mason as candidate. However Mr Scargill also has enemies; like Mr Mason he is regarded as cocky, though like Mr Mason he is admired for his energy and intelligence.

Barnsley seems to me tamer than I remember it; the conversation is less rich. I recorded in 1961 this scornful rebuke by a barmaid (not at The Queen's) to a salesman who had made improper suggestions: 'Listen to me, young feller. If I got you into bed I'd make you tremble so much you'd have to go back by taxi. It's the same with all you men, you only get the idea when you've got some beer inside you. Now my late husband, he really was a man. He didn't need beer. He could do it on bread and jam. Aye, he could do it on bread and jam.'

I was interested, not to mention amazed, to read in *The Times* that Barnsley has been the subject of a research project entitled 'The Book in the Community'. The Book Marketing Council of the Publishers' Association despatched to this town a team to pave the way for a 'book promotion' next April. The head of the Council is quoted as saying: 'We looked for a town of manageable size, with a sense of community rather than established bookselling and book-

D

reading traditions, a town with local newspapers and other media that would be interested and active, and we felt that support from local library services, local societies and local government, including the education authorities as well as the retail trade, would be vital.' *The Times* report ends gloomily: 'BMC statistics show that only 2 per cent of leisure spending is on books, compared with 39 per cent on drink; and that is a national figure, not Barnsley's.'

I know nothing about the publishing trade or how it can hope to sell books. But I thought it worthwhile taking a look at the local bookshops to find what Barnsley people are buying before the 'promotion' next year. The only bookshop I found was W. H. Smith's, who have taken a large two-storey premises in the shopping centre. (Smith's and Boot's are among the stores that tend to take space in these shopping centres.)

The Barnsley W. H. Smith's has two window displays. One is entirely filled with 'top name toys', the other is almost entirely filled with electronic computer gadgets, 'six exciting games to test your skill', programmed video systems and watches, plus, in the bottom left-hand corner, one copy of Smith's 'Book of the Month', Graham Greene's *Ways of Escape*. Going into the ground floor shop one discovers newspapers and magazines, Christmas cards, toys and greetings cards, paints and other artists' materials, 'gift ideas', like garden kits, kitchen gloves, candles, chess sets, sports bags, ice buckets, children's bricks, pens and typewriters, cigarette lighters, field glasses, radios and masses of paper plates and cups, and – right at the end – a sign pointing upstairs to 'records, Christmas ideas, gift vouchers, books'.

Upstairs the book section comprises one third of the space. The books are themselves divided into the categories of Transport, Motoring, Do-it-Yourself, Gardening, Hobbies, Sport, Natural History, Atlases, BBC Publications, Nursing and Medical, Textbooks, Dieting, Cooking, Children's, Biblical (Twenty-one Bibles of which only one, called 'School Bible', used the Authorised Version), Art and Architecture, Poetry, Fiction and Non-fiction. In the poetry section there are no collections or even selections of Milton, Wordsworth, Coleridge, Tennyson and Yeats but a big display of '*Selected Poems II* by Erica Jong, author of *Fear of Flying*'. Non-fiction displays biographies or memoirs by Robert Morley, John Mills, Frank Muir and Val Doonican. The paperback non-fiction has none of the

Penguin history, biography or current affairs books one usually finds in a W. H. Smith's. The hardback fiction contains nothing by the classic novelists. Paperback fiction includes one Dickens, one Jane Austen, several novels by good modern writers like Orwell and Greene, though nothing by Evelyn Waugh. All in all I should say that of 'leisure spending' at W. H. Smith's in Barnsley, about fifteen per cent was on books. The spending on what might be called good books – the classics, and modern titles that might be reviewed in *The Times Literary Supplement* – amount, I should estimate, to less than one per cent of the turnover of the shop. I do not write this in criticism of Smith's local managers; their job is to make money and not to improve the public mind. Whether it is desirable that Smith's have so large a group of shops – in many towns and in railway stations amounting to a monopoly – is a subject outside the scope of this book. Anyway, I want Smith's to sell mine.

23 October – Barnsley – Doncaster   I boarded a bus for Doncaster, expecting to have to pay at least a pound, and was taken aback to be charged 24p. An official of the bus company told me that Barnsley subsidises the bus fares out of the rates, so that the lowest fares are still as little as 3p, or 2p for children, compared to the lowest fares in London of 15p and 12p. Two good results of this are that Barnsley people will travel to work, unlike the people of Liverpool who insist on having a job next to their home. Low fares have also brought people back to public transport; this company has just added twelve new vehicles to its fleet. But why should the subsidy come from the rate-payers and not from the car-owners who get an enormous, disguised subsidy from the tax- and rate-payer in building and maintenance of the roads system? I suppose the answer is that politicians dare not offend the car-owners, still less the car-workers.

You leave the bus in the station, walk up the steps and find yourself in Doncaster's very own Arndale Centre. As I am now a connoisseur of these places, I can proclaim this by far the most hideous. The centrepiece of the 'Mall' is a revolving statue of a man and a woman, naked and gilt, with their arms thrown up in the air for joy, and their loins pressed tightly together. One arm of the man holds the woman's waist, apparently in an effort to stop them both falling on to their backs. As these preposterous figures revolve, a shower of water falls on them from the Arndale Centre ceiling.

I cannot pretend I am glad to be back here in 'Donny'. It reminds me too much of writing about the South Yorkshire coalfields. Actually going down a mine was not quite as frightening as I expected, perhaps because fear was dispelled by pure physical weariness; you come out feeling as though you had run twenty miles or scaled a mountain. Another time I was sent by the *Manchester Guardian* to write a report on the Yorkshire miners' refusal to work with Hungarian refugees from the recent uprising. I came away convinced that the miners were right to refuse outsiders, partly for safety reasons and also because they form a hereditary village community that likes to stick with its 'own kind'. The *Guardian* would not publish the story. Even to this day, and in spite of the Race Relations Act, the great majority of the pits refuse to take immigrants. This tradition dates to 1922 when the British miners expressed solidarity with the South African miners who started a revolution on the Rand under the slogan 'Workers of the World Unite for a White South Africa'. The miners were quelled by the bombs, artillery and infantry of South Africa's army, but later the South African Socialists joined with the Nationalists to impose white supremacy in the goldfields.

Once, I heard news of a strike at one of the pits near Doncaster and went to investigate at the nearest pub. Yes, the miners told me, they had just been called out and were now going along to a pit-head meeting. Did I want to come with them? We walked to the pit, chatting jovially of this and that, and joined the crowd at the back to hear the ranting of the shop steward, a Communist. About half way through his address he spotted me as a journalist, picked up a newspaper and set it on fire, meanwhile denouncing the capitalistic press. I was kicked out (literally) by two of his Communist henchmen. Back in Doncaster, I went to the offices of the National Coal Board and asked for information. I was shown into a room where three public relations men sat drinking tea. The phone rang and a secretary took the call. 'It's the *Evening Post*,' she said, putting her hand on the speaker mouthpiece. 'Tell them there's nobody here,' said the chief public relations officer, who then blandly asked me how he could help. I asked if the Board had issued a statement about the strike. 'There isn't a strike,' he said. 'But I've just been there,' I answered. He thought for a bit and then gave me a bit of advice: it would be better not to write about it.

The head of the South Yorkshire National Coal Board was W. H. Sales, scourge of the Communists, and a man of gravity. He looked like the actor Jean Gabin and had the same habit of dangling a cigarette from his lower lip. Many years later Sales was tried and convicted for taking bribes from Poulson. He had also done quite well out of the NCB and us the tax-payers and coal users. According to Michael Gillard and Martin Tomkinson, the authors of *Nothing to Declare: The Political Corruption of John Poulson*,

When he [Sales] worked at Doncaster he frequently used to ring up a very expensive hotel just outside the town and inquire, "What is the most expensive item you have on the menu for hors d'oeuvre, for main course, for dessert?" and order what was most expensive for the party. Eating and drinking would continue well on into the late afternoon and the NCB virtually kept this particular establishment in business.

Once again, we get this insight into the nationalised industries simply because Sales happened to know Poulson, who happened to go bankrupt. For all we know, the same luxury at the tax-payers expense is enjoyed throughout the nationalised industries, the civil service and local government. Thinking of people like Sales, I begin to forgive those bitter Communists who had kicked me out of the rally. Were they not right to detest their new masters, the Coal Board?

I was here in Doncaster on my last day with the *Manchester Guardian*. Three years earlier I had joined on three months trial. When the three months were up, the editor told me to look for another job. I could not find one. Then, in Cheshire, I hit on a story that made the front page: a sow had killed and eaten a fox in its sty. At any rate that was my story. The widow who owned the sow was deaf, and simply nodded assent to my questions. After this first success, I started to get more stories into the paper and stayed on indefinitely as a kind of freelance. I cannot have had a permanent contract, for one summer I took three months off to travel the Balkans. Now in May 1958, I was leaving for France and then to Vienna to start up a press service with two other *Manchester Guardian* journalists. (The plan never took shape. One of my colleagues got married and needed a steady job. The other was murdered in Paris.)

At the time I left, I was still the newspaper's Yorkshire correspondent and therefore I had to report on the opening of a railway repair yard in Doncaster. I dimly remember a tour of the works, a speech, some cocktails and sitting down to lunch. I had a hangover and tried to put it right with wine. The man next to me also had a hangover. He was about twenty-two, rather thin and haggard. I told him that I was just leaving the *Manchester Guardian*. He told me he had just been sacked from a Yorkshire evening paper. We drank to the seemingly dismal future. Then I suggested he took my job. He brightened at this and we had some more drinks. I rang up Manchester and told them that if they were really lucky they might just be able to get a brilliant young journalist who was getting offers from every paper in Fleet Street . . . We grew more and more happy until next morning I woke up under the carpet in his sitting-room. I left for France, and my job on the *Manchester Guardian* went to the young Michael Parkinson.

24 October: Bawtry   To Bawtry, the southernmost village in Yorkshire, bordering Lincolnshire and Nottinghamshire. 'It grew up round the old A1,' I was told by a local, which shows how little people know of their history. King Harold stopped at Bawtry in 1066 on his way from Stamford Bridge – where his troops had defeated and killed the Norwegian King Harald Hardrada – to Hastings. Talking of Harolds, the staff of Yorkshire television have asked the former Prime Minister Harold Wilson to head a consortium, on the grounds that he is the most distinguished living Yorkshireman. The most distinguished? I wonder if he is even as famous or popular as Freddie Trueman, the cricketer, Harvey Smith the horseman, or, come to think of it, Michael Parkinson.

On Friday nights in Bawtry an auction is held of used cars. There are dozens of buyers from London and other big cities – men in leather or padded jackets and anoraks, all with the grey, joyless look of the motor trade. To one who knows nothing of cars, they seemed to be going cheap. A Ford Cortina must be a bargain at £60 as long as it starts and possesses four wheels. Apparently many London dealers come on the train to Doncaster, take a taxi to Bawtry, buy a car which they drive down to London, clean up and sell in a few days more for a healthy profit.

East Anglia

LINCOLN – ELY – KING'S LYNN – EAST DEREHAM

NORWICH – LOWESTOFT – SOUTHWOLD

ALDEBURGH – WOODBRIDGE – FELIXSTOWE

BURY ST EDMUNDS – CAMBRIDGE

25 October – Lincoln   I came once, briefly, to Lincoln on work, but I did not have time to go up the hill to see the Castle, the Cathedral, and other historic wonders. Not for the first time on this journey, I felt ashamed of my ignorance of my country. Lincoln was one of the cities that quarrelled with King John over taxes and privileges; he was going to Lincoln from King's Lynn when he took sick and died. John appears as a villain in *A Short History of Lincoln* by Sir Francis Hill, but the more I read of him, the more I think he was one of the best of our sovereigns. 'John was the true son of the King who devised writs to bring business to the royal court of justice, who watched over the Exchequer and supervised the justice his judges administered to the shires . . . No King has ever known England better than John, for no king has ever been so continuously moving up and down its roads.' That is the judgment of Doris Mary Stenton in *English Society in the Early Middle Ages.*

There is the John who interests himself in the administration of justice, is ready to listen to the cry of those whom contemporary practice would bar from immediate access to his presence and make available the new judicial practices to his Irish subjects. There is the John who can organise defence and attack on the grand scale, so that it seems as though English naval history must begin with him. There is the John who introduces new fat pennies to take the place of an outworn currency, who sees the possibility of a Merseyside port and founds Liverpool.

Doris Mary Stenton was writing in 1950. Since then, most of the institutions founded or fortified by King John have gone. Our Navy is down to a couple of sloops; our fat pennies are turned into slender pence; and Liverpool as a port is no more. Needless to say, modern English and Irish people do not enjoy the right of complaint and access to government such as our ancestors had to King John.

It used to be said that King John was an enemy and exploiter of Jews. In fact, he wrote to those who lived in the diocese of Lincoln:

Henceforth, we commit the Jews dwelling in your city to your charge; if anyone attempts to harm them do you always protect them; for in future we shall require their blood at your hands if through your default evil happens to them, which Heaven forbid; for we know that these things happen through the foolish people of the town, not the discreet, by whom the folly of the foolish should be restrained.

The attacks on the Jews in Lincoln, Norwich and York were inspired by the enemies of the king, by the barons and what was eventually to become the parliamentary faction. The nastiest outbreak in Lincoln occurred in 1255 when a Christian boy was found dead in a well, and the story spread of his having been seized and crucified by the Jews in derision of Christ. A Jew denounced his fellows, saying that ritual murder was practised each year. He was hanged. Other Jews were taken to London and some of them executed. The boy victim came to be known as Little St Hugh and his story occurs in Chaucer's *Prioresse's Tale*. Not long ago, the owner of Jews' Court, next to the twelfth century Jews' House, constructed a 'well' in his basement, and charged admission to see the supposed place of martyrdom of Little St Hugh. This commercial enterprise failed; Jews' Court became a slum and was bought by the Corporation. It now houses the Craft Centre of Lincolnshire and Humberside Arts.

The people of Lincoln opposed a good king, John, but caved in to the worst king in our history, Henry VIII. In October 1536, some 40,000 Lincolnshire people, led by the clergy and gentlemen, gathered here to protest against the Act of Supremacy. The king sent them a letter: 'How presumptuous then are ye, the rude commons of one shire, and that one of the most brute and beastly of the whole realm, and of least experience, to take upon you, contrary to God's law and man's law, to rule your prince whom you are bound to obey and serve and for no worldly cause to withstand?'

The rebellion collapsed and some of its leaders joined in the plunder of monasteries.

For thirty years of the nineteenth century, an MP for Lincoln kept up the anti-monarchic tradition. This was the arch-reactionary Colonel Charles Sibthorp, who hated industrialism, the factory system, Free Trade, Catholics, the Crystal Palace and foreigners, therefore the Prince Consort. He crowed like a cock in the House of Commons when bored by one of the Manchester radicals. He was a great foe of the railways, and it is thanks to him that the main line to Newcastle by-passes Lincoln. Instead the city now has a main road next to the Cathedral. The traffic in juggernaut lorries threatens to shake the building into collapse . . .

A pleasant pub here, The Wig and Mitre, is marred by a ghastly plaque: 'This is to certify that Simons Design Services Ltd has gained a Premier Award in recognition of human and social responsibility and environmental quality in respect of The Wig and Mitre Public House Lincoln.' This infernal document is signed by Peter Parker and David Broadbent, respectively President and Chairman of something calling itself the Business and Industry Panel. Presumably this is the same Peter Parker who is running down our railways. A nice revenge on the city of Colonel Sibthorp! Can one not now go to a pub without suffering 'human and social responsibility and environmental quality? Come to think of it, plaques such as that could drive one to drink.

26 October – Lincoln – Ely To Matins in the Cathedral. A dignified service using the Authorised Version and proper liturgy. I notice however that almost the whole congregation is over forty, in contrast to that I described at St Nick's in Durham. In the debate on mutilating the liturgy, people do not sufficiently stress the poetic and magical element in the old version. Take the line 'The sea is his and he made it: and his hands prepared the dry land.' The words 'and he made it' are, strickly speaking, repetitive and unnecessary but they help to give the sentence divine wonder. Compare that with the excerpts from Michael Wharton's 'Bevindon New Testament' which is scarcely more ludicrous than *The Good News Bible:* 'Please provide facilities, Jesus commented, for infants of pre-school age to associate with me whenever feasible. They can play a relevant part in the life of the future world community.'

By train to Newark to Peterborough to Ely. For the first time in more than a month of travel, I found some difficulty in getting accommodation. The White Hart had a room for only one night. Of course Ely is a tourist attraction but East Anglia prospers more than the North. Commercial travellers come here still. The last time I was in Ely, I was the only person in my hotel who was not attending a weekend conference of the National and Local Government Officers, the frightful union which seems to be mostly composed of strident social workers. The regulars in the hotel bar were moaning about the invasion: 'We're always getting these union meetings; it was the railwaymen last week . . . They're NALGO this lot. Just listen to them calling each other "brother" and "comrade" and flashing their rolls of ten and twenty pound notes – our money, mind you. They look so sour and miserable. You can tell what they are by the beards and the bra-less.' The NALGO small talk seemed to consist largely of glottal whines and grievances: 'Like when it's a case of health and safety, and management says no, you've got to get stuck in . . . If he was doing it just to save his face, we might not get any more provincial councils.' And some of the locals sympathised with the NALGO people. A master at King's School – founded by Alfred the Great – complained that there was not enough teaching of economics and business management and too much teaching of Latin and Greek which would not be useful in working life . . . This latter day Gradgrind, incidentally, is just the type who complains of 'Dickensian' conditions – a favourite epithet of NALGO spokesmen.

Ely has always been radical or cantankerous since Queen Etheldreda, its eighth-century founder, refused to consummate two arranged marriages, thus qualifying for sainthood at her death – caused by a throat tumour attributed to an early passion for necklaces. On her saint's day this year, I went to a service in St Etheldreda's Church in London, at Ely Place, to hear a most interesting talk on her life and work given by Monsignor Francis Bartlett. At the end of the talk he described how, when employed at the Vatican, he was given the task of inspecting St Etheldreda's mortal remains, which had once been sealed in a casket and kept by recusant Catholics during the time of religious strife in the sixteenth and seventeenth centuries. Monsignor Bartlett had actually held in his hand the tiny and shrivelled hand of St Etheldreda.

I discovered from John Seymour's splendid *Companion Guide to East Anglia* that Etheldreda's name was corrupted to St Audrey and thus to tawdry, because of the poor quality goods sold at Audrey fairs. There was nothing tawdry about the saint herself; she established a priory that became a fortress of English faith and national spirit against the Danish invaders, and then the Normans. Ely was the last place in England to hold out against William the Conqueror. The partisan leader, as we should call him today, was Hereward the Wake. His deeds were romanticised in a novel by Charles Kingsley, called *Hereward the Wake: Last of the English*, which reads like propaganda for Kingsley's 'muscular Christianity'. He presents the thesis that lowlands or fenlands produce few heroes because these 'being the richest spots, have been generally the soonest conquered, the soonest civilised, and therefore the soonest taken out of the sphere of romance and wild adventure, into that of order and law, hard work and common sense, as well as – too often – into the sphere of slavery, cowardice, luxury and ignoble greed.' Lowland people are therefore first to deteriorate:

In the savage struggle for life, none but the strongest, healthiest, cunningest, have a chance of living, prospering, and propagating their race. In the civilised state, on the contrary, the weakliest and silliest, protected by law, religion, and humanity, have their chance likewise, and transmit to their offspring their own weakliness or silliness.

I doubt if this theory would win the approval of NALGO members; but then they would not have heard of Kingsley, unless as the author of 'sexist, elitist' *Water Babies*.

27 October – Ely Almost six centuries after the death of Hereward, Oliver Cromwell was tythe-farmer, or what we would now call the tax-man, to the Dean and Chapter of Ely, although when war broke out, he led a party of troopers to the Cathedral and drove out priests and communicants, afterwards smashing the popish statuary. He was not an ecumenist.

The great William Cobbett was sent to prison for two years for having written a spirited protest against the flogging, at Ely, of English soldiers by Hanoveran mercenaries. Twenty years later, during one of his Rural Rides, Cobbett came back to Ely, interviewed two of the men who survived the flogging, and made an inflammatory speech from The White Hart. He painted a very unflattering picture of Ely in *Rural Rides*, comparing the bishop badly with those of pre-Reformation days. Unusually for a man of that age, Cobbett realised that English civilisation had been in decline since the Middle Ages. Torture, for instance, was not introduced till the late Middle Ages and was still not as severe as the terrible floggings at Ely. The city flourished during the Middle Ages, but fell into poverty in the eighteenth century; as late as 1816 the starving farm workers rioted in the streets of Ely. No one was killed but afterwards, at the Bishop of Ely's court, five men were sentenced to hang, five to deportation and many to long terms of prison. Such was the justice meted out in Protestant, parliamentary England.

The radical spirit has been revived, in a sense, by the election to Parliament of a Liberal, the chef, dog-food advertiser, and 'TV personality' Clement Freud, who fancies himself as King Edward VII's double. 'He's enormously popular here,' I was told by an Ely Conservative. 'He's a marvellous constituency man and we'd have to put up somebody really sensational to unseat him.' An ex-Army officer – 'I was in Kenya, chasing the Mau Mau' – spoke still more admiringly of his MP: 'I know I'm a Conservative, but I didn't vote for Mrs. Thatcher. I voted for that other chap, Freud. I know he's a German Jew, but a nicer man you couldn't hope to meet in a day's march.' Well, well, well.

The nice Mr Freud has not too many problems to solve in his Ely constituency. Apart from things like inflation, which hurt us all, the people I meet are most concerned about getting a decent schooling for their children. The grammar schools have been abolished and replaced with what are called village colleges, which seem to vary a lot in standards of teaching and discipline. 'There are five round here,' I was told by a father, 'and frankly I'm over the moon that I've got my daughter into a good one. Two of them are little more than legalised brothels.' He exaggerated, I trust.

The farmers complain a lot about frost, trash (weed) in the beet crop, manganese, and 'stress', which seems to affect the vegetable kingdom as well as human beings. But farmers with hundreds of acres of wheat, potatoes and beet no longer even pretend to be out of pocket, or anything other than stinking rich. And they cannot resist the temptation to swank about their Mercedes, their holidays in Barbados and how much they got for the last sale of land. They all frankly enjoy life round Ely, especially the many people you meet who have come here from places like Yorkshire and South Wales. London, Cobbett's 'Wen', has little attraction: 'I go there once a year for the Smithfield Show,' I was told by one farmer 'and all I see of it is from the taxi between Earl's Court and Liverpool Street. I couldn't live there or even work there.' The main anxiety of the farmers concerns the discontent of the labourers. 'Frankly they're not paid enough;' I was told. 'Some of the big companies in the farming business want to pay them more. With mechanisation you don't need many employees but those that there are should get a bigger share of the profits.' This farmer is no doubt satisfied that the farmworkers union has just put in a 100 per cent pay claim.

28 October – Ely   The Jerseys munch in the meadows beside the Ouse; Friesians keep to the hillside among the chestnut trees; and tomtits search for food in the cracks of an old brick wall by the Bishop's Palace. The Cathedral itself is a wonder beyond description, perhaps the greatest artistic achievement in England's history, so it comes as rather a shock to learn that all the £25,000 a year needed for urgent repairs comes only from private donation, and nothing in subsidy from the state; a useful reminder of cultural and spiritual values in a society where the Arts Council pays £305,000 a year to the Royal Court Theatre, much of which sum, as revealed by Auberon Waugh (*Spectator*, 8 December 1979) finances a Young People's Theatre Scheme including a course of lectures by Anna Raeburn on counselling, Angela Phillips (of the National Abortion Campaign),* Maureen Colquhoun (described as an ex-Labour MP, feminist, lesbian), Rose Robertson (Parents Enquiry for GAY Teenagers), Hazel Slavin on contraception and Lucy Toothpaste (Rock against Racism). When you are standing in Ely Cathedral, such things as the Arts Council and NALGO appear in perspective.

Beautiful though the building is, it can also inspire sombre thoughts. In the delicate Lady Chapel, where Cromwell's troopers knocked the heads off every statue, I thought of Pol Pot, that twentieth-century Cromwell whose Khmer Rouge madmen are said

* She is one of the *Guardian* women who praised the sacrilege of the Papal Cross. See *Liverpool*.

to have knocked off the heads of most of the Buddhas and dancing girls in Angkor Wat. Nothing changes; certainly not for the better. Ely Cathedral was begun about two hundred years before Angkor Wat, and the Lady Chapel was finished in 1349, the year when the Black Death struck England. Yet the Black Death was a mild affliction compared with what the modern Cambodians suffered under Pol Pot. At least people then had the chance of survival. I thought of Ingmar Bergman's movie *The Seventh Seal,* set at the time of the Black Death, in which, at the end, the knight rides out on the sea-shore to meet the horseman Death, and overhead the cloud forms into a mushroom cloud, and a jet plane forms a vapour trail – a master stroke of anachronism.

The sky over Ely is criss-crossed with the vapour trails of Air Force planes; one can seldom forget the thought of a horror worse than the Black Death and Pol Pot combined. During the last war East Anglia was covered in bomber bases and now has been chosen to form the site for many batteries of the Cruise nuclear missiles which, it is hoped, could wipe out Eastern Europe, should the need arise. In many East Anglian villages, polls have been taken on whether or not to allow these bases, and so far the vote has been favourable; the American Air Force are generous spenders. The Bishop of Ely, the Rt Revd Peter Walker, has expressed concern about 'the way we can assume that in the end there is no choice about this matter . . . and the way we can internally acclimatise ourselves to the thought of nuclear war, and by talking about ways to survive, lose sight of the monumental and incalculable destruction that would be the actuality.' The enemies of the Cruise missile plan have put out a poster, which you see in several windows in Ely, showing a nuclear mushroom cloud and the caption: 'Is the wind blowing in your direction today?' Like most people, I hardly need reminding about the danger of a third world war. I am guilty of what Bishop Walker calls 'internally acclimatising' myself to the thought; how else can one stay sane in face of the awesome danger?

Walking along the tow-path this morning, I noticed two anglers, float-fishing, who let the ends of the rod dip in the water, instead of keeping it raised in readiness for a strike. It occurred to me that there was some other place I had recently been where the anglers used the same lazy practice. It was Dalat, in Vietnam, where I had been back last April: the Vietnamese fishermen always dip the end of the rod in the water.

29 October – King's Lynn On the train to King's Lynn, I wondered again at the sheer variety of this country's splendour. Two weeks ago I was walking the fells of Grasmere, and now I enjoy a completely different but no less enchanting landscape of rich brown earth fields, where the seagulls wheel behind a plough, of dykes, windmills, poplars and farmhouses – all shimmering in that East Anglian light which has made this the home of English painting. Just as the fells are superior in their grandeur to the mountains of Switzerland or Austria, so this flat country of Norfolk is somehow grander than Holland or Belgium. I read in the papers today that Michael Parkinson is off to make his fortune in Australia. I envy him Sydney and Melbourne; but Australia has no proper countryside. Charles Darwin remarked on the ugliness of the continent and its monotony. I once met an English woman who came back from Australia although she greatly admired the people. Why? 'I just couldn't stand all those dead trees,' she replied.

A couple in the compartment are kissing; an ordinary sight one might imagine, except that, when I come to think of it, this is rare enough to be worthy of notice. Twenty-five years ago, young people were always kissing and spooning in public, or necking as it was called. Now there seems to be no intermediary stage between getting to know one another and full sexual intercourse. Or does it mean what I sometimes suspect has happened, that all the pornography and the propaganda for sex has turned people against it? Now that sex is no longer romantic, mysterious or in any sense naughty, it may have become just boring. In the United States, that fountainhead of absurd trends, the latest craze is for celibacy. Even young married couples, scarcely returned from their honeymoons, are 'into celibacy' for the sake of the personality. I was brooding on this when I saw that the male of the kissing couple was wearing an earring, and come to think of it, had very smooth hair and a woman's haircut. All very strange.

The lady at my hotel said 'Room 12A. You're not superstitious, I hope.' As a matter of fact I am, but did not dare to admit the fact. I became still more alarmed by the sign posted on the mirror: 'ILLNESS. Should there be an emergency and you require a doctor during the night, assistance can be found by contacting the occupant of room 4 which is situated on the ground floor through the door left on the bottom of the main staircase.'

King's Lynn is a noble town surrounding the vast Tuesday Market Square, which somewhat resembles those *pleins* in Amsterdam. Indeed there are parts of King's Lynn – for instance, the brick alleys between seventeenth-century houses – that could be the subject of many a painting by Vermeer and Pieter de Hooch. This was once the busiest port in the country, after London, and it has seen a revival in recent years due partly to good trade in the region and still more to the wrecking of ports like Newcastle and Hull. I am told it is common to see the flags of as many as twelve countries flying in King's Lynn.

Of the two fine old churches, St Margaret's seems to have suffered most, what with a gale in 1741, flooding in 1978, and pigeons. 'The pigeons at St Margaret's are a menace' reads a sign (to which someone has added: 'NOT . . . they are all God's creatures'). The sign goes on to explain that in 1977, some 8½ tons of pigeon manure were removed from the West Tower; the gutter beneath the eaves of the chancel was blocked by the dead bodies of pigeons. About 600 birds live and nest on the building, contributing to its 'splitting, sinking and leaning'. I hope King's Lynn does not make the error of certain Italian cities which brought in Ethiopian pigeon hawks only to find that their droppings were larger and more corrosive than those of their prey.

In a pub I meet two women with badges – 'Save Lynn Jobs'. They are threatened with redundancy by the Dynatron factory and will lose jobs worth £78 a week. One of them is moaning about another woman who said to her 'You've got a car, haven't you? You've got a TV, haven't you? You've got a washing machine, haven't you? Well why don't you just go on the dole?' People here just cannot get used to the fact of having been priced out of the market. It is now the Koreans, the Hong Kong Chinese, the Taiwanese, perhaps even the Indians who are going to get the cars, the TVs and the washing machines . . . King's Lynn used to be Bishop's Lynn and belonged to the Bishop of Norwich. Its conversion to King's Lynn predated the Royal Family's acquisition of Sandringham as a country house, but the town has close ties with royalty. The Queen Mother especially likes King's Lynn and has done a lot to raise money for things like the restoration of St Margaret's Church. There is also some scurrilous gossip still concerning King Edward VII, whose sexual frolics at Sandringham, as elsewhere, command a prurient fascination. A middle-aged barmaid told me of how she was born out of her age: she should have been Lillie Langtry. It is instructive to find how the amours of past royalty and politicians – Parnell, or Dilke or Lloyd George – are so much more interesting than the much more frequent and less discreet affairs of present-day men of state. They were exciting, I suppose, because they offended against a morality that we have abandoned.

30 October – King's Lynn – East Derehem – Norwich The excellent bi-weekly paper, the *Lynn News & Advertiser*, carries a good story from Fakenham, whose local Council decided to plant a tree in the Upper Market Place and, fearing vandals, protected it with a heavy iron cage with spikes on top: 'Last weekend, the vandals bodily removed the tree guard and carried it further up the market place. The tree remained unscathed.'

I got off the bus at East Dereham, inspected the sights and went for a drink in a pub that chanced to be run by a couple from London. They liked the draymen here compared with the 'bolshie buggers' in London – but found that Norfolk could be frustrating: 'If you want something done, like fixing a door, you have to get in a southerner. The self-employed people here will work enough for their beer money and then take the rest of the week off. They just don't turn up.' About two minutes later, a bald, bearded man entered the pub and called for a Guinness. He was a casual barman, and the landlord asked him:

'You're coming in on Sunday evening, aren't you?'

'Am I? What for?'

'You said you'd come and mind the bar. You said it on Monday, don't you remember? You were wearing a blue sweater and smoking a pipe.'

'To be quite honest, I'd forgotten all about it. But now I'll put it in my diary.' He fumbled through some of his coat pockets but obviously did not possess a diary.

The couple are full of good-humoured jokes against the local people: 'We play in a darts tournament against other pubs. In one of them the ceiling is so low that they've dug a pit in front of the board so you can throw properly. Another pub has the dartboard behind the fruit machine, so you're throwing over the shoulder of a man who's trying to win a quid's worth of tokens.'

The talk turns to the animals which provide much of the country's wealth. Goats are prized these days: they are sold to the Arabs in London for feasts at the end of Ramadhan. But goats are intractable. 'Have you ever tried to get one into the back of a car? And geese are difficult too. There's a man near us who has three of them – Freeman, Hardy and Willis. They tried to escape last week but they're so fat that even on taking a long run they only just cleared the bungalow and they came down to earth half a mile away.'

The paper that day had carried an item on 'Churkey', a new Norfolk hybrid of chicken and turkey, but everyone in the pub said it was old hat. The conversation turned to the coypu, the massive water-rat which has spread and multiplied in the county over the last fifty years. Was it edible? Opinion divided. Not till later in the day did I learn of another addition to Norfolk wild-life, the zander, a fish that was introduced to the Ouse in the 1960s and now is a prime target of anglers. It looks a bit like a pike and may be the 'pike-perch' I have eaten in Warsaw.

I buy the evening paper, whose front-page headline, next to the photograph of a mushroom cloud, talks of a nuclear threat to Norwich, described by some boffin as the most threatened city in England. This may be true but is not, surely, a reason for papers to make our flesh creep. I remember in Manchester, in 1957, or there-abouts, how the *Evening News* carried a headline like 'We will A-blast North-West: Khrushchev.' On reading this, one Lancashire man killed his wife, his children and then himself. If he had waited till the later editions he would have seen something like 'Killer Rain Hits N-W Roads' and a tiny paragraph on an inside page saying that Khrushchev had said that if attacked, Russia was capable of destroying any city in Europe.

31 October – Norwich This is the biggest city for a hundred miles but has somehow escaped the destruction of other places its size. The reason for this is largely negative: the Norwich Labour Party, which ran the city during the heyday of the developers, was not taken over by crooks and 'public relations' men. When I came here in 1961, after twenty-seven years of Labour control of the city, I found that the leadership of the party was liked and respected even by local Conservative politicians.

Bad luck as well as good sense have helped to preserve so much of what is ancient and beautiful in Norwich. When steam power revolutionised the textile industry at the end of the eighteenth century, this ancient textile town had no source of coal in the neighbourhood and could not compete with the new, growing industries in Yorkshire and Lancashire. Norwich underwent a depression and took on the character of a market town. People could not afford to knock down their houses and build in the Gothic style; and by the time Norwich's fortunes began to improve in this century, the Tudor, Jacobean and Georgian styles were back in favour. It is one of the local axioms (I reported nineteen years ago) that 'if there's a boom or a slump, Norwich won't feel it till long after the rest of England.' England then was right at the start of the long, disastrous boom in which money and energy poured into road-building, property speculation, mergers, take-over bids and asset-stripping, but not into sound productive industry. Norwich was not caught up in that false boom, which is why she is now less hurt by the present slump. 'Norwich people pull together,' an engineering contractor told me. 'In my firm the employees understand that their interests coincide with the management's.' Would that were true of the rest of England.

31 October – Norwich – Lowestoft – Southwold   Alas, I cannot linger in Norwich (I am meeting my wife and children for a weekend break at Southwold) but manage the time to revisit the Castle and see the fine collection of paintings. To say they are almost all local is not a disparagement since Norfolk painters are surely the best in the history of English art. Best, that is, as a school of art, for apart from Crome, none was really outstanding. But they show the landscape before it was ravaged by industry and the motor car. (*Pace* the art critic Richard Cork who once condemned poor Constable for having depicted things like haywains and Salisbury Cathedral rather than working-class conditions.)

I went by train to Lowestoft where I had some time to spend before getting a bus to Southwold. Since it was lunchtime in a fishing port, which is also a busy seaside resort, I thought I might purchase some fresh fish and chips, but found only emporiums of the jumbo beef-burger and fried chicken. The decline of fish and chips is another matter for sadness and one I cannot explain. When I was last in Lowestoft in the summer I went to inquire into the troubles of the fishing industry. Was it true that imports were pushing down the value of home-caught fish? Was it true, as industry spokesmen said, that 'men are fed up at seeing the threat of their livelihood grow day by day?' I used to report on fishing from Grimsby and Hull, and recall from that time how seldom it is that fishermen ever agree on what is wrong with their industry, so I was not surprised, here in Lowestoft, to hear the official version denied. A fish merchant, sorting plaice into plastic tubs, told me: 'You've been hearing long-shoremen's talk. A load of bullshit. There hasn't been a Dutch or Belgian or Danish ship landed here in five years. Only boats from Lowestoft are accepted here. It's true that some are owned by the Dutch but the crews are local people. What's wrong with the fishing industry? It's not cheap imports. The real explanation is the high cost of fuel. These boats were designed for speed at a time when fuel was cheap. The Dutch boats are modern, designed for high cost fuel . . . The other reason is that people don't buy fish any more. We're not allowed to fish for herrings now, and if we were we haven't got the boats any more equipped to catch them. And people's eating habits have changed. Twenty years ago if we got a good catch of herring, we could sell 50 stone to a fish shop and they'd get rid of them. Now, if we got a boatload in, we wouldn't know what to do with them. Housewives don't want to buy herrings. Kitchens these days aren't designed for cooking fish.' It is a piece of social history that deserves proper study.

1 November – Southwold I went to the common to see the tree which was planted in August to mark the eightieth birthday of the Queen Mother who has known the town since she and her husband, then Duke of York, used to preside at boys' club festivities here. Yes, it is still there, which is quite an achievement for Southwold. At the planting ceremony, which I attended, Mr E. B. Hurren, the town mayor (as his office is now called), said that the site, which is sheltered by houses, would give the tree the chance to survive; this was in answer to critics who said it was 'daft' to plant a tree on a common. Indeed his address was a catalogue of the mishaps that had befallen trees planted on royal occasions, from the Jubilee oak for Victoria 'that didn't last long' to an oak for the Duke of York in 1932, and a coronation elm for his coronation five years later. The first of these trees apparently vanished – along with a gold coin, a silver coin, and that day's *East Anglian Times*, which had been planted beneath it. After the third disaster, in 1936, the boys in the camp clubbed together to buy the clerk of Southwold a book called *The Care of Trees*. Very facetious, but, as Mr Hurren knows only too well, the position of Southwold, battered by north-east winds and the sea itself, is not conducive to trees or much beyond gorse, bracken and marsh reeds.

There is quite a gale this evening, and talk at The Lord Nelson turns to a favourite Southwold topic. 'That was the year The Swan was lucky: all the chimneys fell but nobody was hurt. The Red Lion lost theirs too . . .' 'I used to live in a house that when the chimney moved in a storm, the whole house moved with it. There were four fires serving that chimney . . .' 'Our chimney here has a steel support, so I expect when a storm comes the chimney will stand but the house will come down round it . . .' 'They used to know how to build in those old days. They lined everything with rushes. We took up our flooring and found the bundle of reeds still there, 300 years later. Now they tell us to save heat with polystyrene; but they knew better 300 years ago . . .' 'Yes, the chimneys, for instance. They were lined with lime but soot attacks lime so they put on another lining of cow dung. Nothing gets harder than that . . .' 'Yes, if you look at old timber it may look worm-holed on the outside but it's sound inside. They had to buy all the timber from Portsmouth. All the new timber went to the Navy . . .' 'There was someone in here today who'd seen a man hit by a falling slate but it only got his shoulder.'

In 1953, the ocean broke over the sea wall and flooded the town with much loss of life: one of the pubs on the estuary shows the high-water mark. When film companies want to do *David Copperfield*, especially the shipwreck and drowning of Steerforth, they do not consider Great Yarmouth where it was set, but Southwold, whose present lifeboatmen maintain the tradition of Peggotty.

A dozen Southwold men live entirely by fishing – a large proportion, since during the winter months the population of the town shrinks to a thousand. They leave before dawn and return in the late morning with plaice, codling and dabs, which are sold fresh in the local shops – an unusual thing even in fishing ports, when so much of the catch is sold to some distant middleman and then sold back to the fishmongers several weeks later. (In Ireland it is even worse: at Clifden, on the Connemara coast, I was told that the nearest place to buy fish was in Galway. And this was a Friday!). Some Southwold people have joined one of the trawlers at Lowestoft, which used to be a herring port before catching those fish was banned, and now does medium distance fishing as far as Iceland. A Southwold girl told me a heart-rending tale of what the fishermen endure: 'My brother ran away to sea – he left his car at Lowestoft docks – because he likes the life so much. But often they go out ten or twelve days and come back owing the company money. They get £35 a week to be paid to their wives and may get another £20 but often they get nothing more.' But as I remarked at Lowestoft, one needs to be sceptical about fishermen's grievances.

Nor can I wholly sympathise with another Southwold grievance: the buying of houses by Londoners and outsiders to use as 'second homes', which are closed except for the holiday season. This tendency over the last twenty years has put up the price of houses twenty-fold, or far more than the rate of inflation, and made buying a home an impossibility for local young people. Some of the purchasers have gone in their old age to live in their second homes and eke out their lives on the sale of their previous homes; but this has given the town a certain atmosphere of senility. Hence the cruel graffiti at Southwold's nearest railway station: 'Harwich for the Continent. Darsham for the incontinent.' Southwold welcomes retired people but cannot abide the rich who leave their second homes empty.

'I fully sympathise with the Welsh who burn down English second homes,' said one fierce young man of what might be called the better class. 'If I had the courage I'd go and burn down a house at Walberswick' – the twee, neighbouring village which is the second home of many a Hampstead actor, potter and William Morris socialist, as well as Clement Freud, the popular MP for Ely.

Some blame the Heath regime for having offered a subsidy to the purchasers of a second home and would like instead some kind of a swingeing tax. To my mind, it would make more sense to impose a double or treble rate on owners of second homes, thus easing the burden on those who actually live and work in the town. I heard a local shopkeeper remark: 'The rates here are terrible. Do you know, in the first half of the year, the council pestered me for £234. If I'd been living in a fisherman's cottage and had a title, I'd have been all right.'

But one cannot blame the buyers of second homes. Inflation and the collapse of productive industry have made it impossible to invest or save except in property. The economy of the 'second image' is found at its worst in the countries of Eastern Europe like Poland, Czechoslovakia and Yugoslavia, where the new bourgeoisie save for their future, and that of their children, by purchasing or erecting villas in the countryside – while the peasants drift to the cities.

Southwold is far from being a mere retirement place for the middle classes. In fact, it is one of the places round here where industry thrives. As the heavy industries of the Midlands and North are now in decline or have vanished, so East Anglia has resumed the place it enjoyed in the fourteenth century as the richest part of the Kingdom. Agriculture remains the base of the wealth, but most of these small towns also possess some kind of industry. In Southwold this is the Adnam's brewery.

The Campaign for Real Ale and other advocates of traditional brewing agree that Adnam's bitter and old are two of the best beers in this country. Obviously this is in large part due to brewing by old-fashioned methods. It is fun to go round Adnam's and hear the homely details of running a family business: how, for instance, the yeast was brought from a Norwich brewery thirty-seven years ago, only a few hours before that brewery was destroyed by bombs; how yeast renews itself and the surplus is sold to make Bovril and Marmite, though some would like the surplus dumped in the sea as sustenance for the fish. The fluoridation of water, which started in Southwold in 1964, created trouble; apparently it was put into the water supply first thing in the morning, so that Adnam's, who start work at the same time, had two or three brews spoiled by the chemical.

The success of Adnam's is not just attributable to the taste of their beer; it shows up the folly of modern economists. During the late Fifties and early Sixties, the majority of the breweries were bought up and merged into the giant Six, which in turn diversified into property and manufacturing. The Labour Party's Manifesto of 1963 promised to nationalise brewing. Both capitalists and socialists believed that brewing would benefit from 'economies of scale', that production would rise and prices fall, as explained at the time by Lord Vaizey, the Wilson-ennobled economist. Under this pressure from left and right, most of the small brewers sold out to the Six.

The result was not just bad beer but a swift decline in efficiency, a fall in profits, and a steady increase in price. An Adnam's pint, in Southwold, costs 40p compared to the 55p charged by some of the big brewers in London and other cities. The failure of the Six is partly attributable to bureaucracy, restrictive practices by the unions, and transport costs in getting beer from a few central breweries to the pubs. The financial director at Adnam's said to me that the biggest single cause of inflation in the industry had been the prices and incomes policy; whenever the time drew near to raise prices to meet the rising costs, companies spent like mad to qualify for the price rise.

Those Trotskyists who have wormed their way into power at the Campaign for Real Ale – these pests like to attach themselves to a going campaign – have found to their horror that all the good brewers are hostile to trade unions. A director of Adnam's made the policy clear: 'We don't allow our staff to join a trade union. We don't allow union representatives to address the staff on our premises, or in one of our pubs. And to hold a union meeting in a church hall simply isn't on. Our wages aren't high by national standards but we've increased our staff to 115; we have a Rolls Royce of a pension scheme, and if we did raise wages considerably this would cause a great deal of upset in the rest of the community.'

Southwold is free not only of trade union wreckers but most of the hellish features of modern England. There is only one chain store in a town which provides three excellent bookshops, two good fish-mongers, various food shops, cheap hotels (two of them owned by Adnam's), pleasant pubs (most of them owned by Adnam's) and, in summer, a repertory theatre. An inspection of the war memorial shows that a lot of Southwold people have borne the name Gold-smith, but I am told the town is not responsible for the millionaire grocer from whom I received a writ a few years ago – or rather, should have received a writ: the document was delivered by mistake to Richard West, the *Daily Telegraph*'s philatelic correspondent.

When last I wrote about Southwold, in the *Spectator*, I called it a favourite town of two of the greatest Englishmen of the century – Eric Blair (George Orwell) and Clement Attlee, our last true Prime Minister, only to be corrected by a reader who said that Orwell had stayed here only because he had a room in his father's house, that in fact he hated the town and had sent it up in *A Clergyman's Daughter*. Since I cannot face re-reading that dreary book, I must take it as true that Orwell disliked this town. But if so, I think he deceived himself. In *The Road to Wigan Pier*, Orwell wrote brilliantly of 'the cult of northernness', the idea 'that the industrial work done in the North is the only "real" work, that the North is inhabited by "real" people, the South merely by rentiers and their parasites.' Orwell noticed what now is a frequent phenomenon – the cult of the North among southerners. He recounts how a friend of his, brought up in the South but living now in the North, was driving him in a car through Suffolk. He glanced disapprovingly at a beautiful village and said: 'Of course most of the villages in Yorkshire are hideous; but the Yorkshiremen are splendid chaps. Down here it's just the other way round – beautiful villages and rotten people. All the people in those cottages there are worthless, absolutely worthless.' Orwell quotes from another southerner, now living in Lancashire: 'I am in Clitheroe, Lancs . . . I think running water is much more attractive in moor and mountain country than in the fat and sluggish south.'

Perhaps Orwell suspected that he himself half subscribed to the cult of Northernness. He was an honest man and he may have come to regret his unkind portrayal of Southwold, written a few years earlier. Certainly he would have hated Walberswick which then, as now, was a haunt of middle-class socialists, 'the bearded sandal-wearers and fruit-juice drinkers and birth control fanatics' he so despised. He also despised the jamborees of the Duke and Duchess of York. But I do not think he despised the Southwold brewery workers and fishermen.

2 November – Southwold – Aldeburgh The gale goes on but the weather is bright, so I take the opportunity to make this next stretch of the journey on foot. I head for Aldeburgh, twelve miles to the south. Ideally I would have made this whole journey on foot, on a bicycle or, like William Cobbett, on horseback; however I do not get on with horses, quite apart from the problems of fodder and stabling; bicycling is extremely hazardous in modern traffic, and walking on modern roads is unpleasant. You can, of course, walk dozens of miles at a stretch on moorland or country paths in the style of John Hillaby who published a book on the subject. But such a *Journey through Britain*, to use his title, would mean avoiding what is, alas, the typical England of motorways, 'metropolitan areas', new towns and sprawling suburbs and, in the countryside, agro-technology. In West Suffolk, for instance, the vast fields of corn and root crops are just as rigidly fenced and unwelcoming as grazing land for the cattle. A walk in the countryside usually means the side of the road with, on one side a bank and a barbed fence, and on the other a stream of hurtling lorries and cars. Most parts of the modern country afford less safe and agreeable walks, and less good scenery, than Hampstead Heath or Regent's Park. In fact, even a walk through the London streets is safer and more enjoyable than an average walk in the country; which is sad, because walking remains by far the best means of exercise and relaxation. It is also a sensible and cheap way of getting about. Thank heavens, the idiot craze for jogging has not caught on in this country, in spite of attempts to encourage it by the *Sunday Times*. That newspaper sums up the folly of jogging. Those of the senior staff who enjoy company cars may drive them to work though living as near as Islington. Quite apart from wasting petrol, they miss out on the chance of some exercise to work up an appetite for the next expense-account meal; or to work off the hangover from the last one. It is no use pleading bad weather because, as Charles II was first to remark, in England there is no day of the year when a man may not be outdoors in comfort.

The first seven miles of a walk south from Southwold are some of the finest one can enjoy in England. The common and marshes between the town and the River Blyth offer a wonderful view in all directions, only slightly spoiled by the water-tower. There is a golf course at the Southwold end, some football pitches, and sometimes anglers in the dykes. Although this is not yet a sanctuary, there are many birds and I had the intense joy yesterday of seeing a swan in flight. It had been foraging in a dyke about thirty yards away when it took the decision (as I was later to see) to move to a dyke at the side of the path – only a short distance but one that involved going downwind. Why it did not walk the distance, I cannot say; perhaps swans cannot walk? At any rate, this one decided to fly. For the take-off it faced upwind, built up a powerful wing-beat and slowly rose in the air, scarcely moving forward at first, then gradually heading towards the sea, until, after fifty yards, it dipped down its right wing and was swept in a wide arc to the south and back to the west until, two hundred yards away, it was once more facing into the east wind. Slowly it fought its way towards where I was standing, reached the ditch, lowered its body slowly onto the surface, then dropped with a splash.

I crossed over the footbridge and went down to the river mouth where a few people were float-fishing for bass, then walked south along the beach. There is a footpath through the marsh, but this can be heavy going in wet weather; also you get a good view from the sea wall of both the sea and the marshes. And so to Dunwich, the sunken city which once was a major seaport, a bishopric and a thriving town. In the eighth century it paid a tax to the king of 3000 herrings a year.

After Dunwich I started to walk along the cliff until I came to a sign saying 'private property'; I turned back, not too unhappy; the wind was pitiless and the horizon marred by the Sizewell nuclear power station. I found a path which led for two-and-a-half miles to East Bridge through a bird sanctuary. Being short-sighted, I failed to see any bird more interesting than a jay, and I would not have seen him but for his screech. At East Bridge I resisted the lure of The Eel's Foot, an Adnam's pub, and headed on to Leiston. The small road becomes a main road and stays so till Aldeburgh.

I dislike Aldeburgh, but not for the reason that some others do. Some dislike it because of the music festival; because it was once the home of Benjamin Britten and Peter Pears and E. M. Forster, and is near the home of Jeremy Thorpe. It is often implied by some who hate Aldeburgh that those who come to the festival are enthusiasts not for Britten's music so much as his well-known sexual preferences. I think this is unfair. Whatever one thinks of Britten's music, it is patent nonsense to say it appeals only to homosexuals. Nor did Britten himself parade his sexual habits after the fashion of recent, strident bores continually 'coming out of the closet' to which we all wish they would go back, slamming the door. It is also suggested that those in the Aldeburgh set are pretentious and hoity-toity towards the locals;

certainly there was a case of this at a recent birthday party at Snape for Peter Pears when fireworks were lit at the stroke of midnight. The locals, who had not been warned of this (let alone asked to the party) rushed into the street thinking that World War Three had begun with a strike on the nearby bomber base.

But Britten himself, I am told, was well-liked in Aldeburgh. Certainly he belonged there; he based one of his best operas, *Peter Grimes*, on a story by Crabbe, the Aldeburgh poet. He and his music were quite as much part of Aldeburgh life as the Beatles were of Liverpool life; and nobody has suggested that they were affected or hoity-toity, although they have long ago left the city that brought them fame. It seems to me that Britten and the Beatles are just another example of how the vitality of the country has passed from the old industrial north to the south and east. The Beatles enjoyed the Indian Summer of Liverpool's fame; their cellar is demolished, but people come from around the world to hear Britten's music at Aldeburgh.

Then why do I not like Aldeburgh? I find it an unfriendly place, with neither the gaiety of a northern seaside resort nor the village atmosphere of a place like Southwold, which closes as a resort in winter. The hotel where I stayed is owned by Ladbroke's, the betting people. Radio One blared through dinner; service was slow; the customers dreary. I went to a famous old pub to find a crowd of rugby supporters telling bad jokes. They complained of the lack of a Space Invaders machine. No pansy opera lovers, these.

3 November – Woodbridge   Here is another small town in Suffolk where people appear to be satisfied with their life, not eaten away by envy or grievances about their imagined rights. 'Suffolk is really looking up', says a middle-class gentleman. 'Things seem to be getting better here rather than worse, like in the rest of England. People don't like the unions, that's one thing, but they don't want the country mucked about by big business. They're very conservationist-minded. They want the railway service restored instead of so many cars.'

The locals in what might be called a working-class pub are equally sanguine, in spite of the country's economic trouble. A 'bricky', a bricklayer, told me: 'The only person who ever balanced the budget in this country was Oliver Cromwell. I say that though I'm a

Catholic.' He and his fellow brickies work much of the year in Holland where you are paid £4 an hour, after tax. 'But you need to work thirteen hours a day' he said. 'They have so many holidays there that sometimes it isn't worth it.' That kind of talk does not suggest that the English have lost the will to work.

When I was last in this pub, the postman said to the publican: 'I'll be calling in tomorrow with cod, some plaice and a bit of eel.' And later the publican told me: 'Sometimes I don't know if this is a pub, a fishmonger or greengrocer. I go out on Thursday and get some vege- tables off a friend, and then the customers get to hear of it and I'm getting orders for carrots, caulies, a few pounds of runners. There's a lady comes down from Lowestoft with some fish and soon she's taking orders all over the place. That's the thing about a small community. It's cheap and you know everyone. If I go to the bank in the morning, I'm bound to meet ten people in the street to yarn with, besides the people in the bank . . . If there's anything wrong with anyone in the family, the doctor comes round to the house in fifteen minutes.' That last statement sounds incredible to one, like myself, living in central London, where doctors now never come round to the house.

This town on the Deben flourished during the Middle Ages, constructing boats, and trading in coal and corn, with a little piracy on the side. It flourished again in the eighteenth century, so that most of the houses date to a time when architects had an eye for beauty, and builders still knew the rudiments of their trade. The poet Edward Fitzgerald lived here and entertained Tennyson at an inn, which still has framed lines from the *Rubaiyat*, as well as a juke box and maddening football machines. What a marvellous poem that is! And how much pleasanter Persia was in Omar Khayyam's day than under the Ayatollah, who would not approve of Omar's book of verses, his jug of wine, or his Thou, whoever she may have been. The surly thugs of the Ayatollah have smashed most of the old Persian monuments, just as Cromwell's thugs destroyed much of St Mary's at Woodbridge. Fitzgerald was on the committee of restoration. The churchyard also contains the bones of John Clarkson, one of two brothers who played worthy parts in fighting the slave trade, though John, as Governor of Sierra Leone, was treated with much ingrati- tude – not the first nor the last kind man whose heart was broken by Africa.

Like so many towns in East Anglia, Woodbridge is close to an

American air base, but the noise is not quite so disturbing now that the Phantom jets have been replaced by the quieter A10 'tank-busters'. The Yanks are less boisterous than their predecessors in the Second World War. They are also poorer compared to the English civilians, who now buy them drinks instead of cadging from them. Throughout East Anglia there is a sale for dishcloths marking the British and US bases during the Second World War, and everyone over forty-five has stories to tell of those days. For instance: 'They [the Americans] used to go out and come back in formation and when they got over the coast they switched all their lights on. One night they must have lost thirty or forty planes – Jerry had sneaked in behind them and had a field day. They're still digging bits of Flying Fortress out of the ground.'

4 November – Woodbridge In Woodbridge, as in Southwold, industry thrives as it fails to thrive in the North and Midlands of England. (British Leyland is once more threatened with closure.) While Liverpool, Newcastle and Glasgow scarcely produce any ships in spite of subsidy from the taxpayer of £5 billion per annum, the people of Woodbridge have recreated yards for the building of small boats and yachts. They cashed in on the craze for yachts and launches which started up in the Fifties and goes on, in spite of recession. A lady at one of the yacht companies told me that many people were now stuck with mortgages on the yachts they could not resell. The price of fuel discouraged motorboats, and fibreglass was bad for trade because of its durability; yet nevertheless the Arabs who cruise off the south of France are still in the market for motorboats, and the faster the better; there is a move back to wooden boats; and rich people do not appear to be worried by recession, so there is still a trade at the top of the market.

At his boat sale and repair yard, Andy Seedhouse told me: 'Yes, it's been a bad year. There hasn't been much of a change from motor to sail – they're two different sports, but lots of people are going over to wooden boats.' Incidentally, Mr Seedhouse is one of the many you meet round here who comes from the Midlands or North, in his case Wolverhampton. 'I'm one of those people who came for a fortnight's holiday and stayed. To be frank, I couldn't stand it at first. I thought it was slow, and I was the one who was going to change it. Now it's changed me.'

The great number of yachtsmen and boat people in Woodbridge accounts for one of the town's remarkable businesses, Small Craft Deliveries Ltd. As its name suggests, it began in 1959 as a service for taking yachts and other small boats from local yards to the customers down the coast. Soon they were taking bigger boats to ports on the Continent; and in the last few years they have taken vessels of up to 2000 tons to Iran, Venezuela, Pakistan, Burma, Saudi Arabia and the Solomon Islands. Although most of the crews are local men and the business is run from a modest office down by the river, the tone of the operation is high-powered. When I walked in, one of the partners was on the phone to a colleague in Corsica concerning delivery of ten tugs from South Korea to Saudi Arabia. The business has suffered from the recession, particularly because this government has stopped giving vessels as aid to countries like Gambia and the Solomon Islands. Nevertheless the firm has built up a profitable and useful service while so many British businesses are dying of inanition. It must also be fun to sail small boats round the world – and get paid for it.

5 November – Felixstowe – Bury St Edmunds   This little Edwardian seaside resort has been transformed over the last twenty years into one of the busiest towns in Britain. Why it was once a haunt of the *haut monde* I fail to understand. It has none of the architectural charm of Woodbridge, Aldeburgh or Southwold. The country behind the beach is dull; and the view over the Orwell to Harwich is nothing to get excited about. Yet the Kaiser came here on holiday; as did much of European royalty. The town had a scandalous fame when Mrs Simpson took a house here while waiting for a divorce to come up at Ipswich; her lawyer, Theodore Goddard, had said that a Suffolk town would provide the secrecy which she could not expect in London, and indeed no newspaper printed the fact that she shared her Felixstowe house with the Prince of Wales. After his abdication, the King did not return to Felixstowe, which turned into a more proletarian seaside resort, somewhere between Southend and Aldeburgh in social as well as geographical terms. The house where the Kaiser stayed is now occupied by the Suffolk social services department. The new fame and prosperity of the town are due to its startling emergence as a port.

Like most of the towns on the estuary of a Suffolk river, Felixstowe was a port in the Middle Ages, exporting grain and wool, and receiving goods like coal from the north of England. It was used by the Royal Navy in both world wars and still had occasional barges into the late Forties. Its revival began with the London dock strike of 1949, when the great and good Prime Minister Clement Attlee sent in troops as strike-breakers: I was a national serviceman at the time, but failed to get in on what was considered a cushy number at strike-breaking. In spite of Attlee's courage, the Transport and General Workers won the day and consolidated their power on the docks of London, most other ports, much of the land adjoining ports, as well as most airports. Most British seaports and Heathrow airport are now notorious throughout the world for slowness, restrictive practices and, worst of all, thieving.

The success of the strike at the Port of London meant that shipping companies looked round for ports that were not controlled by the unions. A Felixstowe landowner, H. Gordon Parker, who had recently bought the old docks, started to trade on the Continent with Scandinavian exporters of timber, paper and lager beer; also with the British services NAAFI in Germany. As I was told in 1973, when Felixstowe was still only a small port: 'We tried most things . . . spuds from Spain and Greece, livestock, general cargo in every sense of the word. We've had art works come through, highly sophisticated electrical machinery, and swarf, you know, the dust from gold. We've had tanks of crocodiles, giraffes, elephants and lots of race-horses.'

During the Sixties and early Seventies, Felixstowe was the pioneer among British ports of 'roll-on, roll-off' road cargo, and also containers – taking ships from across the Atlantic. By the end of next year, it will be the largest port in Britain for this kind of cargo and, in terms of traffic, one of the largest ports of any kind. The old Felixstowe Port and Railway Company was bought up a few years ago by European Ferries Limited who own, among other things, the Northern Irish port of Larne, and Townsend-Thoresen, two of whose ferries, the Viking Venturer and the Viking Victory, were in the news this August by breaking the French fishermen's strike and blockade at Le Havre. The managers of the port had an anxious time after the Labour Party came back to power in 1974 when it was feared that the company might be forced into the state Dock and Harbour Board, but common sense prevailed and Felixstowe was allowed to flourish.

Some salesmen from Felixstowe recently went to Japan and acquired new business. 'The Japanese were over the moon when they heard of a British port which had only one strike in the last seven years, and that by default,' I was told by one of the delegates. That strike was in fact a demonstration by workers against their shop stewards who had gone to the House of Commons to make a protest without having consulted their members. The reasons for the success of labour relations here are not easily summarised. All the workers are members of one trade union, the TGWU, but all jobs are controlled by the company, at a uniform rate. At Felixstowe there is not the problem of other ports, notably Southampton, where crane-drivers or warehousemen may work for different private companies, offering different rates and, often eager to poach employees, causing jealousy. Most employees are local men, without the traditional grudges and grievances of London dockers. Most have a good education and sense enough to see they are well off. And although no one admits as much, the dock company will not hire agitators and politicians. It is a far cry from Liverpool, one month ago on this journey.

The Felixstowe docks should not be considered as altogether a benefit to the country. Extensions have taken over some of the marsh land used by birds for nesting; the lorries and juggernauts that come off the ships have made life hellish for many East Anglian villagers; nor do I like the idea of a whacking great bridge on the Orwell. Nevertheless, it must be said that the port is kept distinct from the town of Felixstowe, which remains much as it was, although richer.

Just before leaving the town, I made a pleasant discovery. I had gone to the railway station, which now is unmanned, to find out the time of the next 'pay' train to Ipswich from Lowestoft. It was due in forty minutes, at 11.55 am, and I was wondering how I would pass the time till then when I saw signs of life in the corner of the station. It was a little pub called The Witching Hour, a splendid place with a big open fire, pictures and mobiles of witches, nude calendar advertisements for a Felixstowe Chinese restaurant, Adnam's beer, a jovial barmaid in smock and mob-cap, and best of all, plenty of regular gaffers and old dears, cosily chatting: 'It's going to be rough on the Rotterdam boat this morning . . . Terrible weather. I only got up because it's boring in bed . . . Depends who you're with, darling . . . Awful crops this year. Sort of stuff you'd have given your

E

cattle in our youth . . . I see that peanut vendor's been given a kick in the behind [Carter had just lost the US election]. Shows what Hollywood can do for a man . . . [looking out of the window] Watch out everyone, the Major's approaching.'

It did not seem possible that such an agreeable pub could belong to British Railways. Nor does it. 'It's a free house,' the barmaid explained. 'All British Rail owns is the land. We pay them a rent. There's another place like this at Manningtree.' And come to think of it, the Woodbridge station houses a café and bed and breakfast place. Why do not British Rail let all their unmanned stations? Better still, why do they not allow private pubs and cafés on all stations, manned or not, and even in buffet and restaurant cars? This might not ensure pubs as excellent as The Witching Hour but it almost certainly would provide refreshment places that were cheaper, pleasanter and more efficient than the average British Rail buffet. The British Rail catering service is not only bad but pricing itself off the market. We have recently suffered a bombardment of boastful praise for British Rail breakfasts – at £5.50. That is what one would pay for breakfast, sleeper and ticket on Thai Railways, an excellent organisation that British Rail might study.

Cheered by the conversation, and Adnam's delicious beer, I got on the pay train to Ipswich, and changed there for Bury St Edmunds. It was market day and the lorries were noisy with lowing and grunts. The stalls were as busy as everywhere else in this time of depression. Nobody buys new goods when you can get them cheap. 'Gannex Quality Men's Slippers. Originally £9.00, now £3.75.' There's nostalgia for you. Lord Kagan, whose friend Harold Wilson once sported a Gannex coat, has just pleaded guilty to theft from his famous company.

Bury St Edmunds may serve as a peg to append certain remarks on the Peasants' Revolt, of which the sixth centenary will be marked next year. In June 1381, John Wrawe, a former priest, and his band entered and looted Bury St Edmund, hunted and captured the Prior of the Abbey, jeered and taunted him all night, then cut off his head in the morning. His head was placed on the pillory next to that of his friend Sir John Cavendish. The crowd amused themselves by pressing together the lips of the two men or having Sir John whisper confession or secrets into the ear of the monk. When Parliament met in

120

November, five months after the brief revolt ended, Bury was the only large town in the country not to be given an amnesty for the crimes committed in June. The official statement said that the citizens were excluded 'because of their outrageous and horrible misdeeds long continued, and will not have their share in the general pardon, nor take part in it'.

Already we have had warnings that the sixth centenary of the Peasants' Revolt will be the occasion of socialist pageants, NALGO and NUPE rallies, Trotskyist TV series and, no doubt, a National Theatre play with lords and archbishops killing and sodomising farmhands. 'When Adam delved and Eve span, who was then the gentleman?' are lines we shall doubtless hear a lot of in 1981. And of course, our modish historians will attempt to find parallels between the rebellion of June 1381 and today. There were indeed similarities, but not of the kind that comfort modern socialists.

The Peasants' Revolt, like most such revolutions, came at a time of rising prosperity, largely due to the Black Death. Labour was so scarce that wages increased and villeins, or serfs, as modern historians call them, were able to get employment as free men. The increased bargaining power, or clout, of the labouring classes encouraged a radical spirit, which found expression in politics and in religion. The many priests or failed priests who took part in the Peasants' Revolt were forerunners of Protestant rebels against the luxury and corruption of the church. In London, the Peasants' Revolt produced a violent battle which had its origins in an old dispute between those guilds dealing in food and drink and those dealing in manufactured goods. It was what we would call an inter-union dispute. This was a common cause of revolt in every age until our own. The French Revolution occurred when the price of bread had risen so high that it accounted for more than half a working man's wage. In England, incidents like the Gordon Riots occurred when bread was intolerably dear. Nowadays bread and all food represents only a small item of anyone's personal budget.

The immediate cause of the Peasants' Revolt was the raising of a poll tax to pay for the long war in France. Although this tax was what we would now call 'graduated', the Commons believed that the lower classes were not paying their share now that 'all the wealth of England has gone into the hands of the labourers and workmen'. The labourers and workmen resented the new tax and lied as to the number of adults, eligible for the poll tax, in their household. An early history of the Revolt told how the collector of poll tax came to the house of Wat Tyler and asked three groats for him and his wife and also for Alice his daughter. When Tyler's wife said that Alice was only fourteen and not therefore liable for the tax, the taxman took the girl in his arms 'and most uncivilly and dishonestly took up her clothes and bared her before her mother saying he would see whether she had any pubes upon her or no . . ' That scene is bound to come in next year's celebrations.

The hero of the Peasants' Revolt was the child king Richard II who rode out unarmed to meet the rebels at Blackheath and later, at Smithfield, persuaded them to return to their loyalty and their homes. The villains of the story were the King's advisers and Parliament, already becoming too powerful. The later overthrow and murder of Richard II marked the beginning of the decadence of the English nation.

6 November – Cambridge The Peasants' Revolt in Cambridge took the form of a Town versus Gown riot. A mob looted college plate, jewels, glass windows and all the books which were then the university library. These were burned, under the orders of a crone named Margery Starre, who is said to have shouted: 'Away with the learning of clerks! Away with it!' Somehow I get the impression that Margery Starre, or her spirit, lives on in modern Cambridge. It is a dour, cold city. I did not appreciate or enjoy my studies here as an undergraduate, although I was later heartened to find that Wordsworth and Malcolm Muggeridge felt the same, and for much the same reasons.

Almost everything that one hears of Cambridge is disagreeable. It was here that Professor Anthony Blunt, a quintessential Cambridge man, recruited his gang of upper-class Stalinist pansies. The 'Cambridge Rapist', before he was caught, inspired as much terror and newspaper articles as the 'Yorkshire Ripper' himself. It turned out that the 'Cambridge Rapist' had been inspired to his crime by reading pornography about rape; but one does not hear this admitted by advocates of publishing licence. Cambridge is also the centre in England for heart-transplant surgery, which I have always thought repugnant to man and God. Indeed, my hostility to South Africa is caused more by Professor Christiaan Barnard, than by the apartheid system. I knew that the liberal movement in Czechoslovakia, the so-called 'Prague Spring' of 1968, was doomed when it started heart-transplant surgery. I was the only journalist to report this event from Bratislava. The deputy editor of a local newspaper gave me the inside story: how a man was surprised in bed with the wife of a travelling salesman; how he climbed out of the window just as the husband returned; how he fell off the ledge and was taken, half dead, to a hospital; how his heart was cut out and placed in the chest of a gypsy woman, on whom the surgeons wanted to do this experiment; how she in turn died after a few hours. Reporting this, in *Private Eye*, I said that the donor must be the first man in history who in the course of one day had two of his vital organs throbbing inside two different women, neither of whom was his wife.

Kent and the South Coast

LONDON – ROCHESTER – CANTERBURY

FOLKESTONE – RYE – BRIGHTON

CHICHESTER – PORTSMOUTH – SOUTHSEA

7 November – London – Rochester Back to London, en route for Kent. It is worthy of note that it is only during my brief visits home to London that I see examples of violence and aggression; a customer abusing a bank clerk, a drunk roaring to kill the barman who had taken 'a liberty' of an unspecified nature. Outside London, the English remain as gentle as when Orwell said, in a very good essay, that this is the easiest country in which to push somebody off a pavement.

A trip down the mouth of the Thames always reminds me of Conrad's *Heart of Darkness*, the novel about a voyage up the Congo. The narrator, Marlow, begins his Congo tale to a party of friends on a yacht moored in the mouth of the Thames, and he muses on the resemblance between the two rivers that open up their respective countries. Although England now has a mighty Empire and sends her ships to all parts of the world, 'this also', as Marlow remarks, 'has been one of the dark places of the earth.' He goes on to describe how England must have appeared to the Roman officials, eighteen centuries earlier: 'Sand-banks, marshes, forests, savages, – precious little to eat fit for a civilised man, nothing but Thames water to drink.' He imagined

a decent young citizen in a toga – perhaps too much dice, you know – coming out here in the train of some prefect, or tax-gatherer, or trader even, to mend his fortunes. Land in a swamp, march through the woods, and in some inland post feel the savagery, the utter savagery, had closed round him, – all that mysterious life of the wilderness that stirs in the forest, in the jungles, in the hearts of wild men.

Conrad understood nearly a hundred years ago what is only too evident now, that England will not forever remain a rich and imperial nation; her light 'is like a running blaze on a plain, like a flash of lightning in the clouds. We live in the flicker – may it last as long as the old earth keeps rolling! But darkness was here yesterday.' We live in the flicker today, of North Sea oil perhaps, awaiting the darkness once more 'as long as the old earth keeps rolling', as long as nuclear war does not strike both Congo and Thames. 'The horror! the horror!' that Kurtz experienced on the Congo is present too on the Thames: 'The offing was barred by a black bank of clouds, and the tranquil waterway leading to the uttermost ends of the earth flowed sombre under an overcast sky – seemed to lead into the heart of an immense darkness.'

8 November – Rochester   The local newspapers tell of a pub closing in Rochester, and a spokesman for Medway Licensed Victuallers Association says that 'Price increases have been saturated and people are cutting out luxuries like drink. I can see many houses going to the wall. This could be the end of the public house as we know it.' His union wants legislation to give more flexible hours to pubs and to stop 'preferential treatment' for clubs which can use big profits from gaming machines to undercut prices. The implication of this is that England would grow like Australia, where most of the drinking is done in clubs, like those of the Returned Servicemen's League, to the constant clatter of scores of one-armed bandit machines. But in fact most pubs these days are already equipped with one-armed bandit machines as well as football and 'Space Invader' machines. But machines are no guarantee of good business. In Rochester there are pubs with every kind of machine but no drinkers. Older people, I think, tend to dislike them, and nowadays it is only the old and the young who go to pubs, because parents of young children cannot afford luxuries. Restaurants too have suffered. In a town like Rochester where there are no 'executives' on expense accounts, people must pay for their own meals out and shop for the best bargain. A Cockney I met here was loudly denouncing one flashy restaurant in the High Street. 'They got greedy, they did. Cut their own froats. You can get a better steak at The Greasy Spoon. That's the caff where the drivers go.'

The predicament of the pubs is in part a result of the merging of breweries with all the consequent waste and expense; people like Adnams are still doing good business. It also suggests that drink is something that people cut out if they want. Oddly enough the drop in drinking has come out simultaneously with the launching of a great new sociological industry devoted to fighting alcoholism. Dozens of books have appeared on the subject; two or three quangos have published reports; the Bishop of Birmingham, ever the first to catch on to trends, has said that alcoholism is now the most serious problem facing England. Since the statistics show that people are drinking less, sociologists have had to give weirder and weirder definitions of alcoholism. A report I saw recently on the North West of England said there had been an enormous increase in women alcoholics; this statistic was reached by defining an alcoholic as one who drinks more than three pints of beer a week. In effect it defines an alcoholic as one who sometimes drinks alcohol. This propaganda, like that about cigarettes, serves only to make people dependents or addicts; it suggests that drinking is something one cannot give up without therapy from professionals; it rules out the idea that people might exercise will-power. It is only quite recently that tobacco came to be thought of as addictive, with the result that it became addictive. I used to be an 'addictive' smoker and found it a struggle to give up, but now that I know I am not an addict, I can smoke when I want and give it up when I want; indeed, far from getting withdrawal symptoms of craving I feel an active dislike of cigarettes. I sometimes suspect that even the hard drugs, like heroin, although generally lethal, are not quite as addictive as doctors tell us. I spent several days at heroin clinics for children in Saigon and saw no symptoms whatever of 'cold turkey', of people 'climbing the wall' in the agony of withdrawal. Between the world wars, several million Americans were regular users of heroin which they took in the form of tablets imported from Germany; but when the supply was stopped by the war there were no reports of mass 'cold turkey'.

Oddly enough, the kind of people who say that three pints of beer a week makes a woman an alcoholic are often those who want to legalise marijuana. I have seen films on the BBC in which it was stated as proven fact that marijuana has no possible bad effect on humans – which is pernicious nonsense. It is because of their proven and recognised bad effects that marijuana and similar drugs have been condemned by all societies in countries where they are grown. Anyone who wants to see a society where marijuana is widely and freely consumed can take his life in his hands and visit Kingston, Jamaica, the most violent city in the world.

8 November – Rochester This is the town where Dickens spent most of his childhood and near which he died. It is the setting for *Great Expectations* — which I consider his masterpiece, because although there are no great comic grotesques like Micawber, Pecksniff or Sarah Gamp, the straight characters come to life as they do in no other novel except possibly *David Copperfield*. Pip is a self-portrait, as David Copperfield is only a half-likeness. Joe Gargery is a good and lovable man; we believe in him as we cannot believe in, say, Mr Wickham. Estelle is clearly a far more attractive woman, physically, than pathetic Dora or solemn Agnes.

The Dickens House – at least it is not called the Dickens Heritage Centre – is short on letters and written matter and goes in for pictures and models and taped recordings. Inevitably, we are given a lesson in social history. 'The word Dickensian has two contrasting meanings. Here we see its first meaning – hearty, good cheer, substantial meals and the fellowship of family and friends.' Then we see a picture of a man wearing tattered clothes in the rain. 'Dickensian also means dark, dirty, grim, grotesque, sordid . . . the mid-nineteenth century had much that was Dickensian in that sense.' Oddly enough, because of the pulling down of the doss houses in London, more people now sleep out in the streets than did in Dickens's time; you can see them just behind Dickens's house in Doughty Street, in an alley mid-way between the *Sunday Times* and Camden Social Services centre.

Certainly Dickens disliked the 'dark, dirty, grim, grotesque and sordid' but he also liked making the readers flesh creep. Also he saw his villains – Quilp, Fagin, Bill Sykes, Uriah Heep and the rest – as evil men deserving of punishment, and not as victims of an unjust society. Indeed he complains in *David Copperfield* that the prison conditions were too soft for Uriah Heep. As a matter of fact, I do not think Dickens was any kind of social reformer in our sense of the words. He feared the proletariat as a revolutionary force, as one sees from *Barnaby Rudge* and *A Tale of Two Cities*. The most admirable characters in his books are respectable merchants, lawyers and other professional, middle-class people; he was not sentimental about the working class, or aristocrats for that matter. His child heroes, like Oliver Twist and the young David Copperfield, are pitied because they have fallen beneath their station and have to endure the company of their social inferiors, most of whom are presented as cruel and mean.

In fact, I believe that his sympathy with children was Dickens's strongest social concern, no doubt inspired by his own notorious servitude in a blacking factory. As Pip in *Great Expectations* says: 'In the little world in which children have their existence, whosoever brings them up, there is nothing so finely perceived and so finely felt, as injustice.' Apart from the dreadful Yorkshire schools, like Dotheboys Hall, Dickens most hated depriving children of childhood by sending them out to work like Oliver and David, or by shouldering them with adult responsibilities, like Little Nell. In his concern that children should not be turned into little adults, that they should enjoy the love of family and the magic fanciful world of fairy tales and of Christmas, in short those things we associate with his own *Christmas Carol*, Dickens was not in line with modern thinking.

The modern race of educationalists, as they call themselves, want to turn small children into joyless prigs like themselves. Children's books must be purged of religious tales, of elitist princes and princesses, 'racist' Little Black Sambos, and any suggestion of separate male and female roles. At an age when children are still dreaming of high adventure and romance, they are now issued with pills and French letters and told how and when to use them.

The Dickens House has an extract from *Hard Times* in which Mr Gradgrind is questioning Little Sissy Jupe, who has been reading to her dying father.

'And what,' asked Mr Gradgrind, in a still lower voice, 'did you read to your father, Jupe?'

'About the Fairies, Sir, and the Dwarf, and the Hunchback, and the Genies,' she sobbed out; 'and about . . .'

'Hush!' said Mr Gradgrind 'that is enough. Never breathe a word of such destructive nonsense any more, any more. Bounderby, this is a case for rigid training . . .'

The Gradgrinds are with us yet; can one imagine some child being allowed to read of the Dwarf? Or the person of restricted growth?

The hotel where I stay put on an old-fashioned music hall tonight. Like yesterday's evening of folk song it was both well attended and fun, the average age for the music hall being double the previous night's. The Marie Lloyd songs are immortal. There was one I had never heard before called 'A Yard of Lace' – about a Jewish shop-keeper who tries to sell a customer almost everything except what he wants.

9 November – Rochester Remembrance Sunday is not neglected in what is a major naval and military town. There was a naval battle here against the Dutch as late as 1667, and Pepys was sent down to discover how the foe had got through our defences. The Royal Engineers have their depot at Chatham; the names of the regiment's dead from all our nineteenth-century wars are inscribed on the west wall of the Cathedral. Here we kept the one minute silence before singing the no less traditional 'O God, our help in ages past'.

There is something wrong with a country which does not remember and honour its dead, even those who are now thought to have died in an unjust war. It was depressing but not surprising to hear that President Hillary of Ireland, a Fianna Fail hack of the worst order, refused to attend a Church of Ireland service because he did not commemorate foreign wars. Scores of thousands of Catholic Irishmen joined up in 1914 to defend not just our own two islands but Belgium and Christian civilisation. Indeed the response to recruit-ment in Ireland was greater even than England's because it was seen as an affirmation of Ireland's new-found place and dignity in the Empire. Sir Roger Casement, and other Fenians living and plotting in Germany, found it hard to recruit even a single man from Irish prisoners-of-war, who rested loyal to their country and, yes, their King.

The infamous Easter Rising of 1916, which built an Irish Republic on murder and terror, has left a legacy of implacable civil hatred which poisons the island from end to end. What kind of a country can wipe out the memory of those who fell in Flanders and France – the only memorial is neglected and covered with weeds – while naming the streets of Dublin after Connolly, an embittered shop steward, and Pearse, a proto-Nazi obsessed with daydreams of execution, blood and wounds? While the Southern Irish betray the memory of their fallen heroes, and honour instead the agents of Germany, there cannot be peace or unity in the island. Nor in Zimbabwe, either. On the day Mr Mugabe announced a ban on remembrance services there were forty-two killed in Bulawayo during a tribal fight between Shona and Matabele.

10 November – Rochester – Canterbury On to Canterbury. Nowadays, any train compartment without a corridor is covered with digusting graffiti, like a public lavatory. Among the pornography, there is almost always a Socialist Worker scrawl and some kind of fascist filth, in this case 'Roses are reddish, violets are bluish, if it hadn't been for the Nazis we'd all be Jewish'. I am told that this is a new twist to an old rhyme with the words 'if it wasn't for Christmas etc'; which is a harmless joke. Somebody showed me a new fascist magazine with pretensions to some intelligence; it was full of cranky ravings against the Jews, who seem to have taken over from non-white immigrants as a target for these unpleasant people. I suppose it will not be long before this country gets right-wing terrorist outrages such as occur now in France and Italy.

11 November – Canterbury I took a taxi to Howletts to see John Aspinall's famous zoo where two keepers were recently killed by tigers. I did not actually get as far as the tiger cage, partly because the taxi was waiting and partly because of a private phobia which needs some preliminary explanation. About six years ago there came out a thriller called *Harris in Wonderland*, written by Richard Ingrams and Andrew Osmond, the editor and one of the founders of *Private Eye*. The character Harris was an unsuccessful and rather boozy freelance journalist, who had lost his employment with most respectable papers because it was thought that he worked for a fort-nightly scandal sheet. He spent much of his time in Africa and South-East Asia, and was now engaged in exposing a crooked businessman and writing a book on an international mining com-pany. Now everything so far said about Harris was equally true of somebody not a million miles from myself. And indeed the large and famous solicitor who in the book chases and tries to kill Harris, was not unlike in appearance the solicitor for the international mining company from whom I received a complaining letter.

Last year, I was told that Messrs Ingrams and Osmond were writing a sequel to *Harris in Wonderland* in which Harris had gained the enmity of an Anglo-French grocer and, while in Rhodesia, had picked up the trace of a fugitive earl, one of the grocer's acquaintances at a London gambling club. The book, so I am told, reaches its climax with Harris trapped in the tiger cage of a Kentish zoo run by the owner of the gambling club. Not wanting to mix my real with my fictional life, I thought it was wiser at Howlett's to stick to looking at harmless creatures like deer. Which is a pity, because I have felt most interested in the zoo since I read John Aspinall's book *The Best of Friends*.

He founded the Howletts zoo (he has a second at Lympne) with the proceeds of a considerable win on Prelone in the Cesarewitch Handicap. Although Mr Aspinall, in his work for wild animals, has received considerable help from friends such as Jim Slater and James Goldsmith (whose brother Edward is also a keen ecologist) he wrote *The Best of Friends* partly to raise more money because, so he says, 'The great crash of 1974 has savaged my fortune and crippled my ability to fund a private collection of wild animals which has now bred into a horde of 350.'

The cost of feeding the beasts is prodigious, including, for instance 5000 lbs of apples, 5000 pints of milk, 2500 bottles of Ribena per annum, besides such occasional items as 100 lbs of lychees and 40 lbs of uglis. One day when two of the bears escaped and raided a neighbour's orchard, they had to be lured back with a bucket of green chartreuse – six bottles' worth from the local pub. Sweater-grabbing, a famous game of Mumbah the gorilla, is also expensive, wrote Mr Aspinall. 'He has destroyed dozens of my finest cashmeres during the last year.'

Such anecdotes, and the glossy pictures of Mr Aspinall splashing about with his tigers in his swimming pool, should not be taken to mean that his book and his zoos are frivolities of a man who looks on animals as a jolly, exotic hobby. He is a serious, even fanatic zoologist, whose writing is spattered with terms like 'primal biotope'. His observations on the gorillas in his care are an important complement to the recent observation of wild gorillas by George Schaller and others; they give the final lie to the slanders made on the gentle and dignified creatures by Paul du Chaillac, the first explorer to see them alive. He also dispels some myths concerning the tiger: it will

131

lick human blood from a wound without getting a taste for human flesh; a mother will let a human being, at any rate Mr Aspinall, play with her new-born cubs; and the tiger does not turn hostile with adulthood. The killer Zeya, which Mr Aspinall had to shoot after the last fatal mauling, was an exception.

Obviously Mr Aspinall has a deep emotional bond with his animals. He writes of a female gorilla: '. . . she came and embraced me with an overt display of affection which typically included a gentle drumming on my back. I answered her gurgles with my own and we both bathed in the joys of rapprochement.' The death of another gorilla inspired him to verse:

> Kulu is dead,
> His females look for him:
> Moulla, Shamba, Baby Doll.

And he wrote of another animal friend:

> I swear to you now my tigress
> Your offspring shall live on
> Through Zsa, Zombie and Zola,
> Through Zemo and Zorra and Zon.

At times when reading his book, I started to wonder whether John Aspinall knows to which species he himself belongs, particularly since most of his family have animal-sounding names. It is easy to get confused between Toumbi, Founa and Shamba (gorillas), Ugh (a bison), Bassa, Jamunda and Damian (Aspinall's children) and Min (his second wife). When little Bassa learned to ride on the back of Ju Ju, a female gorilla, the only danger, so Mr Aspinall says, was 'due to Bassa's inability to "cling" in quadrumanal fashion like a true Pongoid.'

The animals sometimes turn nasty: the gorilla Gugis, a mother's boy, returned Mr Aspinall's kiss with a bite on the cheek. But Mr Aspinall says that even in childhood he always preferred the more dangerous animals: 'It is difficult to be uplifted by a Dalmatian or a budgerigar . . . Without wildness there can be no ingredient of fear, and without fear, even fear of a nip from a ferret, or a peck from a jackdaw, there must be a lessening of respect.' Since nips and pecks no longer meet his need for fear and danger, the adult Aspinall chooses to live among such formidable beasts as the tiger, rhinoceros

132

and, most ferocious of all, the honey badger. He much prefers wolves to dogs; and gorillas to chimpanzees, for a reason that tells us much about himself: 'Chimps are too close to us in temperament and disposition. They invite condescension. English people of my background have been brought up to disdain excitability and emotional volatility.'

Perhaps chimpanzees remind Mr Aspinall of human beings, or rather those human beings he calls 'urban biomass' or more simply 'the lowest social echelons'. He says such people 'usually have the greatest contempt for other organisms' and should not be let free into zoos. It seems that members of the working class who come to the Aspinall zoo are likely to suffer unpleasant experiences. Two paperers who discovered gorillas under the bedclothes 'downed tools and fled'. A coalman who had been charged by a playful tiger 'was found on his knees blubbing out the Lord's Prayer'. (Having been charged in Addis Ababa by a playful lion, I feel considerable sympathy with that coalman.)

Love of nature, more than class prejudice, has turned Mr Aspinall into a partisan of 'wild *politik*', a movement to save world wild-life by cutting the human population to 200 million. To Mr Aspinall, it matters more to save dwindling species such as the tiger and the gorilla than to feed hundreds of millions of mouths of the 'great urban biomass'. He believes that the crimes of man against other species, crimes that started nearly a million years ago with the discovery of fire, now threaten the very existence of life on this planet. As a gambler, he understands that the odds are against the world accepting 'wild *politik*'. Marxism and all the main world religions, except for Buddhism, are anthropocentric, as of course is the 'great urban biomass . . . which has never understood – and probably never will – the justice, the beauty and the relevance of the natural world.'

Up to this point, I agree with much of what Mr Aspinall has to say; but how to reduce the world's human beings to 200 million, or about the population now of the United States? As Mr Aspinall sadly remarks, modern medicine has removed the traditional 'cullers' like typhoid, malaria and bubonic plague, while nuclear war he does not even consider, perhaps because of the damage it might do to other species besides mankind. The solution he suggests is that 'medical research should be funded into abortion, infanticide, euthanasia and birth control'.

And who decides who are the lucky 200 million who kill instead of being killed? Unfortunately, Mr Aspinall ducks this question, contenting himself with the bland suggestion that if he was leader of the United Kingdom he would introduce *Jus animalium* and *Jus herbarum* – a couple more additions to the statute book. Or has Mr Aspinall got a secret, stupendous master-plan to wipe out nine-tenths of the human race? Perhaps so, for he asks rhetorically at the end of the book: 'In a thousand years or a million years will the road to Canterbury be thick with pilgrims come to weep at my shrine?' A few lines later, one sees it is really this book that will change the course of the world:

. . . a premonition seizes me as I write that the understanding that I have will pass to many, will grip my heirs, wrench them from their lasts where they cobble their ruin in blindness. A whole earth is what I seek, nothing less than a whole earth – a whole security. Gambler that I have always been, brave man that I am, I tremble with fear before the oncoming storm.

I still think I was wise not to go too near the tiger cage.

12 November – Canterbury   I have an Everyman *Canterbury Tales* in which the respectable parts, such as the Knight's Tale, are edited into easily comprehensible English, leaving the bawdy parts like the Miller's Tale in the safe obscurity of fourteenth-century dialect. In fact, it is easy to pick up the language after an hour or so, just as German or French returns when you visit the country. And what an enjoyable book it is! It has been rightly said that most of the hundreds of thousands of people who went on pilgrimage in the Middle Ages were neither seeking a cure – like those who now go to Lourdes – nor specially pious – like those who now go to Walsingham – but what we would now call tourists. Of Chaucer's pilgrims, described in the famous Prologue, three-quarters are worldy and some are wicked; they are representative of the nation, then and now. And then, even more than now, the English were passionate travellers.

In the age of the motorway and the jumbo jet, we tend to imagine that earlier English people knew no horizon beyond their own village or, at most, market town. This is entirely wrong. The old Roman roads, maintained and extended, offered quick and reasonably safe passage throughout England and Wales. Mediaeval kings with their courts spent most of the year in peregrinations about the country, supervising administration, adjudicating in cases of law, and listening to the pleas or grievances of the common people. For this reason, mediaeval kings were far more accessible to the people than are modern prime ministers – isolated by walls of bureaucracy and 'public relations'.

One could comfortably travel on horseback thirty miles in a day, and three times as fast given a relay of horses. Thousands of people went on foot, looking for better jobs, trading or simply from wanderlust. Whereas the unemployed young of modern Liverpool refuse to commute ten miles to work, mediaeval masons would travel all over the country to find employment – a cathedral in Kent or a castle in Wales, wherever the pay and conditions were right.

The pilgrims followed the king's highway and not, as later legend insisted, a special pilgrims' way. The road from Southwark to Canterbury was perhaps the busiest in the country, for it went on to Dover and the Continent. There was huge and constant traffic between this island and the Continent. The Norman and Angevin kings were of course French-speaking; they owned, or claimed to own, parts of France; and Calais, across the Channel from Dover, was held by England until the sixteenth century. But traffic across the Channel was not confined to France. England sold much of its wool and cloth to the Flemish who, in turn, set up in this country as merchants and, incidentally, taught us to drain the fens. Most Englishmen with aspirations to scholarship studied for some time at least in Paris, Bologna, Salerno or, during the late middle ages, in one of the German universities. And hundreds of people journeyed each year to Rome, most of them pilgrims, but some who were caught up in ecclesiastical law cases, and wanted to take their suit to the top.

I mention these things because it is somehow believed that England has only just 'gone into Europe', thanks to the politicians who favoured the Common Market. In fact, the chief result of that foolish enterprise has been to revive old enmities and to start up new ones – over the price of lamb, Golden Delicious apples, fishing rights, agricultural support costs, VAT and the rest. Edward Heath was given a 'Charlemagne Prize' and, as a reward, England now has to foot the bill for a great new tribe of otiose and expensive Euro-MPs and Eurocrats. In terms of friendship and cultural exchange, we know less of the Continent than we did in the Middle Ages. The teaching of modern languages in our schools has fallen by half since the war; a holiday on the Continent now means a package tour to the coast rather than seeing historic cities; there are also the many English who go as *Gastarbeiter* to Holland or Germany.

13 November – Canterbury – Folkestone – Rye In spite of the strength of the pound, there are still thousands of tourists and shoppers from France in all these towns of south-east England; a journalist friend of mine who produces a free shopping handout for travellers on the cross-channel boat and steamer once told me that he is the only editor in the country (except for one Fleet Street man he named) who cannot understand a word of his newspaper. The French are anything but popular: 'they do not try to speak English,' 'they are mean,' 'the youngsters go in the pubs and get the landlords in trouble.' In Canterbury I met an elderly man who interprets for tourists for British Rail: 'I speak enough French to get by' (here he grimaced) 'and I know German, don't I? Five years in their P.o.W. camps. The people I really like are the Poles. If you've got a Pole for a friend you've got a friend for life. The Poles are the grandest people in the world. You'll never subdue them. I'll say outright that I wouldn't mind one of my daughters marrying a Pole.'

The new heroes of Folkestone are Townsend-Thoresen, the ferryboat line which last summer broke the blockade of the Calais and Boulogne fishermen. 'There's a pub in Dover,' I heard, 'that's got a sign up "No French allowed." That's because of the strike. And Townsend-Thoresen are fast. It takes only ten minutes more than the hovercraft.' 'God knows why anyone wants a tunnel. There's bound to be huge queues at both ends and probably strikes.' 'God knows why we went in the Common Market. Anyone could have seen beforehand that something was wrong when the French came over and bought butter and meat and even their own wine.'

The disastrous idea of a Channel Tunnel was given new life during the Heath regime, when the Government favoured every kind of gross, prestige bauble that would benefit property and construction companies at the expense of productive industry. The bureaucratic tyranny that conceived the re-arrangement of counties was eager for new airports, new motorways and ring-roads, and above all the Channel Tunnel. This building megalomania coincided with Heath's dream of England joined in a giant European bureaucracy of business and administration, with Heath himself at the centre, prating of Charlemagne.

Some of the leading Tories were in the construction business. The Rio Tinto-Zinc Corporation, whose horrible mines and smelters have defaced five continents, were asked to produce an estimate for the job on the shaky ground that sinking a mine is the same as drilling a tunnel.

Only last week, I read with horror that Ian MacGregor, the new chairman of British Steel (who was bought for a transfer fee of £2 million) has plans for a 'road and rail crossing of the English Channel, combining both bridge and channel'. His rationale for this folly, according to the *Spectator* (8 November), is that 'if demand for steel does not exist it has to be created.' But the demand for a tunnel does not exist. This stupendously over-priced expert, purchased by Mrs Thatcher, clearly believes in the old Keynesian principle that the cure for depression is hiring the unemployed to dig holes in the ground and then fill them in again – in this case with British Steel plates.

14 November – Rye After twenty minutes by train from Folkestone, one comes into Romney Marsh, which, because of its low-lying and watery character, has been attractive to England's enemies over the last 2000 years. Rye, in spite of its fortifications on a hill, was several times sacked in the Middle Ages, and Romney Marsh was Bonaparte's intended landing place, or so the English feared. They lined the coast with Martello towers and built a military canal – much to the scorn of Cobbett who came here thirty years later:

Oh, Lord! To think that I should be destined to behold these monuments of the wisdom of Pitt and Dundas and Perceval! . . . I think I have counted along here upwards of thirty of these ridiculous things which, I dare say, cost from perhaps ten thousand pounds each; and one of which was, I am told, sold on the coast of Sussex the other day for two hundred pounds! . . . Here is a canal . . . to keep out the French; for, those armies who had so often crossed the Rhine, and the Danube, were to be kept back by a canal, made by Pitt thirty feet wide at the most.

The canal did help to drain the marsh, while the Martello towers were actually used in the Second World War as machine gun posts from which to pot at German aeroplanes.

Cobbett approved of the 'very pretty and large' Romney Marsh sheep, which he said were as white as 'a piece of writing paper': 'The wool does not look dirty and oily like that of other sheep.' The Romney Marsh sheep also pleased Richard Ingrams, who recently published a book on that subject with photographs by Fay Godwin*. 'They are placid, peaceful animals and when they have been sheared they shine in the sun . . .' Part of Mr Ingrams's feeling for sheep as religious symbols may have been a reaction against the fiercer beasts to be found in John Aspinall's other zoo at Lympne, which he built with the help of friends like Sir James Goldsmith. Apparently this zoo was built against the wishes of some of the local councillors who worried that elephant droppings would roll down the hill and pollute the Royal Military Canal. Port Lympne House was purchased before the First World War by Sir Philip Sassoon, who later played host to celebrities such as the Prince of Wales and Mrs Simpson, Lawrence of Arabia, Sir Winston Churchill and Charlie Chaplin. The house of a hundred rooms was decorated with marble pillars and blue-glazed tiles from Spain, windows of Tuscan alabaster, an inch thick, panels of lapis lazuli, and murals from artists such as Rex Whistler. 'Under Aspinall's supervision,' as Mr Ingrams dryly records, 'the Whistler mural has been restored and where Sassoon's celebrities sipped their cocktails there now stands an enormous black statue of a gorilla.'

As one might expect, Richard Ingrams is good on historical gossip round Romney Marsh, from the literary men like Henry James (I have yet to succeed in reading one of his novels) to the Deedes family, who have been prominent here for two hundred years. I had no idea that the father of W. H. 'Bill' Deedes, the editor of the *Daily Telegraph* and a former Conservative Cabinet minister, was a Christian Socialist who sold many family possessions, including Saltwood Castle. The castle has a haunted room. A lady visitor to Lympne Castle, claimed to have seen a Roman soldier, a priest and an apparition which had the body of an eagle attached to the skull of a man. Rye, more prosaically, is haunted by a turkey cock, though some say its cry is made by the ghost of a friar who seduced a nun and was bricked up in a wall for his sins.

'Ghosts of another kind hover about Goldenhurst Farm,' writes Richard Ingrams, getting a dig in at Noël Coward, who lived there for thirty years before fleeing to tax exile in north Jamaica (not

*Romney Marsh. London, 1980.

138

Bermuda, as Ingrams says). This is a bit hard on Coward who used this neighbourhood as the setting for quite the funniest supernatural story in English, *Blithe Spirit*: the ghost of the first wife at one point wants to be driven to Folkestone to see a movie.*

Rye, because it has kept its fine old houses, is sometimes abused as a 'picture-postcard town', or as dead; those who say so should visit a city like Bradford or Manchester which is truly dead. Of course Rye is quiet – as Ingrams says, you can hear people's footsteps at night – but quiet and dead are not synonymous. The writers and artists who live there are no less 'real' than those who write about and describe the Newcastle unemployed and Brixton 'Rastas'; sheep remain valuable even although the textile industry has decayed; after the hiccup of the industrial revolution, it is once more places like Rye that matter.

In November, now that the tourists have gone, one sees that Rye is also a place where people work with their hands, in the manner approved by socialists. They build boats; there are four thriving potteries; and if you go in a pub at night, the conversation is not of Henry James but of mundane employment. These were sailors and odd-job men: 'I've never had a job in Rye. Hastings is the nearest you can get one. Further than that it's not worth it because of the rail fares.' 'Lowestoft's useless, but there's a chance on the ferries in Folkestone and Dover.' 'And there's seasonal work like turkey plucking.' 'You have to go to Norfolk for that.' 'No you can get it here in the Marsh, but I think I'll wait till December to get a job.' 'Of course you can get a job as a kitchen porter . . .' 'Yes, catering attendant they call it now.'

The workers of Rye can be choosy about their jobs: their benefits come from the taxes and rates of the well-to-do and the diligent. The proprietor of a very good small hotel and restaurant told me: 'They squeeze us for £2500 a year in rates, that's without water and so on. That's because Rye people will put up with a lot just for the pleasure of living here. That only applies up here on the citadel.

---

* The following day, at Brighton's Theatre Royal, I saw and greatly enjoyed a rollicking version of *Blithe Spirit*. It was all the more enjoyable, since I had previously seen the play on my first and last visit to the National Theatre. It was directed by Harold Pinter in a style suitable to a Strindberg tragedy or one of his own plays. To make matters worse, I was seated by chance next to Mr Pinter and his lady, and could not seek refuge in sleep.

Two hundred feet down and the rates are halved.'

Like most of the desolate and once unspoiled parts of the coast-line, Romney Marsh has a nuclear power station, at Dungeness. The two reactors have now been closed for some months because of cracks and corrosion: the local liaison committee which was set up to keep the public informed will not give an estimate of the likely date of re-opening, nor any hint of likely danger. The Central Electricity Generating Board has said that its information centre at Lydd must be moved 'to an area with more comprehensive facilities to improve communications with the press and public'. But such information would be released by a group of senior CEGB officers acting as a 'single local authoritative information source to co-ordinate the flow of off-site information'.

15 November – Brighton   Every time I come here I like Brighton less. When Greene wrote *Brighton Rock*, the town may have had some criminal vigour; now it is just shabby. The proletarian trippers now go to Ramsgate, Southend, or even to Worthing; it is no longer smart now that the conference centre is active, and Brighton frequently overrun by politicians, confederations of businessmen, trade union officials, and other horrors; the tone of the place is set by quarrelsome, ageing pansies. High rise buildings have wrecked the façade of the front; nude bathing and a marina have not improved the beach; and the Palace Pier seems to be rotting and waterlogged.

Writing of sex in *The English are they Human?*, published in 1931, the wise Dutchman C. J. Renier ended by saying 'Of course, there is always Paris; London, for those who don't live there, and Brighton for those who do.' When I was eighteen, and training in a nearby army camp, I came down to Brighton for the Saturday dance in the Palace Pier and found that the girl I fancied was a sergeant in the police of the Women's Royal Army Corps. This was unnerving, so I went back to my lodging house. About two in the morning, I woke to find that the other two beds in the room were now occupied by a chorus girl and two Americans, who took her in turns while she talked – about her hats, about what she had told her friend Agnes, about that cheeky sod of a manager, on and on and on.

The hotel where I stayed gave me the smallest room I have had so far on my travels; there was wet paint on the corridor walls; and the price was £15.50. Next morning, I saw how they got away with it. The only other guests were canoodling couples of thirty or forty – adulterous without doubt. So Renier's wisecrack still holds true. Incidentally, his is the most prophetically accurate book ever written on England. He foresaw the collapse of the British Empire, of British industry and of the British will to work, with the country existing simply as a tourist centre, staffed with Mediterranean waiters and cooks.

16 November – Brighton   I went to the Pavilion and once more failed to find it even amusing; its garishness and extravagance are as un-Chinese as they are un-English. Why did the Prince Regent develop this half-baked, ignorant fancy for Asian things when he showed such taste and perception for art nearer home: for Regent Street, Carlton House Terrace, seventeenth-century Dutch paintings and Jane Austen's novels? One cannot help brooding upon that despised Prince Regent and king in a week when our own Prince of Wales is said to have chosen, at last, a bride in Lady Diana Spencer.

The popular hatred of George, which some feared might destroy the institution of monarchy, was made worse by the follies and crimes of his brothers; the whole lot of them seemed to the public rotten. The military Duke of York had a mistress who dealt as a broker in army commissions; when she was later disgraced, the Duke made an ass of himself with the elderly Duchess of Rutland. The sailor Duke of Clarence had ten illegitimate children by Mrs Jordan, an actress, before he married Princess Adelaide. The Duke of Kent, the father of Queen Victoria, shocked even the army of that time by his love of sadistic punishment; and later became a socialist of the Robert Owen variety. The Duke of Cumberland was said to have had a child by his sister, murdered his valet, and married a nymphomaniac. The last of these accusations was certainly true. Even the less notorious Dukes of Sussex and Cambridge were odd to the point that, if they lived now, their names would be constantly in the French and English Sunday newspapers. All seven sons of the mad old king behaved worse than does the blackest sheep, whether ram or ewe, in the modern royal family.

Even without his brothers, George would have been a butt of the artists and satrists who, in those days, enjoyed a licence greater than *Private Eye*'s. His spending on works of art, building, liveries, food, drink and mistresses were such that by 1796, more than twenty years before he became king, George had incurred debts of £600,000 – or more then £10 million in modern reckoning. Although the money of even the richest individual, if it had been shared out, would have made no difference to the misery of the masses, there was no shortage of Willy Hamiltons* then to point the contrast. The long French war and its aftermath produced a shortage of food amounting to famine. Even had England been prosperous and well fed, there is something gross in the menu on view in the kitchen of the pavilion, offering thirty courses of food, each with half a dozen varieties, and wine to match. One thinks of Nero or Caligula.

George paid the price of his greed in fat that had to be corseted if he went out in public; he liked to receive both his ministers and his mistresses wallowing on his bed in a gown as big as a tent. The politicians and still more the military leaders scorned George for his effeteness, which found expression late in life in a number of passions for old, plump women.

Of all his farcical and outrageous follies none was as dreadful in consequence as the marriage that George made in 1795 to Caroline, Princess of Brunswick. It was not that their wedding meant breaking a vow to Mrs Fitzherbert, with whom George had lived for ten years. It was not that the wedding was made for money. These did not matter compared with the personality of the Queen; flashy, foul-mouthed, dirty, perhaps mad, and certainly over-sexed. The marriage broke up after the first night – which nevertheless produced a child. Ten years later the Prince and Princess accused one another of such gross behaviour that a Privy Council committee had to be called to investigate. The Queen went abroad, took an Italian lover, and used to be drawn through the Genoa streets 'wearing a pink hat with several pink feathers floating in the wind, a pink bodice, cut very low, and a short white skirt which showed two stout legs and a pair of top-boots.'†

When George became King, this appalling woman came back to

---

* Labour MP and self-publicist, who has made himself a lucrative slot as a critic of royal spending.

† *George IV* by Roger Fulford (London, 1949).

142

England to take her rightful place on the throne; and such was the king's unpopularity that even a queen such as this found supporters. When the ministry charged her with adultery and scandalous behaviour (not a difficult accusation to prove) a mob followed her coach every day to the House of Lords. When the ministry withdrew its bill, the celebratory feasting and bonfires lasted for three days and nights.

George married, disastrously, when he was heir to the throne. Prince Charles is heir to the throne and, so we believe, is wanting to marry. In other respects, they could scarcely be less alike. Whereas George enjoyed luxury, paintings, architecture and books, Charles is an athlete, an outdoor man, an active officer in the services, and ascetic at table. Charles is as startlingly thin as George was fat. He is not extravagant in his choice of homes; does not patronise architects, artists or writers. Perhaps we have no Jane Austen around. From what one reads in the gossip columns, Charles admires women; but unlike George, he is most discreet.

George IV and his terrible brothers outraged an England gripped by evangelical fervour. It was the time of Wilberforce, Mrs Bowdler, the 'Saints' (as their enemies called them) who set their stamp on the age of Victoria. Now, when England is under the rule of the new 'Saints', the propagandists for contraception, abortion, gay liberation, the nuclear family, free divorce and woman's right to an orgasm, our royal family is, with a few exceptions, demure (without priggishness), fond of family life, eager for children, and paying at least an outward respect to the faith of its forbears. And the public loves them. It does not want royalty to conform with the times: to divorce, to abort, to 'come out of the closet' as homosexuals. The love and esteem felt for the Royal Family, is due, I would guess, as much to their being a family as to their being royal. Like the Archers on the radio, they stand for family feeling in a world of divorce and neglected children. It is because the public so strongly desires the happiness of the Royal Family that it shows such intrusive interest in Charles's choice of a bride.

Here is a point to consider, that there has never been a time in our history when the Crown was so popular, and the members of Parliament so despised.

17 November – Chichester   On the train from Brighton I read that a group of vandals in Worthing on Saturday night overturned six cars and spattered the town with Nazi daubings. I do not subscribe to the 'cry for help' theory of crime, but surely this is a protest against the sanctimonious 'multi-racial' twaddle that they are taught in school: they have found out how to annoy their liberal or Trotskyist teachers.

The Britons in what is now West Sussex welcomed the Romans, who made Chichester one of their focal towns with a street pattern that still survives. The centre has a market cross, which is always a subject of argument. During the recent argument in the local *Observer* on what was the safest way of cleaning the stone, somebody looked up and reprinted a letter on just the same subject from Eric Gill, written in 1901. An article about Chichester tells us that since the increase in postal fees 'the Market Cross is used every morning by the clerks of local solicitors, accountants, estate agents and other professional people to exchange their letters.' It is a pleasing idea but I have not actually noticed the custom.

Chichester, like Rye, is often abused as a 'picture-postcard' town. Its pedestrian precinct angers some of the motorists. It also angers a local poet who told me that when John Keats arrived in Chichester on the side of a coach, the streets of the town were alive with horses and sheep and brawling children. Agreed; but are cars their modern equivalent? I notice that Chichester is a popular town with visitors from the 'real' north, who travel hundreds of miles to sample the Gale's beer and even to visit the theatre. Chichester may not be 'real' but its major industry, Shippam's Meat and Fish Pastes, flourishes as it has done for 280 years. They began as suppliers to ships at Portsmouth; when packaging methods improved, they started to tin such exotic foods as boar's head, whole pheasant and curried prawns. Shippam's Chichester Sausages were admired, while potted meats and fish were packed in white porcelain dishes, sealed with melted butter. The company was a big supplier to British troops in the Boer War; a letter from Captain Scott to the company marks his gratitude and respect for the food that sustained if it did not save his life in Antarctica.

The factory thrives, I was told, but worse luck 'We don't have visits any more. The EEC's put paid to that with their strict regulations. You have to have protective clothing and headgear now to go round a food factory.'

The Cathedral has suffered from restoration by the Victorians, who added some rather incongruous marble statues, like those in Canterbury. And some of the recent additions are controversial: a garish John Piper tapestry and a Chagall window which does not inspire much feeling either way. These modern ornaments would be acceptable if it were not for the usual requests for £500 a day to meet the cathedral's upkeep. The Chagall and Piper works are hardly upkeep. Or were they given free?

The diocese has replied to such charges with testiness but no good explanation. Chichester has a reputation for modernism: a friend of mine in the Prayer Book Society described Bishop Kemp as 'one of our greatest enemies'. The leading advocate of the ancient prayer book, David Martin (who, incongruously, is Professor of Sociology at the London School of Economics) claimed the other day in the *Daily Telegraph* that 'When a study by Dr Roger Homan showed that in Chichester Archdeaconry, numbers kept up better with the Prayer Book than with Series 3, he was denounced as "irresponsible".'

Modernism in liturgy and views cannot protect a diocese from involvement in old-fashioned scandal, as happened recently in Chichester. One of the clerics at the cathedral, a scholarly and admired man, had one of those temporary breakdowns that some-times afflict the middle-aged, and was taken before a London magistrate's court and found guilty of indecent exposure. Although this was a quite extraordinary lapse in a blameless career, and although there was no question of sexual advances to anyone of either sex, the cleric found it necessary to resign, or as some would say, he was told to resign by the bishop. No enlightenment on the terms of the resignation came from the bishop or his subordinate, whose name does not need repeating.

The case and the resignation prompted hundreds of letters both to the cleric and to the newspapers, expressing their sympathy and, in some cases, condemnation of Bishop Kemp. Among the letters in the Chichester *Observer*, friends and admirers of the cleric wrote of his courage, kindness, intellectual distinction and humanity, while one correspondent added waspishly: 'Since suspensions and resignations seem to be the order of the day, it is my personal view that the cause of Christianity in West Sussex might be wonderfully advanced if the Bishop and his advisers might be persuaded to add their own names to the rapidly growing list.'

An outsider might say that the case shows up the moral dilemma of modern permissive Anglicans, since the Church is now accustomed to tolerate, even commend, divorce, adultery, homosexuality and other practices that used to be thought of as sins. But there is no understanding of how to react to a case when what is a moral sin, however slight, is also a crime in secular law. If you do away with the concept of sin, you also do away with forgiveness. When Jeremy Thorpe was found not guilty of a conspiracy to murder an alleged former male lover, the bells of his West Country church rang out in rejoicing. But when a Chichester cleric is found guilty of doing something constantly done by actors and actresses on stage and TV, he is hounded out of his living.

18 November – Chichester – Portsmouth – Southsea If the towns of the south coast lack the bonhomie of the North of England, they offer plenty of cultural fare, and this I have sampled whenever possible. I did not hear, last night, the Amadeus String Quartet, partly because I disliked the look of the Chichester Festival Theatre: a come-down after the warm, Edwardian gilt of the Brighton Theatre Royal where I had seen *Blithe Spirit*. Also, the TV offered a double bill of appearances by Sir Harold Wilson and William Rees-Mogg; even funnier than I had dared hope.

But today at lunchtime, I went to a recital in the cathedral – Bach and Beethoven – interspersed by a reading of T. S. Eliot. I had expected *Murder in the Cathedral*, or at least one of the Four Quartets, and was disappointed to hear two of those cat poems. I suppose it is worth knowing that Eliot wrote light verses; however he did not do it well. If you must have light verse read in cathedrals, why not good light verse by someone like Gilbert, Belloc or Chesterton? The answer, I fear, is a kind of patronising attempt to show that even a serious and a difficult poet like Eliot also wrote stuff that was not above the heads of you and me. I thought of William Rees-Mogg on TV last night when he said that his favourite programmes were *Dallas* and *Dr Who*. How comforting that a scholar and wise man like Mogg should also want to know who killed JR! . . . The eternal fear of the English of seeming clever is borne out by the monument here to William Collins, the city's most famous poet:

146

Tho Nature gave to him and science taught
The fire of fancy and the reach of thought,
Severely doomed to penury's extreme,
He passed in maddening pain life's feverish dream.

Arrived at Portsmouth, I went down to inspect what remains of the
Royal Navy: HMS *Victory*, a number of pleasure yachts, and some
kind of sloop. A few years ago Guatemala started to threaten our
little central American colony British Honduras, or Belize as it is now
called. The British Prime Minister of the time – inevitably it was
Wilson – adopted a Palmerstonian posture and sent out a gun boat
to keep the peace, forgetting that it was armed with no weapons less
deadly than nuclear missiles. One of the few false prophecies in *1984*
is to have a cinema audience looking at newsreel film of a British
battleship sinking enemy vessels and gunning down the survivors.
Perhaps Orwell meant that the film was a fake; perhaps even he
could not predict that long before 1984 our Navy would be reduced
to impotence. Nearly a thousand years ago, in 1009, the English
Navy assembled at Sandwich was said to have numbered 3500 vessels;
small vessels by modern standards, but adequate to the country's
defence.

Southsea's marine parade is a great and cheerful surprise: the walk
down the beach with a view over the Solent is one of the best on the
south coast. My small hotel has a gin-dispensing machine and I guess
that the bars round here are full of pink gin-drinking former naval
gentlemen; but I am off the liquor these several days. Drinking
orange juice in pubs puts me in mind of Donne's description of those
'who go to sea if only to be sick'.

Instead of a pub, I go to the Kent Opera's *The Magic Flute* at the
King's Theatre, Southsea; after a meal of the best haddock and chips
I have eaten in years at a place next to the theatre called simply the
Fish Restaurant. I had heard and read good things of Kent Opera,
but I was nevertheless surprised at the excellence of the entertainment. The translator Michael Irwin and the producer Norman Platt
have combined to restore this work to its proper greatness by cutting
out the superfluous coyness and feeble jokes. What a relief it was to
see no papier maché dragon chasing Tamino on stage! The fauna
were reduced to a few lions and bears. The villain Manostatos was
portrayed as a serious rapist instead of a figure of fun. And above all,

147

Irwin and Platt have tackled the Papageno problem. The greedy and timorous hunter of birds is a comic from pantomine – and therefore a welcome figure on stage for fidgety schoolchildren and others bored by Mozart's music. Unhappily, most producers, abetted by Papagenos, ham up the comedy for the sake of the laughs. Yet Papageno's jokes are threadbare. The more one gets to know and love *The Magic Flute*, the more one dreads every appearance of Papageno, prancing around in his feathers, and chiming his bells. In Kent's production, Papageno is played almost straight as a simple workman with little interest in the mumbo-jumbo of the Masonic Order. The Southsea audience, who chatted and whispered and rustled paper throughout the two arias of Sarastro, were nevertheless best pleased by the Papageno scenes. But for once, and rightly, Papageno was not permitted to steal the show.

And this gave *The Magic Flute* unaccustomed clarity. Some people write it all off as a pantomime, only because it is usually played as such. Played straight, in a good translation, the opera comes across as an allegory as noble and true as the music that goes with it. What you read into it is your own business: Maria Teresa overthrown by the Emperor Joseph; the Church versus Liberalism; the Ego versus the Id; or, as I tend to regard it, youth growing to maturity through trial and ordeal. When I saw the Ingmar Bergman film in Salisbury, Rhodesia, the white audience clapped Sarastro's repression of the revolt of the blacks, led by Manostatos, a Moor. I liked the film and thought it almost unique, among modern interpretations of classics, in rightly emphasising sex in *The Magic Flute*. In the trial sequence, Ingmar Bergman suggests that Tamino has to fight down sexual lust for the Queen of the Night's maidens; also that Pamina is attracted by Manostatos. My instinct is to jeer at such a suggestion; but it rings true. Our sexual consultants and modern 'agony aunties' would not approve Mozart's theme: that happiness and maturity come from sexual restraint.

From Winchester to Bristol

19 November - Winchester I went by train to Winchester through the Hampshire countryside that Cobbett loved, and got so angry about. He engaged in debate those Scottish economists and 'pheelo-sophers' who averred that the Norman kings had ruined the villeins in order to keep their hunting rights in the New Forest. Cobbett would have none of this. The damage to Hampshire, he wrote again and again, was done by the modern businessmen from the Wen, the 'Jews and jobbers', above all the Barings, who 'are now the great men in Hampshire'. At Abbotston, on the Itche, Cobbett observed:

ALEXANDER BARING has succeeded the heirs and successors of the DUKE OF BOLTON, the remains of whose noble mansion I once saw here. Not above a mile higher up, the same Baring has, at the GRANGE, with its noble mansion, park and estate, succeeded the heirs of LORD NORTHINGTON; and, at only about two miles further, SIR THOMAS BARING, at Stratton Park, has succeeded the RUSSELLS in the ownership of the estates of Stratton and Micheldover, which were once the property of ALFRED THE GREAT!

He reckoned that in this part of Hampshire, the small gentry were almost gone and the small farmers along with them. 'The Barings alone have, I should think, swallowed up thirty or forty of these small gentry without perceiving it. They, indeed, swallow up the biggest race of all; but, innumerable small fry slip down unperceived, like caplins down the throats of the sharks, while these latter *feel* only the cod-fish.'

The Baring family, over the last 150 years, has flourished in public life as in finance, receiving no less then five distinct peerages and producing generals, colonial governors, scholars and artists as well as (supreme irony) Richard Ingrams's maternal grandfather. But Barings are still at work in Hampshire, where 'under the picturesque pseudonym of the Abbotstone Agricultural Property Unit Trust . . . they have bought a farm at Ashmansworth and now want to cut down 1300 oak and ash trees.' This was 'Piloti' writing in *Private Eye* in July, under the headline 'Baring the teeth'. 'Piloti', whose pen-name conceals one of the country's best architectural writers, went on to say that

Barings are at least consistent: they hate trees no less than they hate old buildings, but it is adding insult to injury to name their 'Property Unit Trust' after the hamlet near the Grange – the Neo-Classical mansion so generously given to the nation by the Hon John Baring after he had gutted it but had been prevented by public outcry from setting off the explosives he had planted in it. He had already managed to destroy George Dance Jnr's Stratton Park while his company demolished its City headquarters by Norman Shaw. Cobbett, as always, knew the enemy.

20 November – Winchester – Salisbury   Cobbett also made strong remarks about Winchester and its Cathedral. While modern tourists are apt to exclaim in wonder on how such building was done without our technology, Cobbett turned the question around in conversation with Richard, his small son:

'Why, papa, nobody can build such places *now*, can they?' 'No, my dear. That building was made when there were no poor wretches in England called *paupers*; when there were no *poor-rates*; when every labouring man was clothed in good woollen cloth; and when all had a plenty of meat and bread and beer.'

Although Cobbett was right to say that England had gone downhill since the Middle Ages, he was wrong to blame the lack of good modern architecture on poor rates and poor laws; because at the present day the labouring man has plenty of cloth, meat, bread and beer, but our architects are still less capable of constructing such a cathedral as Winchester. I do not just mean that they could not conceive of something as beautiful – that goes without saying – but they lack the physical means of putting up such a pile. For one thing, there is no longer a work force qualified in construction skills, as you can see at any building site, and I doubt if most architects now know how to work with stone and wood or even brick. The example of Ronan Point, and many new buildings that have had to be pulled down, suggests that people cannot even build safely or durably using steel and cement.

The extent of England's regression, not just spiritually and artistically but in many kinds of physical skill, was little known in Cobbett's age of industrial democracy and belief in progress. Today, popular wisdom decries even the spirit of the Middle Ages: 'mediaeval', like 'feudal', is now a term of abuse.

It is therefore a joy to go back to a city that still retains not only its mighty eleventh-century Cathedral, and its college built in the fourteenth century, England's golden age, but a pleasant amount of good later buildings, principally of the Georgian period. Of course there has been destruction, and not just over the last thirty years. From *Winchester – 100 Years Ago* by Barbara Carpenter Turner, I learn that the city then suffered all kinds of familiar worries, from war in Afghanistan (Winchester was a garrison town) and the import of cheap French eggs, to road-widening schemes and the demolition of fine old buildings. Recent planning officials have built a shopping 'precinct' and done much damage under the usual pretext of guarding motorists' rights, but a route plan for the city was shelved thanks to spirited opposition from the Cathedral and College, whose headmaster, John Thorn, deserves the thanks of all of us.

Winchester townspeople seem well-disposed to the College, which may have something to do with what Mr Thorn said in a recent article (*Spectator*, 16 December 1978) on 'The New Public Schoolboy'. He largely concurred with the view that boys were much 'easier' in the Seventies than they were in the Sixties: 'They now do what you say, most of the time. They cut their hair somewhat shorter and don't particularly mind if you tell them to cut it shorter still. If they dress in a slovenly way, it is more likely to be through indifference than in a spirit of rebellion against the *bourgeoisie*.' He went on to say that 'the rise in unemployment which accompanied the subsequent lowering of the inflation has made adolescent dropping out a rare and not much admired luxury'.

That sentence might have amused the gentlemen whom I met in a Winchester public house; he had sent all three of his sons to the College (two of them on scholarships) only to see them all 'drop out', or rather be dropped out, before their schooldays expired. It seems

F

that the commonest grounds for rustication is smoking marijuana, or even cigarettes – because, so it is argued, these can lead to mari-juana. Expulsion is now a special threat to the older boys for whom, in these enlightened and liberal days, beating is no longer appro-priate. I also learned that some of the older boys have been sacked for spending the night out with women. It is heartening to find that although homosexuals (or 'homosexualists' as their enemies call them) have taken over parts of the Church of England, the theatres and the Arts Council, they seem to be losing their stronghold in the public schools. This may be explained by genetic self-interest of the English ruling class – determined to breed despite the homosexuals and abortionists.

Until this year, I had last gone to Winchester for a Cathedral church parade, and I still remember the peril of marching on slippery boots down the steep street from the railway station. In those days Winchester was the home of the King's Royal Rifle Corps (not my regiment, I should hasten to add) which has now been merged with others in what the public relations people have dubbed the Royal Green Jackets. An NCO of this regiment moaned to me of how dead the town had become with so few pubs left in the centre, and how the recruits were inferior material: 'They're mostly school leavers who can't find a job. Lads of seventeen or seventeen and a half. They're hopeless when you put them in a tricky place like Northern Ireland. For that kind of fighting you need more mature men of, say, twenty-four.'

An ex-serviceman told me: 'I was in India, up at the North-West Frontier in 1928. In the RAF. You know that part of the world? Where all the troubles are now. We, the English, lost out twice there. Only one man returned. A doctor. I was in the forces until the end of the Second World War, as a pilot, and now I get a pension only a third of the university grants the students get. Did you hear that student I was talking to? He'd never heard of the *Golden Treasury*. He'd never heard of Mr Pecksniff. He'd never read Dickens. Said Dickens was like reading his own obituary. "There is no order of precedence between the louse and the flea", as Dr Johnson said.'

Hostility between the troops and civilians takes many forms. I went this morning to the assize court and heard the end of the trial of a man who had been in a fight with soldiers in Salisbury. The judge remarked in his summing up that 'members of the jury who know, as

I do, the city of Salisbury, or indeed the city of Winchester, know that there has always been a degree of hostility between the towns-people and the soldiery. When it means only an exchange of insults like "bastards" and "wankers", it is not too serious. Even a strike is not too serious. But when someone is attacked with a milk bottle this cannot be tolerated.'

The assizes are held in an ugly modern building grafted on to the Great Hall, which itself shows signs of having been done up and somehow seems as spurious as 'Arthur's Round Table' which hangs on the wall. This part of Winchester up on the hill is not as pleasant as that in the valley, down by the College and the Cathedral.

William Cobbett, who championed the old faith without at the same time confessing it, was shocked by the congregation at one Cathedral service of only fifteen women and four men:

Gracious God! If WILLIAM OF WYKEHAM could, at that moment, have raised from his tomb! If Saint SWITHIN, whose name the cathedral bears, or ALFRED THE GREAT, to whom St SWITHIN was tutor: if either of these could have come, and had been told, that *that* was *now* what was carried on by men, who talked of the "*damnable* errors" of those who founded that very church!

Perhaps Cobbett overdid his indignation. At the service I attended there were more in the congregation than he managed to count. Wykeham's College goes on still. Winchester has not betrayed the injunction written up in the chapel of William of Waynflete, a fifteenth-century bishop and former headmaster, to 'remember the schools and colleges of this country, for which you are in duty bound to pray "that our sons may grow up as young plants, and that our daughters may be as the polished corners of the temple." '

I went by bus to Salisbury, changing at Romsey. The route is designed to serve outlying villages, and it winds and twists in so convulated a manner that you may spend half an hour passing signposts that read 'Salisbury 6 miles'. These are not the dolled-up villages that you find in Suffolk, Kent or the Cotswolds, but raggedy working farms or cottages, next to untidy fields and copses, and streams full of weed and broken branches. It is pleasantly free of agro-technology – the immense, barbed-wired, crop-sprayed fields of super-corn, or factory cattle and birds. Nor is it gentleman-farmer country. The Barings, I think, are not established here. Unhappily there has come a snake to this Eden. The Forestry Commission, which is bad enough in itself – bringing pines and access roads and compulsory purchase – is once more the tool of the multinational companies. At Lockerley and at Farley, both of which I passed today, the Commission has let its land to Shell in order to drill for oil. 'We shall be moving the rig on to the site at Farley this week,' says Shell's 'Community Relations Officer'. I have seen this company at its work at Amlwch, on the Anglesey coast, where a few of the locals dared to protest at a single berth mooring for unloading oil from ships. They claimed, on the evidence of what had happened at Durban in South Africa, that such a berth would result in spillages, and that anyway it would not create local jobs. Shell appeased the island through its 'community relations officers'; it employed a Labour shadow cabinet minister as counsel to argue the company case at a public inquiry; when the site was debated at Anglesey County Council, a busload of 'Amlwch unemployed' were hired to shout on Shell's behalf. Needless to say, Amlwch has since suffered catastrophic spillages; its beaches and fishing have suffered; and unemployment is higher than ever.

This evening I went to hear the Vienna Boys' Choir in Salisbury Cathedral. Although I have spent many weeks in Vienna I never went to one of the Boys' performances, having imagined that they sung nothing but folksongs and schmaltz. Perhaps because of the place, the choir tonight sang almost entirely sacred music, including bits of the Schubert Mass, his twenty-third Psalm and *Die Nachtbelle*, none of which I had heard before, and all of which are most moving.

The programme referred to the troubles endured by the choir during the Nazi occupation of Austria: it is a subject I know about through a curious route. After the Anschluss, the governors of the choir, who were old-fashioned Austrian Catholics and did not approve of Nazism, refused to allow the boys to join the Hitler Youth or to wear Hitlerite uniform. The new authorities therefore disbanded the old choir and recruited a new one from boys in the slums, whose fathers had once been communists but were now joining Hitler's new order. A troupe was formed, trained in singing and decked out in a brownshirt uniform, complete with swastika armbands. In Spring 1939 the new Vienna Boys Choir set out on tour round the world, beginning in New York and moving slowly across

the United States to the West Coast. From there they sailed to the
east coast of Australia, where they continued to give their concerts,
moving gradually westward till they reached Perth. They finished
their last concert and were about to board ship for the Fatherland
when Britain, and with her Australia, entered the war. The boys
were at first interned but their plight attracted the sympathy – or
political mischief – of Archbishop Mannix, the Catholic Archbishop
of Melbourne, and a rabid Fenian, who had been banned from his
native Ireland during the First World War. He brought the choir to
Melbourne and had them billeted out among the Catholics of the
city. There, in Melbourne, the choir grew up and eventually stayed. I
met about four of them shortly before their annual reunion dinner in
1971.

They were, by appearance, easy-going and beer-bellied
Australians; but underneath they were still upset, or at any rate
puzzled. All of them had been dutiful Nazis and all, so they said,
supported the German army throughout the war. Yet none went
back to live in Vienna. They felt somehow ashamed of having
escaped the bombs and shells and the Russian invasion. During that
tour of America, some of the boys were sent back to Austria because
their voices broke: all of these died on the Russian front. And saddest
of all, when the real Vienna Boys' Choir visited Melbourne during
the 1960s, these veterans of the Nazi Vienna Boys' Choir wanted to
give them a tea of pasties and cakes; but the master in charge for-
bade this tainted gathering. As for the Nazi choirmaster, he served
his years in an Australian internment camp and was last heard of
training a choir in South Africa.

21 November – Salisbury Several cathedral towns have claimed to
have been the inspiration of Barchester; but Trollope himself made
it clear in his *Autobiography* that he got the idea for these clerical
novels in Salisbury Cathedral close. Even if Barchester also has hints
of Wells or Winchester (where Trollope went to school for a time and
was most unhappy), I think that Salisbury ought to be taken as the
epitome for Trollope's vision of life in rural southern England. For
those of us who abhor Westminster politics, the Barsetshire books
have a charm and seriousness which are not to be found in the
Palliser books – for all their melodrama and racy villains. Although
politicians make an appearance in Barsetshire – including Plan-

tagenet Palliser of the other series – none is a central character
except for the sponging MP who nearly ruins the Revd Mark Robarts
of *Framley Parsonage*.

Yet the Barsetshire novels, so rich in detail of work, money, class
relationships and social attitudes, tell us a lot about the political
issues which bothered people and influenced them in electing
members to Parliament. The Pallisers, who controlled seats in
Barsetshire and the neighbouring county, were Whigs, so that the
Duke of Omnium, the head of the Palliser clan and the richest man
in the county had the patronage of liberal MPs. Most of the sym-
pathetic clergy, like Archdeacon Grantly, are high Tories, while
Bishop Proudie and his terrible-tempered wife are 'modernists', and
by implication liberals, although I believe that Trollope does not say
so explicitly.

If Barsetshire had been Lancashire rather than Wiltshire, and
most of the characters had been starving mill-workers rather than
clergymen or farming workers, it would be fashionable to call Trollope's books 'political', just as Dickens is now, wrongly, portrayed as a
socialist and reformer. It is somehow accepted these days that
'politics' is about industrial disputes, class war and violent change;
yet rural, southern England was and is just as important in politics
and economic life as the industrial north.

'It is a comfortable feeling to know that you stand on your ground,'
says Archdeacon Grantly, who is a man of wealth. 'And then you see,
land gives so much more than the rent. It gives position and
influence and politician power.' Land in those days, the 1860s, was
more than a source of wealth from crops or livestock or speculation.
It provided subsistence for most of the population of all classes. It
provided the country's favourite amusements like shooting and fox-
hunting. Its rents provided the marriage endowments and legacies
that figure so large in Trollope's novels. Nobody could declare, after
reading one of the Barchester novels, that rural England then was
less materialistic than the industrial England of Manchester men like
Mr Gradgrind. Even the parsons of Barchester thought constantly of
the size of their livings; the wealth, or lack of it, of prospective sons
and daughters-in-law; the cost of a second horse or the children's
clothes.

The Church of England was not in those days set apart from the
rest of society. Parsons aspired to be landowners and country gentle-

men; their sons might as easily choose a career as squire, army officer, civil servant or politician, as follow their fathers into the church. The older generation of parsons still enjoyed wordly amusements like fox-hunting, whist and bottles of port, though such things were offensive to Mrs Proudie.

Trollope's contemporary, Karl Marx, referred to the 'imbecility of country life', from which he hoped that man would escape to new and eventually socialist cities; he did not foresee that industry could survive only as long as finite fuel. Life was indeed harsh for some of the Barsetshire poor, although conditions were much improved since Cobbett had toured England, thirty years earlier. The brickworkers of Hoggleston were the poorest of all the poor in Barsetshire, though scarcely more so than Josh Crawley, whose torment and prosecution for theft form the story of *Last Chronicle of Barset*.

Yet even the Hoggleston brickworkers had some advantages over the modern country folk. Each village in Barsetshire had a school, so that children did not have to travel miles each day to some distant comprehensive. And children were actually taught to read and write rather than take part in 'creative play'. In those days, educational theories verged on the other extreme. '"What" said his [Dr Thorne's] sensible enemies, "is Johnny not to be taught because he does not like it?"' Today, in those schools attended by Barsetshire children, Johnny is not taught to read, even although he might like it.

And in their medical treatment, the Barsetshire poor are much to be envied by modern readers. Young Dr Crofts visits *The Small House at Allington* several times every day because he loves the patient's sister; but he also visits the sick in the poorest homes of his practice, for an annual £100. In modern England few doctors will visit the sickest patient, even a child; and who can blame them, given the state of the National Health Service? In Barsetshire, parsons did those ministrations of comfort to troubled, unhappy or lonely people, that now are performed by social workers; or not at all.

The postal service was prompt in Barsetshire. This was a subject close to the heart of Trollope, who worked many years as a post office inspector, and gained his knowledge of south-west England from making sure that letters went punctually to even remote houses. Letters arrived the morning after posting except at Framley which chose not to receive Sunday mail. Neighbouring Plumstead chose to accept Sunday letters, thanks to the agitation of Archdeacon

Grantly, who liked his fierce correspondence.

The train service which then connected Barchester with Paddington, rather than Waterloo, was frequent and quick. There is a good scene at Paddington in *The Small House at Allington* when John Eames punches Adolphus Crosbie and sends him sprawling among the papers of 'Mr Smith's bookstall'. Few people probably know how ancient is the monopoly in our stations of W.H. Smith. When W. T. Stead, as editor of the *Pall Mall Gazette*, published his exposé of child prostitution in 1885, great crowds assembled to buy copies off the press; but circulation fell and the *Pall Mall Gazette* was almost ruined when Smith's refused to stock it at railway stations.

There was never a ban on *The Jupiter*, as Trollope, who hated the paper, called *The Times*. Their Religious Affairs Correspondent, as he would now be called, is a priggish and meddling radical called Tom Towers who starts the campaign, described in *The Warden*, to deprive Mr Harding of his sinecure. *The Jupiter* also exposes Mr Robarts for wasting money on hunters and having the bailiffs in. When Tom Towers arrives at a Cabinet Minister's party, he is fawned upon by the politicians present.

At the end of *The Last Chronicle of Barset*, Trollope replies to those critics who said that 'I have described many clergymen . . . but have spoken of them all as though their professional duties, their high calling, their daily workings for the good of those around them, were matters of no moment.' In his defence, Trollope says that his aim has been 'to paint the social and not the professional life of clergymen'; and that is the painting from which we get so much enjoyment.

Yet Trollope did not ignore the debate or spiritual crisis within the Church of England over the period of the Barsetshire novels; a division which still persists, though we may not be aware of it. Trollope was writing when Darwin's books had disturbed the very foundation of Christian belief; when even those who resolved their doubts were critical of the old-fashioned attitudes of an Archdeacon Grantly. Some Victorian clerics followed Newman into the Roman church but, as Trollope pointed out, most funked the crossing.

There is a Catholic convert in *The Way We Live Now*, but none in the Barchester novels. We do have very high clergymen like the Revd Caleb Oriel in *Dr Thorne*:

He delighted in lectures and credence-tables, in services at dark hours of winter mornings when no-one would attend, in high waistcoats and narrow neck-ties, in chanted services and intoned prayers, and in all the paraphernalia of Anglican formalities which have given such offence to those of our brethren who live in fear of the scarlet lady.

None lived in greater fear of the scarlet lady than did Mrs Proudie, the militant low-church wife of the meek Bishop of Barchester. '"Idolatry is, I believe, more rampant than ever in Rome," said she; "and I fear there is no such thing at all as Sunday observances." "Oh, not the least," said Miss Dunstable with rather a joyous air; "Sundays and weekdays are all the same there." "How very frightful!" said Mrs Proudie. "But it's a delicious place,"' says Miss Dunstable, an heiress, and no respecter of persons like Mrs Proudie. '"I do like Rome, I must say. And as for the Pope, if he wasn't so fat he would be the nicest fellow in the world."'

The Proudie, or 'modernist' element in the Church of England, is once more critical of the Pope, but for a quite different reason. Pope John Paul II, who is opposed to divorce, contraception, abortion, women priests and 'liberation theology', is thought a reactionary by the modernist wing of both the Anglican and the Roman Church, and indeed by some nonconformists. Those, like the Revd Ian Paisley, who still feel strongly on things like Sunday observance, are closer now to the Pope on matters of doctrine and discipline than they are to most of the Protestants in these islands. The divide in the Christian church these days is no longer a question of theological niceties like transubstantiation, the infallibility of the Pope, or vernacular worship; it is between those who believe in, and those who do not believe in, the fall of man.

The Proudies, taking over the bishopric at the start of *Barchester Towers*, somehow remind me of Harold Wilson and Marcia Williams taking over Ten Downing Street in 1964, after 'thirteen years of Tory misrule'. Their Evangelical passion to cleanse the see of worldliness, sinecure, chanting and other Romish practices, was, in clerical terms, the equivalent of Wilson's 'white heat of technology' and his dislike of the 'candyfloss society'. And did not Wilson employ men like the repulsive Mr Slope, the Bishop's chaplain and Mrs Proudie's pet until he disgraced himself by lechery? The Proudies represented what would later be called the progressive wing of the Church of England, in sympathy with the Liberal Party in Parliament. There were few actual dissenters then in office – they did not sweep into Parliament until 1905 – although one was a judge of assize where Mr Crawley was due to stand trial.

The low-church Evangelicals were keen on missionary work in what one would now call the 'Third World'. *The Last Chronicle of Barset* was published in 1867, two years after the end of the American Civil War, in which Archdeacon Grantly 'thought that the Southerners were Christian gentlemen, and the Northerners infidel snobs; whereas Mrs Proudie had an idea that the Gospel was preached with genuine zeal in the Northern states.' It is not known whether Mrs Proudie supported Lady Rosina de Courcy's favourite 'mission for putting down the Papists in the west of Ireland', but she did interrupt a lecture on missionary work in Papua and New Guinea ('the lands of which produce rich spices and glorious fruits') shouting 'Christianity and Sabbath-day observance. Let us never forget that these islanders can never prosper unless they keep the Sabbath holy.' No wonder that Josiah Crawley, whose quarrel with Mrs Proudie produces a glorious chapter, should write to the Dean: 'The special laws of this and of some other countries do allow that women shall sit upon the temporal thrones of the earth, but on the lowest steps of the throne of the Church no woman has been allowed to sit.'

22 November – Salisbury   Of all the old cities of southern England, Salisbury must be the best off for cultural events. Apart from the Boys' Choir, which was an outside arrival, the city has two plays in repertory and even a film at the local cinema – *One Flew Over the Cuckoo's Nest* – which might appeal to someone's intelligence. This evening I went to a concert of Salisbury's Orchestral Society: or rather the first half, since dinner finishes early at The Red Lion hotel. The soloist in the Weber Clarinet Concerto must have been a professional; he was very good, and survived even the passage when the clarinet is supported only by three french horns. Things can go wrong for french horns in the greatest of orchestras. The City Hall is full for the concert, most of them friends and family of the players, I should imagine. And scarcely a common accent heard. Salisbury is one of those towns where the public school manner and voice are un-tainted by TV American, Trotskyist cockney, Linguaphone Lanca-shire or any other spurious tones adopted by guilty sons and daughters of the professional class. And with the accent, goes the traditional bray of the upper classes, the nervous pauses and un-finished sentences: 'Yes . . . splendid! . . . Oh really . . . I wonder if this lady would mind . . . An orange juice? Really? Nothing a bit er . . . stronger? No! Splendid!'

23 November – Salisbury – Bath I look up an old friend, Christopher Reynolds, from Salisbury, Rhodesia. As a matter of fact, I have known him almost a quarter century since I was employed by the *Manchester Guardian* and he was the *Daily Mirror*'s Manchester showbiz correspondent, who used to regale us with scandalous tales of the stars: 'So she asked me back to her dressing room and she said "Chris, darling, while we talk, would you mind rubbing this cold cream onto my breasts" . . .' I was once turned down for a flat in Withington when the estate agent heard I was a journalist. 'We had one of your lot in the flat before – Mr Christopher Reynolds. He and his friends chopped up the wardrobe for firewood.' He went to Africa where I met him again in 1977 – many years, drinks and marriages later.

Already one talks of Salisbury, Rhodesia, in the past tense. It was bound to end in atrocities or corruption, and so far the latter has been more in evidence, though I fear the former will come. Rhodesia, which lived through fourteen years of sanctions and actu-ally built up a balance of payments surplus, is now crying for aid from the West – and for what? To pay off the crooked new bour-geoisie. African colleagues we knew as chronic debtors have bought themselves houses in Borrowdale or Highlands; the civil service is near to collapse; thugs like Tekere, who recently stood trial for murder, are sure to attempt a *coup d'état*. 'It's turned sour,' says Chris, who has recently left, for the last time. 'It's no fun any more. Just another corrupt African state.'

Inevitably we compare the two Salisburys. The African Salisbury is lower class, less cultivated, and much more drunken, but probably closer to Salisbury, Wilts, than it is to most English cities. Both Salis-burys retain something of England long ago. When I first went to Salisbury (Rhodesia) in 1964, I hated the whites for their philistine arrogance to a people they neither knew nor bothered to understand. (On that visit, I did not go out to the countryside where one finds a different types of white.) But by the end of the 1970s, the whites of Rhodesia – even the townpeople of Salisbury – had proved themselves

through war and adversity, and what is more, now knew the countryside and the people who lived in it. Whereas, formerly, they had
been rude and touchy with English people, they now regarded us
with the ease that comes from self-confidence. They even treated us
with pity; and they were right, for England had meanwhile changed
for the worse. It was always dispiriting to read in the Salisbury
Herald of strikes and riots in England; of football hooliganism, the
breakdown of education; the ever-increasing power of the state over
the individual and the family. Saddest of all was to read the
announcements by politicians that economic sanctions would sooner
or later bring the whites in Rhodesia to submission. Our politicians
are so accustomed to buying votes with tax reductions and spending
sprees, with cars, washing machines and package holidays, that they
cannot imagine a people like the Rhodesians who hold to other
priorities. I did not support Smith's unilateral declaration of independence; it was bound to fail and only lasted as long as it did thanks
to the folly and arrogance of Westminster. Nevertheless, I came to
admire the Rhodesians and even Smith, a masterly politician deserving a better cause. There was much that I did not like in Rhodesia;
but also something of value that long since perished in English public
life.

'Welcome to Ba-ath, Sir' says the posturing beau to Mr Pickwick.
Jane Austen hated the place as well. Perhaps we are lucky that Bath
now attracts only the rich and not the fashionable – who are better
employed in London, New York or St Moritz. Bath now has the most
expensive hotel in England – or so I read in the *Daily Mail* – and may
have a hotel-cum-mineral-water complex under the ownership of a
group which includes Eric Levine, the distinguished lawyer to Sir
James Goldsmith and others.

24 November – Bath – Bristol In the Roman baths, I read these
lines from an eighth-century Saxon poet:

> Bright were the buildings, Bath-houses many,
> High forest of pinnacles, War-clang frequent.
> Mead-halls many, Merriment frequently,
> Till all was o'erwhelmed, by fate unrelenting.

Today they are filling in a votive spring, along with the coins and
jewels tossed there for luck. The plans to restore Roman Bath are

worthy of praise, if only to counteract the prevalent denigration of what the National Theatre portrays as *The Romans in Britain*. They may not have been very likeable people but they favoured this country with better government than it has had for most of its history; certainly better than that it suffers today. The postal service was quicker then from London to Bath.

I have always liked Bristol better than Bath; better indeed than most places in England. From an early age I thought of it as the port of departure for the West Indies, sea battles against the Spanish, pirate ships and treasure islands. I seem to remember a game like Monopoly in which the prices were chests of pasteboard pearls, doubloons and pieces of eight. I also seem to remember coming to Bristol to see my uncle Lockwood West in *Alf's Button*; his actor son Timothy is a big-shot in the Bristol as well as the London Old Vic. (And Tim's wife Prunella Scales almost redeemed *The Hollow Crown* which I saw in Bath last night; it was dreadfully hammed by the other actors.)

When I came to this city twenty years ago, the theatre world was active. I think it was threatened by Arnold Wesker with some sort of 'working-class' drama, or other modish nonsense. Nevertheless, Bristol was fun; or rather Clifton was fun. This must be the finest suburb in Britain, built of the same warm stone as Bath in nine-teenth- as well as eighteenth-century style; and stretched on the side of a hill over the Avon gorge, rather than sunk, like Bath, in a humid valley. Compared with Clifton, Hampstead is dull and pretentious. The New Town of Edinburgh, although architecturally fine, is too dour for English tastes. Clifton comprises the zoo and school of that name; part of the university and much of the BBC, which here in Bristol has always enjoyed a kind of autonomy from the dead rule of Langham Place and Lime Grove. Even the local papers seemed alive and cared about Bristol; the young reporter, Tom Stoppard, who showed me around was soon to win fame as a playwright. I enjoyed myself greatly and afterwards wrote an article calling Bristol 'Britain's best city'.

The judgment still holds, for if Bristol has lost much of its charm, so has the rest of Britain; and Bristol has gone downhill at a slower speed. Indeed, compared to some of our cities, Bristol has got off lightly. Like most ports, Bristol was bombed in the war, and the damage was used as a justification by politicians and planners to knock down the much larger number of buildings spared by the Luftwaffe. During the 1960s – that decade of wrath for historic England – Bristol Corporation destroyed most of the inner city to make way for the usual ring roads, shopping centre (a stinker, called Broadmead), speculative office blocks and grandiose 'leisure facilities'.

From 1960 onwards, a Bristol antiquarian, Mr Reece Winstone, kept a diary of the change which he published each year in cyclo-styled form. That very first year witnessed the final demolition of Bristol's only Norman house. The next year, 1961, marked the removal of all the Georgian and pre-Georgian houses of Vine Row and old Park Hill – to make room for University buildings. A complete mediaeval church, St Augustine-the-Less, and the Bishop's Palace went in 1962, along with several old streets. After only a few demolitions in 1963, the ball-and-chain men in 1964 accounted for Georgian houses in Prince Street, St Thomas Street, Stokes Croft, Dowry Parade, Bridge Street and Henleaze Street as well as Victorian and Edwardian monuments like the Harbour Master's House, Gingell's Victoria Street building, the Royal Exchange building, the Hippodrome Tower and the Empire Theatre. The needs of the University and the ring road builders led to the pulling down of the eighteenth-century St James Square, much of the Kingsdown hillside and a seventeenth-century lead shot tower.

In 1969 and 1970, says *The Fight for Bristol,**

the cluster of timber-framed houses at the bottom of Christmas Steps and in Narrow Lewins Mead were cleared to allow widening of the Inner Circuit Road, thus wiping out the last area of the centre of Bristol where one could stand entirely out of sight of any but eighteenth century or earlier building.

In the following two years, demolition continued of many fine nine-teenth-, eighteenth- and even sixteenth-century buildings. By this time Bristol had suffered damage ten or twenty times as bad from her own local government as she had from German bombers; more damage in one decade than in the previous twenty. To understand the full folly and crime of British politicians and planners, one needs, to visit West Germany (or indeed East Germany) to make compari-sons. There towns such as Aachen, which suffered eighty or ninety per cent destruction, have been rebuilt and restored to look like they

* Edited by Gordon Priest and Pamela Cobb, The Bristol Civic Society, 1980.

were before the war. Of course wooden or timbered houses have gone for good – although those that were spared are now jealously guarded – but most of the stone and brick buildings proved easy to re-assemble. Ports like Hamburg, which suffered the fire-storm raids, are far more attractive now than the port of Bristol, for the simple reason that Hamburg's government has not been in the hands of fools and philistines.

The final demolition of central Bristol – to bring it in line with Bradford or Birmingham – was stopped by the protest of civic-minded, educated and middle-class people who here have the self-confidence to defy the political demagogues and their property business friends. A plan to replace the eighteenth-century Kingsdown suburb with high-rise council flats on the hilltop was blocked by a coalition of local residents, lawyers, journalists, even a few honest architects. In the same Kingsdown district, in 1972, the protesters started a new fight against the plans of the Hospital Board to clear a site for its own standardised brick flats. Architectural students who measured some of the old building to cost rehabilitation were handed over to the police; hospital workmen stripped the lead off many buildings and knocked down thirteen houses to stop their occupation by students. However the fight was at last won.

The conservationists, as they came to be called, succeeded in stopping a council plan to fill in the harbour for office blocks or to build what the PROs for the city called 'a lagoon system'. The conservationists won a still more worthy victory against the infamous English Tourist Board, which had backed, to the tune of £1000 per room, a plan to 'develop' the Grand Spa hotel, overlooking the Clifton Suspension bridge. The plan, which started off as a modest refurbishment of the hotel ballroom, had grown into an eight-storey bedroom and car-park 'complex' along the side of the cliff over the beautiful gorge. Sir John Betjeman was one of the expert witnesses who testified that 'it is incredible that such vandalism could be con-templated to one of the most beautiful views in Europe.'

After reading this catalogue of destruction it is sad to reflect that Bristol has suffered far *less* than most great cities of England.

The wrecking of Bristol and the dispersal of residents from the centre to high-rise flats or distant housing estates has brought the usual problems of broken families, hooliganism and loneliness. Way back

165

in the early Sixties I read the report of a sociological survey which claimed that one Bristol housing estate – on a windy hillside – had five times the national rate of stress, suicide, drug addiction, murder and so on. Since then almost every survey done has claimed the same distinction for the housing estate under study; and has offered the same solution of more and more, better paid social workers to care for the victims. The sociologists, like the politicians, refuse to see that people were much happier living among their families and their friends in the old city communities, even in houses that could be called slums. And even a slum can be rebuilt at far less cost than goes to creating the new, high rise, or housing estate slums.

In Bristol, as everywhere, the running down of the inner city has led to an increase of crime and disorder, as all the remaining houses are taken over by transient people, some of them criminals. In City Road, at three in the afternoon, I was hailed within minutes by two hideous tarts. The centre of Bristol at night is risky. A few weeks ago, a drunk was clubbed to death with a traffic beacon outside the Law Faculty; this week a torchlight parade of women will march in protest against the attacks on their sex. It is law and order, as much as unemployment, that exercises the minds of people in England; everyone knows this except the politicians. Rightly or wrongly, people everywhere seem to believe that life and property are now less safe than they used to be ten years ago. 'When I was a boy in Clifton,' a man of my own age told me, 'there used to be only one policeman. He was called Pegler, and used to ride on a bicycle. But I wouldn't cross the city centre at night these days. You can't leave a car there.'

The breaking up of the old city has made Bristol less democratic, particularly in the matter of education. 'If you were wanting to move to Bristol,' said one man, who assumed that this was my purpose, 'you've got to get your children into one of the four good comprehensives. They're all in what you might call good catchment areas, where business and professional people live. Any other comprehensive school, and you'll find your children mixing with undesirables – you know what I mean. And even one of the four good ones may be ruined by bussing. In the old days, of course, you had the grammar schools in the city itself. They all took a high proportion of scholarship boys, so they were socially mixed. You couldn't get there just because your parents had money. Now the grammar schools have turned into comprehensive schools and they're terrible. Except of course Bristol Grammar – that's where I went to school – which has gone private and doesn't give scholarships any more.'

The ruination of Bristol is probably less grave than that of other English cities; it angers me more because it was so gratuitous. Bristol was fine before the destruction began. Even now, people believe that our English cities were smashed in the Blitz or by socialist planners during the Attlee Government: in fact the wrecking did not begin until fifteen years after the war, during the vile regime of Harold Macmillan. Of all the horrors inflicted on Bristol, the Labour Party can only be blamed in full for comprehensive schools, and even they were the work of 'social democrats', like 'terribly nice' Shirley Williams and 'Reg' Prentice who, not content with the harm he did as a Labour Minister, crossed the floor and began a second disastrous career as Social Services Minister for the Tories.*

25 November – Bristol   It has been the misfortune of Bristol that her trade and industry have frequently been concerned with goods that the rest of the country considered wicked or wasteful. As early as the eleventh century, Bristol was both the market and the port for the sale of English slaves to Ireland and even further abroad, 'particularly young women whom they [the merchants] took care to put into such a state as to enhance their value'.† Under the influence of St Wulfstan, Bishop of Worcester, the Bristol merchants were moved to desist from the slave trade and turned instead to the export of cloth to France, Spain and Portugal, in exchange for the wine of those countries. As the only large town in the west coast of Britain, Bristol maintained links with Ireland and therefore was called upon by King Henry II to help in the task – enjoined on him by the Pope – of removing heresy and abuse in the Irish Church, especially the sexual depravity of the west Munster clergy. The city of Bristol was given the right of settlement at the place we call Dublin.

At the start of the fifteenth century, when new techniques in the building of ships encouraged adventure into the four ends of the

---

* His first and characteristic step as a Tory Minister was to appoint 200 snooper bureaucrats to detect social security scroungers. This at a time of cuts in government spending. He was rightly sacked in January 1981, along with Arts Minister Norman St John Stevas.

† James Savage, *History of Carhampton*, pp xvii–xx.

G

earth, Bristol became our main port for merchant-explorers, especially towards the newly discovered Americas. Besides gold from the Indies and furs from the north, the Bristol merchants brought back tobacco, a mild narcotic that grew so popular that Bristol, with Nottingham, now produces most of the country's cigarettes. Bristol also returned to the slave trade, dispatching Africans (and in Cromwell's time Catholic Irishmen) to work on the sugar, tobacco and cotton plantations of mainland America and the West Indies. The ships left Bristol for Africa with a cargo of cloth, gunpowder, rum and trinkets to purchase the slaves to carry on the notorious 'middle passage' to Kingstown, Charleston or New Orleans, where they were reloaded with sugar, tobacco or cotton to take home to Bristol.

Irish settlement, wine, tobacco and slavery have all in their ways brought trouble as well as profit to Bristol. The Dublin venture collapsed when time after time the Irish breached the protective pale and slaughtered the settlers. Tobacco has had its powerful critics from James I, who wrote a tract on the subject, down to the new breed of puritans who want to stop people enjoying a smoke with their coffee and wine after dinner.

Anti-smoking fanatics like James I preceded the foes of strong drink. In the Middle Ages, wine was considered both wholesome and necessary to enrich the blood and expel bad humours. Bristol vintners supplied the highest in church and state throughout Tudor and Stuart times and even during the rule of Cromwell's Puritans, who did not identify drink with the Devil; indeed the troopers who smashed our churches were usually drunk. The abuse of liquor was first perceived as a social menace when William of Orange endeavoured to pay off his English debts by granting the right to distil and sell gin to various cronies from Holland; soon the poor of London and other cities were 'drunk for a penny and dead drunk for tuppence', as shown in the Hogarth pictures. The Methodists were the first reformers who made strong drink a major part of their sermons, and John Wesley himself gave special attention to Bristol as entrepôt of the wine and rum trades.

Back in Rochester, I mentioned the growth of the Alcoholism Industry – the new profession devoted to fighting strong drink – and at the same town, referring to Dickens, I mentioned the way that modern social reformers want to deprive children of all that is

168

joyful and magic in childhood. One recent news item neatly combined these odious trends. 'Children should be taught how to drink
alcohol, their parents would be the teachers . . . That was the
controversial proposal put forward yesterday by Bill Saunders,
director of the Alcohol Studies Centre at Paisley, Scotland' (*Daily
Express*, 18 November 1980). Speaking at Strathclyde University Mr
Saunders apparently went on to say that:

A suggested age to start would be twelve onwards with perhaps a couple of
glasses of wine with a meal or a half pint of shandy. As youngsters get older
they can graduate to a pint of shandy so that come their eighteenth birthday, their organs will be capable of absorbing a certain amount of drink
and they will be able to take three pints without getting drunk or falling
down.

The amazing Mr Saunders, whose Study Centre gets £30,000 a
year as a grant from the Scottish Office, was backed in his views by
one Douglas Allsop, the Executive Director of the Scottish Council
of Alcoholism (there's glory for you!). However his thesis annoyed
Alcoholics Anonymous. 'The gist of what they said was that I
should be shot,' Mr Saunders said later, and went on: 'Alcoholics
Anonymous treat alcoholism as a disease. They believe the only
solution is prevention. We know that the majority of people use
alcohol sensibly.'

The great G. K. Chesterton made the same point more
amusingly, and without the benefit of a grant from a government
quango: 'The dipsomaniac and the abstainer are not only both mis-
taken, but they both make the same mistake. They both regard
wine as a drug and not as a drink.' But unless you regard wine as a
drug, and a very addictive one, there is no way to get money and
jobs from stopping people drinking it. Most of the money spent on
research into drink is quite simply wasted: for example, the discovery that men who drink at lunchtime work less well in the afternoon. Pertinent findings are kept quiet – such as the fact that
women, for hormonal reasons, are more susceptible both to intoxi-
cation and liver disease from alcohol. This discovery bears out the
popular wisdom that young women who drink tend to get maudlin
and aggressive, whereas older women – those past the menopause –
make excellent drinking companions.

Two hundred years of attacks on drinking have not affected the

Bristol wine trade, which this year recorded an increase in sales of about 12 per cent, or almost the same as the loss in national sales of beer.

26 November – Bristol Unlike the drink and tobacco trades, Bristol's traffic in slaves was suppressed by moral reformers – some of whom felt compunction at therefore putting people out of a job. When the Revd Thomas Clarkson rode into Bristol one evening in June 1787 to start his inquiries into the 'middle passage', he suffered qualms: 'I began to tremble at the arduous task I had undertaken of attempting to subvert one of the branches of the commerce of the great place which was before me.' His inquiries took Clarkson to drinking dens used by sailors: 'These houses were in Marsh Street, and most of them were kept by Irishmen. The scenes witnessed were truly distressing. Music, dancing, rioting and drunkenness were kept up from night to night.' But Clarkson had to admit that the merchants and shippers engaged in the slave trade were not all personally evil or cruel; indeed most were pious. The whole merchant class of the city opposed abolition. When the first motion for the suppression of the slave trade was put to the Commons in 1789, a petition of protest was sent by the Mayor, Commonalty and Burgesses of Bristol, and another from the Master, Wardens and Commonalty of the Merchant Adventurers. There were petitions from the West Indian merchants and from the principal manufacturers, shipbuilders and general traders. Bristol hired lawyers and 'representatives', or what would today be called public relations men, to advance their case and to plant pro-slavery articles in the more venal newspapers. Their argument was that three-fifths of the trade of Bristol depended on slavery; that abolition would not benefit Africa because other countries would take up the trade; that abolition of slavery would destroy our colonies; that Britain would suffer in naval strength.

Much the same arguments were used to defend the manufacture of Concorde aircraft: that thousands of Bristol jobs depended on it; that other countries like Russia and France would take over our lead; that cancellation would damage our balance of payments and cause us to fall behind in aerospace science. All the Bristol MPs supported Concorde and one, Anthony Wedgwood Benn, was at one time the Minister who approved this monstrous gadget. This time Bristol hardly needed to hire lawyers and 'representatives' to obtain good publicity for their commerce; the national press wrote adulatory rubbish about the Concorde in return for the full page advertisements bought by British Airways – and paid for, of course, out of the tax-payer's pocket. Just to insure a favourable press, British Airways offered free Concorde flights to dozens of sycophantic hacks.

The Concorde aircraft was not the only Bristol industry to have vexed conservationists. The Imperial zinc smelter at Avonmouth, owned by the Rio Tinto-Zinc Corporation, came to be known to the readers of *Private Eye* as 'Rio Tinto Stinks'. The opening of the plant in June 1968 had been the cause of rejoicing in Bristol. A special supplement of the *Western Daily Press* bore an advertisement for Imperial showing a happy mother and baby. 'It is true' said the caption 'that we have just put into the operation the world's largest blast furnace for smelting zinc and lead,' and then went on to boast of the by-products from sulphuric acid. 'So we help mother to keep her hair in place (father too). And to clean the oven. Then get the right amount of cream on her hands. Repel flies. And freshen the room. And when baby is dowsed in talcum powder or soothed with cream, our zinc is in both products. If he cuts himself we are in the adhesive plaster . . .'

The guest of honour at the official opening was Harold Wilson, who was then under attack in the country – above all in Bristol, where he had turned down plans for a new dock. Although he made a speech praising RTZ and the British metallurgical industry, he was afterwards met by a hostile crowd at the station who shouted 'Resign!' and even 'Resign pragmatically!' (Wilson in those days was much praised as a 'pragmatist').

Soon after the opening of the smelter, Avonmouth people started to notice a foul smell which seemed to come from Imperial's chimney. Housewives complained that fumes discoloured their washing; people with bronchial troubles got pains in the chest; garden plants grew withered and stunted. Air pollution around the industrial estate was so bad that the Medical Officer for Health would not approve plans for houses in the locality. Even the Alkali Inspectorate, which tends to be lenient with pollutant firms, said that the first results from Avonmouth were bad. In 1971, the manager of a local stud farm found that some of the foals were un-

171

accountably lame; the Ministry of Agriculture, the National Farmers Union, Bristol University and an independent neurologist all blamed this on industrial pollution. When I went there in 1971, Avonmouth people poured out their misery over the smelter: 'We used to grow cabbages but now we're afraid to plant anything . . . It turns pink and mauve — you wouldn't believe the wonderful colours.'*

In July 1971, three years after the opening of its main works, RTZ closed three of its Avonmouth furnaces, sacked 900 men and sold its Imperial complex to an Australian company partly owned by Conzinc Riotinto Australia. Late in 1971, the Avonmouth plant was visited by Dr Bob Murray, the medical adviser to the Trades Union Congress who found that 'In the three years since 1968 there had been twenty cases of serious lead poisoning; one hundred workers have been suspended from duty on the lead smelting side because of the high lead levels in their blood; five hundred workers had been recorded with lead in the blood well above the danger level.' He told the *Guardian* that the conditions in the factory were the worst he had seen in twenty-five years: 'There is just no excuse at all for the pollution and the very real danger to workers in the factory.' The late Sir Val Duncan, then Chairman of RTZ, said that conditions at Avonmouth were 'deplorable'. He had earlier called the smelter 'the cross we have to bear'.

Coincidentally, it was the Bristol MP, Anthony Wedgwood Benn, who gave RTZ its immensely lucrative contract to mine for uranium in South West Africa, with then the largest reserves of the ore in the world. The original contract supplying uranium to the UK Atomic Energy Authority has had the effect of hugely enriching the South African government which acts in partnership with RTZ; of swelling the number of whites in South West Africa (Namibia) and therefore blocking progress to black rule; and of giving the South African armed forces the means of producing nuclear weapons. The thousands of English people now working at RTZ's South West African mine have christened a new extension 'the Wedgwood Benn shaft'; they enjoy the joke, if it is a joke. It is fair to say that the fat-

* I told this story at length in a book called *River of Tears: Rio Tinto Zinc and the Politics of Mining* (London, 1972). The publishers went bankrupt shortly afterwards and the book is unobtainable, so I thought it worth repeating the gist of the Imperial story.

headed Benn has done more for the cause of white supremacy in South Africa than any man since Cecil Rhodes.

27 November – Bristol Isambard Kingdom Brunel gave Bristol wonders such as the SS *Great Britain*, the first steamship to cross the Atlantic; the Great Western Railway; above all, the Clifton Suspension Bridge over the Avon Gorge. All these engineering inventions were at some stage commercial failures. The *Great Britain* went aground in the Falkland Islands where it rested till 1971, when it was salvaged and towed back to Bristol—which now has no docks. The first great steamer is now just an 'amenity' among the sailing yachts, the floating pubs and the warehouses-cum-exhibition halls. One of these is now an Industrial Museum. A placard inside says:

Several small ports like Gloucester have today managed to attract what is left of the "coastal" shipping trade but Bristol City Docks, like its great rivals on the Mersey and the Port of London are now almost completely empty. Nevertheless the decline which Brunel's *Great Britain* made inevitable still took 120 years to come into effect.

But why did *Great Britain* or anything else condemn the port of Bristol? Or Liverpool or London? Why are three ports dying when Felixstowe and King's Lynn thrive? Why are the once great ports and industries now just museums?

The Industrial Museum has a still more contemptible reference to the Great Western Railway, which once was the best in the world. Beneath one of the GWR jigsaw puzzles, which I was given as a child and recall with much pleasure, the Museum has stuck up this explanation:

James Inglis, the Great Western Railways' energetic manager from 1904–1921, deliberately set out to improve the popular image of the company . . . His publicity agent W. H. Fraser began to use popular slogans such as "the Holiday Line", "the Cornish Riviera", "the Weekend Habit" and "Go Great Western" to advertise the Great Western holiday routes. By 1930 the Great Western Railway had one of the best publicity departments in the country marketing a wide range of publications, posters and jigsaws. The Publicity campaign carefully supervised by the general manager Felix Pole, was remarkably effective even by modern standards and "sold" the GWR to a whole generation. Much of the intense nostalgia felt for the GWR today can be attributed to the company's well planned publicity of the 1920s and 30s.

Only a public relations man could have written that loathsome twaddle, with its jargon of 'selling' the railway and building its 'public image'. In fact the nostalgia felt for the GWR comes from the memory of a cheap, punctual and courteous railway service. Railway fares on the GWR in the Thirties were twenty to thirty times cheaper than those today; inflation has not been nearly as steep. Trains were much more frequent; about as fast; and they served countless stations on branch lines now suppressed. Delays and cancellations were rare enough to invite complaint in the newspapers. Vandals and hooligans were unknown. Anyone who has tried one of the British Rail super breakfasts at £5.50 per head might like to compare the experience with the memory of a Great Western breakfast during the 1930s. My mother says: 'We got on the train at Kemble Junction, at half past eight I think, and went straight to the restaurant car. We started off with a half grapefruit, then corn flakes or real porridge, with real cream, bacon and eggs and sausages, masses of real coffee, and rack after rack of piping hot toast, so we were only just finishing when the train drew into Paddington.' Does that sound like a British Rail breakfast? Or any British Rail meal, even when the staff bother to turn up for work?

The GWR had no trouble in selling an anyway excellent service. It was the Southern Railway, then as now the most criticised of the networks, that hired the first public relations man in the kingdom. British Railways now has a public relations staff of, I am told, at least thirty. Perhaps they think up those coy, lying advertisements: British Rail Cares. The Age of the Train. All accompanied by the grinning mug of some TV comedian.

Brunel's finest achievement, the Clifton suspension bridge, was something like the Concorde in its day. People praised its design, even described it as beautiful; but there was never a hope of profitability. Since then the bridge has become a favourite jumping-off place for suicides. Statistics are hard to find, although it is known that in 1885 a woman who took the 250-foot leap was saved from death by her skirts, which billowed into a parachute. The Clifton bridge has never attracted suicides to the degree of the San Francisco and Sydney bridges, the Eiffel Tower or the Empire State

Building, although the last is deceptive since sometimes a person who leaps from the observation floor is swept by a draught to the floor below, suffering only bruises and shock. Even in England the Clifton Bridge attracts less suicides than the Beachy Head cliffs or a certain apparently well-known place near Luton, where you can drive your car off the road into a deep river. Nevertheless, sixteen people have jumped from Clifton Bridge during the last year alone; and the trustees have begun to erect a barbed wire screen, as well as putting up signs for Samaritans, the charity you can ring in a state of morbid depression.

'The trustees used to object to the idea,' I was told by the head of the Bristol Samaritans, a young lady who goes by her Christian name. 'They thought it was putting ideas into people's heads.' But now the trustees are very disturbed by the increase in deaths. Apparently most would-be suicides make sure of the job by jumping onto the road which you can do almost as easily from the cliff as from the bridge itself; but it is still the bridge that attracts the morbid. Many of those who kill themselves at Clifton have come from as far as London or Cardiff. The lady from the Samaritans said that housing and marital problems accounted for most of the deaths or potential suicides. 'A lot of our clients are unemployed,' she said, although this was not such a problem here as in the North-East of England. 'Even the weather has been against us,' she said. She did not think that people were driven to kill themselves by the fear of a third world war.

The Samaritans are by definition opposed to the 'Exit' group, who have won a lot of publicity with their booklet guiding people on how to commit suicide. And in spite of a number of famous suicides lately – all of them women – and in spite of the toll on Clifton Bridge, it seems that England is not so prone to suicide as other countries in Europe. 'The cynics attribute this to North Sea gas in the ovens,' the lady from the Samaritans said, 'but we like to think we've helped.'

28 November – Bristol When the slave trade was abolished, Bristol turned to other businesses or, as we would now say, diversified. Soon the Bristol people themselves became champions of the African. In 1814, the mayor of the city headed an anti-slave trade demonstration at which there were shouts from the crowd of 'A

175

Negro is a Man!' Bristol people today are very self-conscious about their slave-trading past. The Cathedral has an exhibition upon the shameful subject. Some Bristol people believe there are dungeons under the city centre, where water at high tide rose to the necks of the slaves. The fact that Whiteladies Road leads up to Black Boy Hill in Clifton is taken to mean that Bristol matrons went there to buy slaves at a market. In fact the trade was direct from Africa to the West Indies, and the only slaves brought to Bristol were personal servants of the returning planters. At the end of the eighteenth century, London had a Negro community roughly proportionate to the one today but Bristol and Liverpool, the slave-trading cities, had very few blacks. Today, however, Bristol has many West Indians and an acute race problem. Indeed the events this January in the St Paul's district must be regarded as England's first race riot — unless one includes the mob attacks on Chinese and Lascars in ports like Cardiff soon after the First World War.

The Bristol Labour Party has formed an inquiry into the riots under the chairmanship of Ian Mikardo MP, apparently with the purpose of finding out what happened and how such troubles can be avoided in future. However Mr Mikardo, the eminent East-West trade consultant and friend of the 'German Democratic Republic', has not yet revealed his findings to the Bristol papers. All we know is what we learned at the time: the police raided a club where Jamaicans were smoking marijuana, whereupon a crowd of West Indians smashed up and looted many shops in the St Paul's district; and the police withdrew to avoid 'confrontation'. Various Trotskyist groups and the Campaign to Legalise Marijuana have set up shop in the neighbourhood and may have some influence on the young West Indians, many of whom are Rastafarians. However the Bristol Jamaicans seem to be less rebellious, less criminal, less demented by marijuana than those who remain on that God-forsaken island. Now the trouble seems to have spread from Bristol to Gloucester where last weekend police were driven off by a largely black crowd of rioters. Among the few arrested was a white youth 'who had to be pulled off the glass cover over a Roman archaelogical site'.

Worcester and the Midlands

WORCESTER - BIRMINGHAM

WALSALL - LICHFIELD

29 November - Bristol - Worcester The pleasure of Bristol was
much enhanced by luck in the matter of entertainment. On
Monday I saw the Old Vic production of Ben Travers's *The Bed
Before Yesterday*, which must be the best play ever written by someone of eighty-five. And over the next three days I was able to see the
Welsh National Opera Company in *Eugene Onegin, Il Trovatore*
and, best of all, *The Cunning Little Vixen*. Who would have
thought, twenty-five years ago, that one of Janaček's operas could be
played to a full house in Bristol? In those days the provincial towns
were lucky to get a Carl Rosa *Butterfly*. Apparently *The Cunning
Little Vixen* is already the fourth of Janaček's operas to have been
produced by the Welsh and Scottish opera companies, helped by a
grant from the Imperial Tobacco Company: if that is how the
makers of cigarettes try to obtain a better 'image', then good luck to
them. The huge popularity and the genuine understanding of opera
in this country is one of the very few welcome changes during the last
twenty-five years. Here Britain is almost uniquely fortunate. This
year, so I am told, a Janaček opera was tried for the first time in
France and booed off the stage by that wholly unmusical people.

The train to Worcester was held up forty minutes 'owing to shortage
of fuel': a new excuse in my experience. The delay did not trouble
me, for I was coming to Worcester more from a sense of duty than
from any hope of pleasure. The hideous shopping centre carries a
plaque saying that 'Near this spot above the family music shop

Edward Elgar lived as boy and man in the years 1866–1879'. The memory of this very great Englishman is noted rather than honoured at Worcester Cathedral, which has fallen on evil times.

This year saw the 1300th anniversary of the Cathedral's foundation, an event that was to have been observed with an address by the Revd Philip Potter, the General Secretary of the World Council of Churches – the same Dr Potter who said that the Black Power leaders Stokeley Carmichael and Malcolm X 'have given far more clear and powerful expression to the true meaning of the right hand of God than the Churches'. (Dr Potter could not attend because of bereavement.) The World Council of Churches, I must repeat, has blessed and helped to finance terrorists all over the 'Third World', while giving tacit approval to tyrants in eastern Europe.

The invitation to Dr Potter did not surprise people who know Worcester Cathedral, which seems to be in the hands of progressive clergymen. A leaflet given to visitors says:

When he [Jesus Christ] was about thirty years old he gathered together twelve ordinary men to be his helpers. For the next three years he went about healing sick and troubled people and opening men's eyes to the justice and love of God. This teaching was a challenge to the secular and religious rulers of his day, who executed him by crucifixion . . .

This conception of Christ as a kind of left-wing social worker perhaps explains Worcester Cathedral's embarrassed attitude to the most famous person buried beneath the flagstones – King John, the third Plantagenet, who died of a surfeit of lampreys (or so we were told at school) on his way from King's Lynn to Lincoln. That was in AD 1216, when the diocese was a mere 436 years old. Today, the only reference to John's life and reign is a facsimile of the Magna Carta document which, according to the Cathedral, '. . . established the fundamental principle of freedom for the British [*sic*] people' – a dubious and anachronistic interpretation of thirteenth-century English politics. Poor John, thanks to the liberal historians of the nineteenth century, is still described as an enemy of our freedoms, rather than one of the good Plantagenet kings. (They were almost all good.) John may have ordered the murder of Arthur, his nephew; he vexed the Irish princelings by pulling their beards; and when he was short of cash his agents drew the teeth of Jewish merchants to make them uncover their wealth. Yet John was certainly less wicked and arrogant than most of the barons who forced him to sign the Magna Carta, let alone modern rulers like Lenin, Trotsky, Stalin, Hitler and Pol Pot, whose methods of getting gold out of Jews and millions of others were both more cruel and more scientific than John's. There have been some attempts to rehabilitate John. Even Shakespeare, who tended to run down the Plantagenets, said that Arthur died by mistake, and tried to present John's row with the Pope as an early example of Protestant outrage against the sale of indulgence; although John offended the Irish with horseplay, he did not try to subdue and plunder the island after the fashion of Tudor monarchs; and, as Chesterton said, one should not imagine that John spent his whole time pulling the teeth of Jews 'with the celerity and industry of an American dentist'.

The Jews and other successful financiers survived and flourished in Worcestershire, as William Cobbett noted with disapproval in 1826. From Ryall, near Upton-on-Severn, he wrote:

On our road we passed by the estate and park of *another Ricardo*! . . . This one has ousted two families of Normans, the HONEYWOOD YATES, and the SCUDAMORES . . . The BARINGS are at work down in this country too. They are every where, indeed, depositing their eggs about, like cunning old guinea-hens, in sly places, besides the great, open, showy nests that they have.

However Cobbett approved of 'the finest meadows of which it is possible to form an idea'; he praised the conditions of work at the local glove makers and called Worcester 'the cleanest, neatest and handsomest town I ever saw.'

The only fault of Worcester was being the birthplace of what Cobbett called the 'LITTLE-SHILLING PROJECT, a plan to make a sovereign pass for more than 20s', or in other words the inflationary printing of money, as practised by all British governments for the last twenty-five years. As Cobbett so rightly said of the 'Little-Shilling project', advanced by 'a vile pamphlet writer, whose name is CRUTWELL', 'If, indeed, you could *double the quantity of corn and meat and all goods by the same act of parliament*; then, all would be right; but, *that quantity will remain what it was before you passed the project*; and, of course, the money being doubled in nominal amount, their *price of the goods would be doubled.*'

Another result of inflation is speculating in building and property.

If Cobbett could revisit this once neat, clean and handsome city, he would observe at its worst the result of the 'Little-Shilling project', or rather the 'Little-Five Pee project'. Although Worcester was scarcely touched by bombs in the war, it has since been turned into a hideous concourse of oneway streets, shopping centre and precincts and highrise car parks, with an appalling circular racetrack just outside the Cathedral. All this is blamed on the build-up of traffic crossing the bridge on the Severn; but you have only to visit a city like Strasbourg or Cologne to see that it is not necessary to destroy a city just because it stands on the bank of a river. The authors of the gloomily titled book *Yesterday's Town: Changing Face of Worcester* are forced to conclude that 'the desecration of whole neighbourhoods, streets and individual buildings of architectural merit is lamentable.'

Some might call it criminal; and the perpetrators of all this horror are planning more. A display at the Guildhall sets out the aims of what is called the Local Plan Area:

To show an overall land use pattern within which a practical and co-ordinated form of development can be achieved . . . to enhance the landscape and the preservation and integration of natural features with the layout whenever possible . . . The policies contained within the Recreation Subject Plan should be applied to ensure adequate leisure provision . . . open space including childrens play and kickabout areas . . . sites for community facilities need to be reserved, e.g. leisure centre, public house, church etc.

The monstrous 'structure plan', with its language characteristic of planners and property sharks, has been produced by that still more monstrous entity Hereford and Worcester County Council – one of the mongrel bodies spawned during the Heath regime by that arch-progressive and latter-day Crutwell, the smirking stock-jobber Peter Walker who is, to the shame of Worcester, its present Member of Parliament. The boundaries of the counties of Worcester and Hereford were laid down over a thousand years ago, before the present Cathedral was built, and even King John, who came to the throne two centuries later, would never have had the impudence to consider tampering with this tried system of local government, as Heath and Walker did, using the almost despotic power of Parliament and the Whitehall bureaucracy.

At present the appalling Walker is Minister for Agriculture and

Fisheries, whose rapid decline since Britain joined the Common Market would so have depressed old Cobbett. Soon after Cobbett came to Worcester, the glove manufacturers whom he had praised were put out of business due to the lifting of tariffs with France; Queen Victoria turned down a plea from the city to wear only English gloves. Now the lifting of tariffs, as well as the imposition of EEC rules, bids fair to kill off Worcestershire's famous apple crop, most of which does not conform to the rules of Brussels. 'It's changed the whole landscape,' a Worcestershire farmer told me. 'Where there used to be large apple trees, there's now just little bushes, or things like raspberries and strawberries.' The French Golden Delicious apples are almost all one can buy in the greengrocers of Worcester.

The demolition of ancient cities, the breaking up of our counties and, not least, the entry into the Common Market, were largely, let it be said once again, the fault of a faction calling itself the Conservative Party. For these reasons alone, one is tempted to vote for or at least prefer, the crooks, prigs and sociologists of the Labour Party. For much the same reasons, Cobbett himself deserted the Tories and joined the equally nasty radicals. 'Pitt and his followers were not in the least Tory in the sense of traditional,' Chesterton wrote in his marvellous book *William Cobbett*:

They were only Tory in the sense of tyrannical. If trying to destroy all old constitutional liberties makes a man a conservative, then certainly Pitt and Castlereagh were model conservatives. But it would be hard to say what it was they conserved. There was not a historic tradition, not a single human memory of the past, for which they even showed the faintest sympathy.

Those words exactly describe Heath, Walker, Lord Carrington and, I fear, Margaret Thatcher.

Touring cricket sides used to play their first county match against Worcester; not any more. Cricket is now just a form of promotion for cigarettes and American razor blades. The little Worcester museum has a good display of the weapons and uniforms and mementoes of bravery of what used to be called the Worcestershire Regiment, now abolished: by a Conservative government, of course. Why did they have to dissolve and amalgamate regiments? Why not leave them in mothballs, as happened after the First World War, to be reformed in a time of need? The Worcester Museum has just one photograph to remind us of Edward Elgar, our country's finest composer. There is

also a sign saying 'Closed Thursday, because of the cuts'. Thank you,
Worcester.

30 November – Birmingham   For more than two months now, I
have been dreading Birmingham; perhaps that is why it has come
near the end of my journey round England. It is a place of which I
have no happy memories. I came here first as a child, in the war, in
the course of a long and confused journey from Newcastle to Reading, in trains that were cold, crowded, blacked-out and unreliable in
their movements. After waiting for several hours at Birmingham, I
ventured to ask a woman if this, the train I was in, was going to
Oxford. She answered 'Fight your own battles.' It was the first time I
heard that adenoidal accent. It still grates.

When I first started to come here, to work in the 1950s, I never
considered Birmingham as a place of beauty, or worth preserving; it
did not seem possible that any change could be for the worse. But
Birmingham has got worse, thanks to the Labour Party, the planners
and the property men. Almost the whole of the old city is now a maze
of ring roads, fly-overs, underpasses and hideous high-rise buildings.
The inhabitants of the old slums have been moved to the nastiest
housing estates I have ever seen. I once spent a day in a block of flats
in Stechford, Roy Jenkins's old constituency, following in the train of
some Labour Party canvassers, and using this as an excuse to
question the flat-dwellers about their lives. Everyone that I spoke to
hated the place; some were depressed to the point of suicide. What
depressed me most of all was the recollection that politicians like Mr
Jenkins feel no guilt nor even awareness of what they have done to the
ignorant wretches who voted for them. I did not get the impression
that Mr Jenkins actually liked or cared about his constituents. Sir
Frank Price, the former Labour Mayor of the city, is now a
millionaire, a colleague of Colonel Seifert, boss of the Inland Waterways Board, and one of Jenkins's 'social democrats'. Alas, there was
no John Poulson in Birmingham to tell how it was all done; nevertheless a few of the guilty people went to prison, including a
Birmingham City Architect. A few but not enough, nor for enough
years.

The Labour Party is typical of the moral corruption that seeps
through this horrible city. Once famous industries, such as the
manufacture of motor cars, have been brought low by the greed and

bloody-mindedness of the trade union bosses. I see from the papers that British Leyland men are going to strike at the plant making the Metro car, which was hailed a few weeks ago as the hope of our industry. The taxpayer is squeezed to the point of bankruptcy in order to subsidise British Leyland, not only by direct grants but by tax relief to owners of company cars; by huge investment in roads at the cost of railways; by pegging the cost of petrol and car licences. The last should be £500 per annum.

1 December – Birmingham Wandering round a city I hardly can recognise, I came to a pub that even on Sunday night was crowded and loud with horrible music. The sight of uniformed guards – one man and one woman – reminded me that this was one of the two pubs blown up by the IRA in November 1974. When I came here last, about a year after the bombing, I noted that this pub had become Birmingham's main tourist attraction, and so it has stayed. There are worse amusements in Birmingham than getting drunk in a place where dozens of people were killed or maimed. I found the place creepy. It was not so much the remembrance of what had happened here but the look of the customers. They were all white, for a start, which is odd for the West Midlands; they were tough, young, and distinctly aggressive; I thought at once of some of the 'troopie' bars in Salisbury, Rhodesia, or one of the poor white joints in south Johannesburg; or indeed of some of the bars in Belfast.

I see in the Irish press that the IRA may start what they grandly call a 'campaign' in England, in order to get political status for murderers and their accomplices in the Maze prison. The fellow-travellers of the IRA in Dublin and London are loud in support of surrendering on this issue but some Northern Irishmen, Catholics included, want no deal with the gunmen. The admirable Gerry Fitt, one of the few honest and brave men in the House of Commons, says that he now 'bitterly regrets' having once called for concessions to the IRA; and Fitt is a Catholic and a Republican Belfast man. I am sure he is more representative of his own people than are the left-wing, middle-class Left of Dublin and North London. The proof of this was the failure of previous IRA 'campaigns' in England. Because the Irish community in this country cannot be cowed and intimidated – as they can in Northern Ireland – they are free to express their detestation of terrorists, and their shame that these crimes are committed in Ireland's name. The Irish in England have rightly informed on terrorists to the English police.

The IRA, I suppose, will always be with us: they are the true inheritors and disciples of Pearse and Connolly – those bloody perverted men who founded a state by murder. The Sinn Fein have been compared to the Jacobins and the Communists, but I think they are most like the Nazis. Pearse had Hitler's obsession with blood and sacrifice. The doomed Easter Rising had something in common with Hitler's Munich *putsch*; they were both done as a demonstration, a way of creating martyrs. The IRA thrive, as the Nazis throve, on bloody ballads of street brawls and murders.

You would find it hard in Belfast itself to meet an intellectual friend of the IRA; the fighting is left to the slum children. But fellow-travellers of the IRA abound in the middle-class intellectual Left of Dublin and London, the people who write and read the *Irish Times*, *MacGill*, *Hibernia* (recently closed but reincarnated as the *Sunday Tribune*), the *Guardian*, the *New Statesman* and the *Sunday Times*. The glossy *MacGill* is given to publishing colour pictures of masked gunmen, ambushes and exploding cars – the hard pornography of political hatred – and articles in which incitement to murder is barely disguised by euphemism. For instance, the English bombings, including the two here in Birmingham, were called by *MacGill* 'an economic campaign, designed to bring the Westminster Government into talks with the IRA. An article in last week's *Sunday Tribune* states once again that only terror attacks in Britain will cause our politicians to take an interest in Ireland; a thesis justifying murder.

The people who write *MacGill* and the *Sunday Tribune* may be sincere; at least their hatred is Irish and of the blood. But what can be said of the English friends of the IRA? Some, I suppose, are genuine Trotskyists, hoping to bring society into ruin; some are sincere Nazis who see the Irish as allies against the Jews, or 'Zionists' as they are now called by Nazis. Some are entirely cynical arselickers of Moscow. I see in the papers this week that East German and Russian journalists are arriving in Belfast to write about the hunger strikers; this at the very time when Russian and East German armies threaten to crush the remnants of freedom in Poland, a land which suffered longer and worse from Russian and Prussian despotism than ever Ireland suffered from England. And the Poles have fought heroically for their freedom; they have never stooped to murdering women and children with 'economic campaigns' in Moscow or Berlin.

The *Sunday Times* sent teams of reporters to Northern Ireland when it was fashionable. These journalists, I believe, provided a quite tendentious picture of what was happening, and the IRA were dazed by their propaganda success; if such an organ of the establishment appeared to talk their side, then surely Britain was weak and timid enough to cave in to terrorism. One more 'campaign', the IRA reckoned, and final victory would be theirs. I never understood at the time how so many journalists could be taken in by the IRA, just as before the war they were taken in by the Communists or the Nazis; and how few journalists cared about the appalling war against the Biafrans during the late 1960s — a war backed and financed by Britain.

2 December – Birmingham The thirteenth murder attributed to the Yorkshire Ripper has caused a flurry of protests from feminists. Some lady sociologists, writing from Bradford to *The Times*, suggest that all men are potential rapists; the *Guardian* Women's Page has produced an article demanding that women should be protected with firearms and karate. Another paper carried a guide to the various anti-rape groups which have appeared in this country, no doubt apeing the vogue in America. Even the West Riding prostitutes started a self-defence group, which was much praised by the feminists until it was learned that the idea came from the National Front.

It is heartening to read that various women's groups have protested against and even attacked the cinemas which are showing films about violent attacks on women; there are, I think four such films now on circuit. And Mary Whitehouse has joined the feminists, no doubt to their embarrassment, with another attack on sadistic pornography.

Back in 1963, I was sent by the *New Statesman* to Edinburgh, where the Festival that year was holding a special Writers' Conference, with delegates from all over the world. At that time censorship was the big trendy issue. A few years earlier, D. H. Lawrence's *Lady Chatterley's Lover* had stood trial for obscenity and had been found not guilty. Thanks to remorseless propaganda from TV and the press, juries were tending not to convict even 'hard core' commercial pornography. There were, however, a few remaining restraints on what was considered acceptable and these were made the object of ridicule and abuse by almost every speaker at Edinburgh. The exception was Rebecca West, who argued that since it is hard to portray the passion of love, most pornography tends to concern sexual feelings unconnected with love, indeed the converse of love. Pornography, she insisted, meant the degradation of women by rape or physical cruelty. She reminded the audience, which was unimpressed and impatient, that sadistic pornography flourished during the Weimar Republic and carried on into Hitler's time in the pages of *Der Stürmer*, the Nazi Party's official organ. She might have said that people who read *Der Stürmer*'s sadistic pornography were later enabled to put their fantasies into action by killing and torturing Jews in police cells and concentration camps.

Happily for this country, we have no secret police cells and concentration camps, where sadists can work out their fantasies in the name of the law; but there can be no doubt that pornography leads to sexual crimes. The Moors murderers were one example; and the so-called Cambridge Rapist, now in prison, was found to possess a stack of pornography about rape.

Birmingham has for some reason led the rest of England in tolerance of pornography, as indeed in the whole of the sex industry. This distinction may be attributable to the fact, notorious in legal circles, that members of the Birmingham Bar are paid much more than advocates in the rest of England, which therefore bumps up the cost of police prosecutions. At any rate, some of the major test cases on what is permissible took place here in Birmingham. One involved making a pornographic film with Birmingham schoolchildren as actors. Another concerned a film called *Anal Rape*, which, according to expert witnesses for the defence, was valuable as an 'aid to masturbation'.

3 December – Birmingham Three of the great entrepreneurs of the sex industry began their careers in Birmingham: Mandy Rice-Davies, Kenneth Tynan and Dr Martin Cole. The first of these is certainly not a pornographer – her recently published memoirs are quite demure – but as one of the figures in the Profumo scandal, and one who revelled in the publicity, she set the tone for the 'swinging England' of sexual freedom and daring. The late Kenneth Tynan, who started off his career as a critic and essayist of something amounting to genius, was sidetracked during the Sixties and Seventies into 'liberationist' politics and pornography. He took up with Trotskyists; he preached the need for bloodshed and revolution; he was lucky not to go to prison in France for sending a fake bomb scare to the set where Peter O'Toole was filming. He wrote in favour of 'soft-flag' (flagellatory) books; he was first to say the word 'fuck' on TV; I can recall one dismal night in a tent of Marines in Vietnam where the only available magazine contained an article by Tynan on masturbation. And he put his money where his mouth was; his long-playing erotic pantomime *Oh Calcutta!* made Tynan rich before his death. What talent there was wasted!

Dr Martin Cole studied plant genetics at university, obtaining a Ph.D. – hence his use of the title doctor, for he is not, as some think, medically qualified. After a time in Africa, working on crop problems, he came back in the 1960s to a lectureship in plant genetics at Aston University, Birmingham, where, according to one of his biographical documents, 'his interest in human sexuality began'. He was, so we learn, 'horrified' at the number of pregnant students and the difficulties of their getting abortions. 'Dr Cole tried to alleviate the situation by campaigning actively for sexual counselling, contraception advice, and easier access to abortions.' He founded the Institute of Sex Education and Research, started the Birmingham branch of the Abortion Law Reform Society, helped to found the Birmingham Pregnancy Advisory Service (now known as the British Pregnancy Advisory Service, with branches all over Britain), and the Calthorpe Nursing Home (to provide abortions), and became director of the Brook Clinic in Birmingham.

Although busy in Birmingham, Cole was unknown to the nation at large until 1971 when he made a film called *Growing Up*, intended 'for use in schools as a visual aid in sex education lessons'. It contained two scenes of a man and a woman masturbating, each lasting about ten seconds, and a couple in sexual intercourse. The film aroused controversy in the press, Birmingham Council and Parliament, where it was shown to a group of MPs (one, now a Cabinet Minister, complained of the dirty fingernails of the man shown masturbating). Several MPs denounced *Growing Up*; it was banned in Birmingham schools (though shown in others throughout the country; the woman teacher who masturbated in front of the cameras was stopped from work.

The *Observer* published a very good article on the film by Mary Miles:

Once again as everywhere today, sex is presented as depersonalised, sex for the sake of sex, part of the drill of growing up, 'the done thing'. Anyway, do children really need to have masturbation and sexual intercourse demonstrated? Do you *teach* a young child to walk by demonstration?

I have known [adolescents] show considerable indignation with teachers and other well-meaning adults, who intrude into their private world of sex education. They have their own ways of dealing with the situation – giggling, 'dirty' stories, helpless amusement at any word with a possible sexual connotation. I think these are the natural ways of dealing with changing bodies and feelings in early adolescence.

Indeed, these are the natural ways; but there is no way to make money out of them. Children now have to be sold pornography, abortions, pills and other contraceptives – the last two are sold by the manufacturers to the local authorities, who then try to wish them on the children. (This practice was shown in its utmost absurdity when one of the sex education quangos issued a booklet for schoolboys on how to put on a French letter.)

In spite of some publicity for *Growing Up*, Dr Cole went on to make three other films, including *Impotence and Premature Ejaculation*, to produce a set of slides, *Understanding Sex*, aimed at children of eleven upwards, and to lecture the Modern Churchman's conference at Roehampton. He told the clergymen of his plan for summer camps where young people could 'sleep around', having first been provided with contraception. 'He brushed aside the likelihood of extra distress being caused to parents,' reported *The Times* in June 1971.

Soon after his film was made, Dr Cole was in the news again, when it came out that the Institute of Sex Education and Research was using women as 'therapists' to assist men troubled with problems like impotence.

One of these 'therapists' is his own wife, Barbara. The *Sunday Express* wrote in July 1971:

Dr Martin Cole, the sex-obsessed lecturer in genetics at Aston University tells us that he sits watching television while his wife Barbara gives 'sex therapy' to men in her bedroom. Already as part of the programme of his Institute of Sex Education, Mrs Cole had had sex with more than 150 men. Dr Cole also confessed to taking part in group sex sessions . . . He still gets more than £4000 a year from Aston University, and his institute collects another £3000 a year from £18-a-time vasectomy operations at Birmingham's Calthorpe Clinic . . . Will nobody in the city do anything to stop him dragging its name even deeper in the mire?

Indeed, this time there was action against Dr Cole. 'The London businessman who put up £35,000 to enable Dr Martin Cole to establish the Calthorpe abortion clinic,' reported the Birmingham *Evening Mail*, 'said today that its future was "anybody's guess".' Referring to the 'female therapists', Mr Trevor Heathcote said: 'I never intended that any of the profits of the Calthorpe Nursing Home should go to such work.' The *Evening Mail* reporter added: 'It is understood that the gross profits of the eighteen-bed nursing home in Arthur Road, Edgbaston, exceed £100,000 a year.'

4 December – Birmingham   Abortion is now the fastest growing part of the sex industry, with profits approaching those of pornography, sex counselling, sex aids or even the manufacture of rubber and chemical contraception. The British Pregnancy Advisory Service, which Dr Cole helped to start in Birmingham, now has clinics all over the country offering cheap abortions to hundreds of thousands of girls. They are cheap because of the massive turnover, but still yield a profit which goes, as I understand it, into the salaries of the doctors, nurses and administrators.

The accounts I saw for one year do not specify how the expenditure is divided – the BPAS is registered as a charity – but I am told that a part-time abortionist gets about £20,000 a year. The abortion itself now costs the girl £60, but she is charged £16 for advice on whether to have the abortion. Not surprisingly, the adviser almost always tells her to go ahead with abortion – at the same clinic, of course. The BPAS also runs a service for women wanting a baby by artificial insemination. The donors, generally medical students, sell their semen at £2.60 a go; which shows that money can even be made from masturbation.

In one of his turgid lectures, Dr Cole wrote: 'Teenagers make lousy parents and our concern [at the Institute] is at a pragmatic level in that every baby should be a wanted baby. That kids should wake up to the fact that if they make love there is a good chance that the girl will end up pregnant.' It is no use explaining to people like Dr Cole that girls have always known this, even in the Victorian age; especially in the Victorian age, when they were not confused by pills and coils and other devices. What children resent most, as Mary Miles wrote in the words I quoted, is the intrusion of sex education into their private world. As a result, it is now the fashion for school-girls to get pregnant on purpose and have a baby to spite the sex educators; this came out this January in a survey conducted in – yes, you have guessed it – Birmingham.

As Dr Cole said, rightly for once, 'teenagers make lousy parents.' There was a horrible case this year, again in Birmingham, of a teenage couple who could not supply their baby with clothing or even a mattress, so solved the problem by bashing its brains out against the wall. Their crime was of course blamed on 'society' and a lack of social workers – who of course, like 'counsellors', are incidental profiteers from the sex industry.

5 December – Birmingham   In one of his self-advertisements, Dr Martin Cole wrote that Birmingham offered greater freedom to make films about sex than any place in the world except California. He is probably right. Birmingham has given the fullest expression to all those fraudulent and corrupting notions that have come to us from Central Europe, via the United States, and have now replaced both our Christian morality and our inherited popular wisdom, or common sense. The 'New Ethic', as it is called – godless, humourless, loveless – reigns in the horrible city of Birmingham. Greed and envy are supreme, from the workfloor of Longbridge to the expensive brothels, one of which once offered a free turn with a girl to any member of Birmingham City Council . . .

Not long ago, the Anglican Bishop of Birmingham, Hugh Montefiore, was telling us all that alcoholism is now the gravest problem facing Britain. This week he told the Birmingham *Evening Mail* that the paper ought to publish each day a front-page column of 'good news', recounting for instance the fine work done by most trade union officials, the success of most of our industry, or the improved race relations in Birmingham. But one man's good news may be another man's bad news. How would you classify news such as 'British Leyland to close', 'Porn dealer gaoled for life', or 'Bishop struck dumb'?

6 December – Birmingham – Walsall – Lichfield On this, my last day in Birmingham, I was taken to see the famous Spaghetti Junction of criss-crossing roads on stilts. My guide is a civil engineer, but even a layman, such as myself, can see that the whole horrible thing is falling apart. Cracks and even holes have appeared in the pillars and walls; the bearings or little pads that support the beams are collapsing with ever-increasing frequency; when this happens, apparently, the noise is an earsplitting thunderclap. The whole structure shudders and rocks with the weight of lorries overhead; it is, quite literally, shaking to bits. I was taken up in a crane to see how the workmen try to repair the damage by jacking up the beams and then sliding simple wedges into the crack; it is a strangely makeshift way of supporting a giant road. I also climbed up the three long flights of ladder to Crosshead 44–3, where already a train of engineers, and even the odd MP and reporter, have come to observe the danger. Even for someone who does not suffer, as I do, from fear of heights, it must be alarming to hear these lorries rumbling and shaking a few inches over one's head.

My friend called this 'the worst cock-up in British civil engineering history' – worse than the Forth Bridge disaster, worse for that matter than other disasters abroad. Other motorways do not collapse in this fashion; those that Hitler built for the Germans are still in perfect repair. Even some of our own motorways like the M4 were built to a tried and sound design; but Spaghetti Junction seems to have taken everyone by surprise. Everything now is blamed on the unexpectedly heavy load of trucks in the slow lane; yet an old brick bridge from the nineteenth century which bears part of this traffic has not suffered at all – it was well constructed.*

Spaghetti Junction has not yet been tested to find if any of it contains high alumina cement – the dreaded HAC which was widely used for speed in the 1960s, and later caused the collapse or abandonment of many buildings. The matter is sensitive here, for one of the tunnels in Birmingham's infamous Ring Road fell in because of HAC. At any rate, I am told there will soon be a new,

---

* And now we hear from a new report to the Transport Ministry (published 10 December) that Britain's road problems can only be solved by *raising* the maximum tonnage of freight to a level higher than most in Europe. This idea, if put into practice, would seem likely to bring all Spaghetti Junction down in months rather than years.

most alarming item of news concerning Spaghetti Junction, which might be closed by the time this book appears.

Spaghetti Junction was opened in 1971 by Peter Walker, the right man for the job in every sense. With Centre Point, the almost empty high-rise block in London, it serves as a monument to the folly and greed which gripped this country during the 1960s; and even now the perpetrators have failed to learn or attend to the consequences of their crime. I see from *Construction News* that the Transport Minister, Norman Fowler, has given the go-ahead to another motorway link road, which will cost £57 million. This at a time when our railways are once more threatened with huge cuts and closures, as well as a rise in the ticket price; yet the cost of re-equipping the railways is tiny compared to what has been squandered over the years on subsidising the motor industry and building roads that cannot even stand up. Once more the energy and investment which should be spent in productive industry has been frittered away on property and construction. And let it be said that the motorways, the Spaghetti Junction, and the complex of Ring Roads planted upon this accursed city have made its people some of the saddest in England.

By train, past Aston Villa football ground, to Walsall, which is un-attractive even compared to the rest of the Black Country. Giant pylons march with the motorway over grey fields crossed by stagnant canals. There are rows after rows of terraced cottages, deserted and waiting for demolition – still showing the grates and pieces of furniture that were not worth stealing. Next to the railway station and the Saddle Centre (the Walsall equivalent of an Arndale Centre), I noticed a filthy and vandalised building, the Walsall Science and Art Institute, which once was intended for better things. 'This building was erected,' says a plaque next to the National Front slogans,

by public subscription in 1887, to commemorate the Jubilee Year of reign of Her Majesty the Queen Victoria. In 1897, the sum of £2,500 was raised by public subscription to establish a District Nursing Institute to provide free nurses for the poor, in commemoration of Her Majesty's glorious reign.

The statue of Sister Dora, who was a famous Walsall nurse (at least famous in Walsall) grew so corroded during the nineteenth century that it had to be replaced by a bronze replica in the 1950s.

Pubs in Walsall tend to divide into 'men only' bars, with a lady barmaid, and a 'women only' lounge, with a male barman; 'I think you want the other room,' I was politely told. This may mean that Walsall has never accepted equality of the sexes, or that the women live in fear of men since the reign of terror carried out by the 'Black Panther', who did for the region what the Ripper had has done for Yorkshire.

The town is also famous for John Stonehouse, the former MP for the North division, who got a false passport by using the name of a dead Walsall man, then faked his drowning off Miami Beach and went to hide in Australia. He was caught, put on trial and sent to prison for fraud with one of his Bangladeshi businesses. At his trial he claimed that both Harold Wilson and Edward Short (another Labour Party leader) had asked him to put work in the way of friends of theirs, Joe Kagan and T. Dan Smith, who both afterwards went to prison. Those Asians who had invested in Stonehouse's bank may not think of him with affection, but I have heard him described in generous terms by a Walsall West Indian: 'In Jamaica we say that if a man sees something and grabs it, good luck to him, as long as he doesn't get caught.'

When Stonehouse resigned his seat, a by-election was held, which the Conservatives won by a big majority. The Labour candidate, David Winnick, who went on to win the seat in the general election, is one of the left-wing prigs now dominant in the party. 'He has a prissy voice, a thin smile and a way of appearing to walk without moving his legs above the knee,' I wrote after meeting him; also noting that he made a career in the worthless quango, the UK Immigrants Advisory Service, whose squabbles and sexual intrigues have often been chronicled in the columns of *Private Eye*.

In the last general election, David Winnick became MP and soon his constituency, or rather the town of Walsall, was much in the news because of the fight by its Labour Council to thwart the efforts of Mrs Thatcher to bring down the level of public expenditure. A few months ago, Walsall Council voted to grant £16,000 out of the rate-payer's money towards some quango, *even although the quango had been abolished*. It was as if the money had gone to give that quango a decent wreath and funeral. And soon after this act of petulance, Walsall Council announced that from now on it would not appoint local officials unless they subscribed to socialist views. No Tories need apply. Such patronage is common abroad; and even in England some of the inner boroughs of London compete with each other to hire Labour stalwarts to gain their votes at local elections – I know of people offered jobs on this principle. But Walsall alone has made this principle open and unabashed; and prim little Winnick stood by his council when it was criticised in the House of Commons.

The bus from Walsall broke down in the sooty, lugubrious wilderness of the Cannock Chase, a place of stopped canals, concealed mine shafts and worked-out quarries. 'I've got no gears,' the West Indian driver complained to base on the radio. 'The gears is faultin'. The whole bloody bus is faultin'.' He grinned at the girls at the bus queue and asked them to give a push. A new bus came, but it went in the wrong direction and soon I was walking to Lichfield under a bright wintry sun.

Another bus came along, with the same West Indian driver. 'You don't need to pay, man, I remember your face.' Lichfield was even more pleasant than I remember it from my last visit, twenty-three years ago. This may mean only that it has suffered less than other towns at the hands of property men and local government crooks. The shopping 'mall' is less offensive than some, and little harm has been done to the old part of the town by the close. It is customary to decry the additions to the Cathedral, and especially the rows of statues placed in the West front in the nineteenth century; yet seeing them in the glow of a winter sunset I found the impression charming. Better still, I had come by chance at the time of the children's Christmas service, or Christingle, a custom which has been brought to us from Moravia. The children, hundreds of them, walk up the aisle, each holding an orange, representing the world, two peanuts, representing agriculture, and a lighted candle, representing the Light of the World. This and 'While Shepherds Watched' were moving; I felt ashamed of my base journalistic urge to ask whether the oranges came from South Africa.

7 December – Lichfield   Dr Johnson said in praise of Lichfield, his native town, that its inhabitants were 'the most sober, decent people in England, the genteelest in proportion to their wealth, and spoke the purest English'. His biographer, Boswell, could not agree with that last item of praise; 'for they had several provincial sounds'; and

194

Johnson himself was always eager for London after a few weeks away. If he were brought back to earth, he would now prefer Lichfield to London.

It is only a bit barbarised. Since Samuel's father, Michael Johnson, had worked as a bookseller (and taken his wares each market day to Birmingham) I thought it a fair test to see how the modern Lichfield was catered for in this kind of shop. At W. H. Smith's in the shopping mall there was not one book by Johnson, or his biography by Boswell; however, Lichfield is well served by a small paperback bookshop and by a splendid second-hand shop, kept by a very Johnsonian gentleman, who is an expert and enthusiast on the works of the Doctor. I bought the Boswell *Life* and was once more refreshed. After two and a half months of travelling in modern England, and coming direct from Brum, that mire of despair and corruption, old Johnson's goodness and wisdom clears the mind. He pondered and ridiculed and refuted every one of the mischievous fallacies that are now paraded as truth in the BBC, newspapers, schools, and even the church. Yet now when he is quoted it is usually for his remark that 'patriotism is the last refuge of the scoundrel'; by which he meant not 'love of country', as we understand the word patriotism, but putting the interests of the people, or mob, above the interests of the King.

Educated people remember Johnson's remarks about Levellers, America and the joys of an inn, but few probably know what he said about printers: 'For when you consider with how little mental power and corporeal labour a printer can get a guinea a week, it is a very desirable occupation for you.' Everyone knows what Johnson said about women preachers, but few remember how much he enjoyed the company of women; how much he valued the friendship not only of bluestockings like Hannah More and Fanny Burney, but simple ladies like Mrs Thrale; how much he had loved and mourned a wife whom everyone else considered ludicrous.

A year or so back I saw a book review written by Miss Jill Craigie (Mrs Michael Foot) beginning 'Marriage, however uncongenial, was considered the only prospect of any worth for a middle-class girl unluckily born during the eighteenth century.'

More recently, I was reading in an introduction by Monica Dickens to *Mansfield Park* that in Jane Austen's day 'women were second-class citizens . . . She was not even allowed to have her own ideas . . . Most women were timid, neurotic, unambitious, pettily vain and scheming, because flirting and fashions and domestic trivia were all they had to think about.' It is commonplace now to claim that until the twentieth century, and probably not till after the Second World War, few women found any sexual pleasure in marriage. After reading this ignorant nonsense written by modern women about women in past times, it is heartening to remember what Dr Johnson said on the subject of love, sex and marriage:

'Marriage, Sir, is much more necessary to a man than to a woman; for he is much less able to supply himself with domestic comforts. You will recollect my saying to some ladies the other day, that I had often wondered why young women should marry, as they have so much more freedom, and so much more attention paid to them while unmarried, than when married. I did not mention the *strong* reason for their marrying – the *mechanical* reason.' BOSWELL. 'Why that *is* a strong one. But does not imagination make it much more important than it is in reality? Is it not, to a certain degree, a delusion in us as well as in women?' JOHNSON. 'Why yes, Sir; but it is a delusion that is always beginning again.' BOSWELL. 'I don't know but there is upon the whole more misery than happiness produced by that passion.' JOHNSON. 'I don't think so, Sir.'

8 December – Lichfield – Manchester.   And so I returned to Manchester, reading of Dr Johnson all the way. Boswell's *Life* is part of the iron rations of any wanderer through modern England. When gloom and anger grow insupportable in Liverpool, Bradford, or Birmingham, one can find relief in earlier writers on England; Johnson, Cobbett, Dickens and Chesterton are the best; and, in our own day, the late J. B. Morton ('Beachcomber'), Michael Wharton, Malcolm Muggeridge and some of the younger writers for *Private Eye* and the *Spectator*, like Christopher Booker, Richard Ingrams, Patrick Marnham and Auberon Waugh. They make England bearable by their mockery. Scorn and laughter relieve the feeling described by Chesterton in his book *William Cobbett*:

Most men with any conviction in a confused and complicated age have had the almost uncanny sensation of shouting at people that a mad dog is loose or the house is on fire, to be met merely with puzzled and painfully respectful expressions, as if the remark were a learned citation in Greek or Hebrew.